Engineers
Inventors
and Workers

Engineers
Inventors
and Workers

By P. W. KINGSFORD

EDWARD ARNOLD, LONDON

Preface

Britain became a great industrial nation because of her ability to make tools and machinery, at first from iron and later from steel. She became wealthy because of her engineers and inventors. Some of these men found out how iron and steel could be used. Others discovered how to make the machines, and the machines to make machines. Others again discovered how to drive the machines; they found how power could be used, steam, electricity, oil.

As well as the inventors and engineers there were the workers, the men on the shop floor and in the foundry. As the tools and machines were invented so new kinds of work and new skills were required from the workers. These men wanted fair wages so they formed themselves into trade unions to protect their interests and improve their lives.

Thus to see how Britain has become the industrial nation it is today, a country of factories, mines, power stations, railways and roads, we have to understand the part played by the engineers and inventors, the way their discoveries were used in industry, and the lives of the men working in industry.

P.W.K.

1963.

Acknowledgments

Acknowledgment is gratefully made to the following for permission to include various extracts from the sources given:

Amalgamated Engineering Union & Lawrence & Wishart Ltd: J. B. Jefferys, *The Story of the Engineers*.

G. Bell & Sons Ltd: Bland, Brown & Tawney, *English Economic History*.

Clarendon Press: Singer and others, *A History of Technology* (Vol. IV).

Gerald Duckworth & Co. Ltd: Cressey, *100 Years of Mechanical Engineering*.

Engineering Ltd: *Sir Henry Bessemer, F.R.S., An Autobiography*.

Institution of Civil Engineers: *Southey's Diary*.

Institution of Mechanical Engineers: *Brandling Papers, Longridge Collection*.

Iron and Steel Trades Confederation: Pugh, *Men of Steel*.

Lady Labouchere: *Darby MSS*.

W. J. C Little, Esq: *Telford's letters*.

Liverpool Public Libraries: *George Stephenson's letter*.

Manchester University Press: Fitton & Wadsworth, *The Strutts and the Arkwrights*.

Sir Humphrey Noble: *Diaries and letters of I.K. Brunel*.

Frederick Muller Ltd: Sir Frank Whittle, *Jet*.

C. A. Parsons & Co. Ltd: Appleyard, *Life of Sir Charles Parsons*.

Passfield Trustees: S. and B. Webb, *History of Trade Unionism*.

Society of Friends Library: *Norris MSS*.

University of London Library: *The Rules of the Grand National Consolidated Trade Union*.

The author is also indebted to the following for permission to reproduce illustrations from the sources quoted:

Allied Ironfounders Ltd: Raistrick, *Dynasty of Iron Founders*.

Amalgamated Engineering Union: *150th Anniversary booklet*.

Edward Arnold (Publishers) Ltd: Hill and Sellman, *A Survey of British History*, Book III.

Basil Blackwell: Andrews and Brunner, *Capital Development in Steel*.

Cambridge University Press: Dickinson and Titley, *Richard Trevithick*.

Constable & Co. Ltd: Appleyard, *Charles Parsons*.

Engineering Ltd: *Sir Henry Bessemer, F.R.S., An Autobiography* (published in *Engineering*, 1905).

The Editors of *A History of Technology*, Vols. IV and V.

The Iron and Steel Trades Confederation: Pugh, *Men of Steel*.

Longmans, Green & Co. Ltd.: Rolt, *Thomas Telford* and *George and Robert Stephenson*.

Methuen & Co. Ltd: Young, *The Complete Motorist*.

John Murray: Smiles, *Boulton and Watt* and *Nasmyth's Autobiography*.

The Director of the Science Museum, London: photographs of exhibits in the Museum.

List of Plates

Contents

CHAPTER ONE

The
Ironmakers

ABRAHAM DARBY, THE FIRST, SECOND AND THIRD

WHEN Abraham Darby the first was born (in 1678) the fuel which had been used for centuries in smelting and refining iron was charcoal. The charcoal burners, the men who made the charcoal to send to the iron furnaces, were well known figures in the woods and forests. So much wood was needed that the forests began to disappear and the Government stopped the building of ironworks and the industry declined.

There were two stages in the manufacture of iron. First the ore was smelted in the blast furnaces to produce pig iron. According to the particular branch of the industry the pig iron was either taken to the forges to be converted into wrought iron in bars and rods or at the furnace it became cast iron by being poured into sand moulds. Wrought iron was used for such things as nails, tools, spades and hoes. Cast iron was harder and brittle and so was used for articles which did not need to stand a strain, pots, kettles, pipes, fire grates.

Both the furnaces and the forges had to be near forests for the charcoal and near streams for the power to work the bellows or the water wheel for the big hammer. They had been scattered all over England, but as the forests were used up the industry had to move to the still thickly wooded counties near the Welsh border. For instance, much pig iron was carried from the furnaces in the Forest of Dean to the forges of the Upper Severn Valley and the West Midlands. There it was converted into bar iron and slit into rods for the nailers. Many of these men set up their own small businesses, particularly in Worcestershire. Daniel Defoe tells us, 'Every farm has one forge or more; so that the farmers carry on two very different businesses, working at their forges as smiths when they are not employed in the fields as farmers. And all their work they bring to market, where the great tradesmen buy it up and send it to London. We cannot travel far in any direction out of the sound of the hammer.'

Abraham Darby's father, John, was such a man, a farmer as well as a nailer and locksmith. The Darbys were always Quakers, strong in their faith, as they needed to be under persecution and imprisonment.

'John Darby was a farmer – lived at a house called Wren's Nest near Dudley in Worcestershire. He had by his first wife, one son and daughter named Abraham and Esther. He put his son apprentice to Jonathan Freeth, a maltmill maker at Birmingham who was a 'Public Friend', and while he was there Abraham Darby and one or two of his master's sons had a gift in the Ministry. I think I have heard that there were four of them in the same shop that worked together in public and used to sit together one evening in the week. After he was out of his time he married Mary Sergeant.'

This was on 18th September 1699, and in the same year, having served his apprenticeship as a smith, he moved to Bristol where he set up with several partners, all members of the Society of Friends, in a small brassworks as a maltmill maker. Among the smaller articles he made were large pots and cauldrons cast out of brass and he began to search for a better way to cast them from iron. A great many of these were imported from Holland for the Dutch were ahead of England in the art of casting. Darby went to Holland and brought back some Dutch workmen. Then one day he found out how to cast in sand, instead of the loam used so far, these three-legged cauldrons, bellied pots. This made it quicker and cheaper than before and Darby thought it was important for we know that he tried to keep it secret by stopping up the keyhole to prevent spying. On the 13th April 1707, he obtained a patent for fourteen years which ran as follows:

'A new way of casting iron bellied pots, and other iron bellied wares in sand only, without loam or clay, by which iron pots and other wares may be cast fine and with more care and expedition, and may be afforded cheaper than they can be by the way commonly used, and in regard to their cheapness may be of great advantage to the poore of this own Kingdom, who for the most part use such wares and in all probability will prevent the merchants of England going to foreign markets for such wares, from whence great quantities are imported, and likewise may in turn supply foreign markets with that manufacture of our own dominions.'

This was a minor achievement in the use of iron but it was to lead to a major one. It happened this way. Darby's partners of the brassworks were not interested in iron casting but he wanted to expand his business. According to Hannah Rose, the daughter of one of his workmen, 'After a few years Abraham Darby wanting to enlarge the Brass Works, and his partners not being willing, he drew his share of it out, and hearing of an iron works at Coalbrookdale in Shropshire, went and settled there about the year of 1709 or 1710.'

Coalbrookdale stood on the Coalbrook, a tributary to the Severn near where it runs through a narrow gorge at Ironbridge. There were probably several reasons why Darby made the move there, which was a considerable one for those days. It was an important coalfield, with ironstone close by, and Bristol got most of its coal from it, brought down the busy Severn waterway. It was also well wooded for charcoal. There was abundant water supply for power. Markets were easily reached by river. Towns such as Shrewsbury, Bewdley, Birmingham, Wolverhampton, were within reasonable distance and Quakers were already in business there.

At Coalbrookdale, Abraham I and his son Abraham II and grandson Abraham III built up a famous ironworks which has lasted to the present day, for the Coalbrookdale Company is now a member of Allied Ironfounders Ltd.

He had a great advantage in the site and natural lay-out. In the iron industry of the time the furnaces were usually widely separated from the forges, so that they would have independent areas for charcoal fuel, and this meant much transport, often by pack horse, of pig iron from furnace to forge. At Darby's works furnace and forge were side by side on the stream, in which pools were constructed to supply power for all of them. The natural gradient meant that ore and fuel could run down to the works by wagon way, the molten metal could run out into the sandfloor, and the finished castings or the pig iron be taken by wagon down to the boats on the Severn. The castings he made were chiefly pots, kettles, boiling pans and also firebacks, smoothing irons, grates, door frames, weights, cartboxes or bushes, pestles and mortars. He smelted five to ten tons of iron a week. During Abraham I's time the forge was little used because he found a big market for his cast iron domestic articles, and the pig iron he produced he sold to other forges.

It was soon after he had settled at Coalbrookdale, in 1710, that he made his major discovery. This was how to use coke instead of charcoal for smelting the iron.

Let Darby's daughter-in-law, Abiah Darby, give her account of the discovery, written some sixty years later:

'He cast Iron Goods in sand out of the Blast Furnace that blow'd with wood charcoal, for it was not yet thought of to blow with Pit Coal. Sometime after he suggested the thought, that it be practable to smelt the Iron from the ore in the Blast Furnace with Pit Coal: Upon this he first try'd with raw coal as it came out of the Mines, but it did not answer. He not discouraged, had the coal coak'd into Cynder, as is done for drying Malt, and it then succeeded to his satisfaction. But he found that only one sort of pit coal would suit best for the purpose of making good Iron. He then erected another Blast Furnace, and enlarged the Works. The discovery soon got abroad and became of great utility.'

Why was this discovery of such importance? This was the first time iron ore and mineral fuel had been successfully brought together. The need for it was urgent and many attempts had been made before. The demand for charcoal fuel had meant the stripping of England's forests and ironworks were moving farther into remote districts where the forests were still untouched. England needed the timber for her ships. As charcoal became scarcer its price rose and the iron industry could not expand. However, from now on the industry could depend on the vast and unused coalfields.

How exactly Abraham I succeeded when other men failed is not clear. Probably one reason was the use of more powerful bellows to produce a stronger blast, thus increasing the

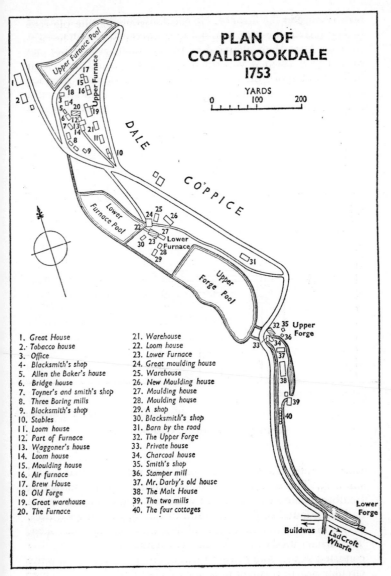

PLAN OF COALBROOKDALE 1753

YARDS
0   100   200

Upper Furnace Pool

Upper Furnace

DALE

Lower Furnace Pool

CO'PPICE

Lower Furnace

Upper Forge Pool

Upper Forge

Lower Forge

Buildwas   LadCroft Wharfe

1. Great House
2. Tobacco house
3. Office
4. Blacksmith's shop
5. Allen the Baker's house
6. Bridge house
7. Toyner's and smith's shop
8. Three Boring mills
9. Blacksmith's shop
10. Stables
11. Loom house
12. Part of Furnace
13. Waggoner's house
14. Loom house
15. Moulding house
16. Air furnace
17. Brew House
18. Old Forge
19. Great warehouse
20. The Furnace
21. Warehouse
22. Loom house
23. Lower Furnace
24. Great moulding house
25. Warehouse
26. New Moulding house
27. Moulding house
28. Moulding house
29. A shop
30. Blacksmith's shop
31. Barn by the road
32. The Upper Forge
33. Private house
34. Charcoal house
35. Smith's shop
36. Stamper mill
37. Mr. Darby's old house
38. The Malt House
39. The two mills
40. The four cottages

[From *Dynasty of Iron Founders*, by A. Raistrick

temperature in the furnace. He certainly bought a new pair of bellow boards for £12 at this time. The coke would stand a stronger blast than charcoal so that the iron would become more liquid when it was smelted and thus could be cast in lighter and more detailed designs. It was in such superior domestic pots and other wares that Abraham I found his main market. The other most probable reason was that, as Abraham

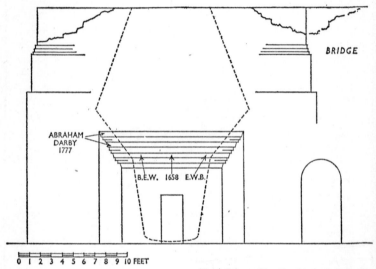

[From *Dynasty of Iron Founders*, by A. Raistrick

Section of old furnace, Coalbrookdale

Darby wrote, 'He found that only one sort of pitcoal would suit best.' This sort was the clod coal found near the surface at Coalbrookdale in which there was little of the sulphur which had been found to be so harmful to the making of good iron. It was in order to remove the sulphur that the coal was coked. The furnace used was an old one which he restored. It probably consisted of a masonry structure at the bottom of which was the circular hearth made of firestone, of about 18 inches diameter and about 5 feet high. Above this rose the furnace shaft to a

16

height of about 20 feet. Leading into the top of the crucible was the blast hole into which the air was forced from the bellows at the back of the structure.

Abraham I had not much longer to live for he died on 5th May 1717, at the age of thirty-nine, but before then he expanded the business considerably, both by building a new furnace at Coalbrookdale, as we have seen, and by taking on leases of ironworks elsewhere at Dolgelly in Merioneth and at Vale Royal near Bolton, Cheshire. He remained an active member of the Society of Friends as Hannah Rose described:

'When A. Darby first came into the Dale he and my father used to go once a month to Newport and meet William Osborne from Wolverhampton, and hold meetings near an Inn, I think, the Swan, and many of the inhabitants would come and behave sober and attentive. The last meeting he was at was in the new house he built in Coalbrookdale. It was not quite finished so not inhabited – the meeting was held in the room now called the best parlour and he was greatly favoured in prayer. My father and mother said they never heard him so fine but he was too ill to sit the meeting out. He died not long after. He died at Madeley Court and was brought to the new house to be buried from there at Broseley.'

Abraham II was born in 1711 and thus was only six when his father died, and his mother died in the following year. The boy was sent with his brothers and sister to a well-known Quaker school in Lancashire where he stayed until he was eighteen. Soon after he left school he was taken in the works and became a partner when he was twenty-one.

In the meantime the works had to be run and it was managed for twenty-eight years by Richard Ford, the son-in-law of Abraham I. He had been trained under Abraham I and in his capable hands the trade of the company grew. There were more pots and kettles for the wholesalers, who sold both at home and overseas, particularly in Africa; there was more pig iron, much of which went to merchants; and as the early steam engines of Savery and Newcomen appeared so the works produced the cylinders and pipe work for them. The company's reputation for iron castings spread. The two furnaces were now smelting more then 12 tons of iron a week.

When the time came that Savery's patent of his steam engine would expire, Richard Ford took over two more furnaces, one at Willey near Coalbrookdale, to meet in advance the increased demand for engine castings which he expected. He wrote:

'The business in Castings of one kind or another is enlarged pretty much here and as the Patent for ye Fire Engine is now Expiring that Business will consequently increase more and where those Furnaces to go on to our Satisfaction, ye Piggs produced (besides other Castings) would not be sufficient for ye Bristol Demands, and as they can't well do without 'em and we should not have 'em to Supply, it may put 'em upon further Experiments which may be of bad Consequence so that a Blast once in a year at Willey for Piggs will be a Fortification against their Attempts.'

By the time Richard Ford had managed the company for twenty years Abraham II was twenty-seven and came into the position of works manager. When Ford died in 1745 Abraham II took over all the management and continued it until his death in 1763. Abraham II made two notable advances in iron making, although they were less important than those his father made. The first of these made the blast stronger and more regular. One of the problems of the iron makers was always that in dry weather the streams were insufficient to keep the furnace bellows working. The early steam engine of Savery and Newcomen made it possible to pump back the water into reservoirs to be used over and over again, and Abraham I was probably the first to see this possibility. His wife wrote:

'My husband Abraham Darby . . . made many improvements. One of Consequence to the prosperity of these Works was as they got very short of water that in the summer of dry Seasons they were obliged to blow very slow and generally blow out the furnaces once a year, which was attended with great loss. But my husband proposing the Erecting of a Fire Engine to draw up the water from the lower works and convey it back into the upper pools, that by continual rotation of the water the furnaces might be plentifully supplied; which

18

answered Exceeding well to these Works, and others have followed the Example.'

Thus it can be seen that just as Abraham I's discoveries in casting iron had helped in the making of steam engines (or fire engines as they were called) so the engines now helped in the smelting of ore in the furnaces by Abraham II.

Abraham II's second discovery was in improving the smelting of the pig iron. Abraham I's market had been in cast iron pots and kettles for which iron smelted with coke was suitable. Now Abraham II found a growing market in another branch of trade. At a time when wood was the universal material for ships as well as for machinery, there was a great demand for nails of all kinds and the men who made them, the nailers, were increasing rapidly throughout the Midlands. They obtained their wrought iron from the forges in the form of rods, which had been cut from the malleable bar iron hammered out from the pig iron received from the furnaces. Abraham I's problem was that the Coalbrookdale pig iron smelted with coke was found unsuitable for nailer's rods. He set to and experimented and after many trials succeeded in making a suitably tough iron from which the impurities were eliminated. The technique he used is not known but the event was described by his wife:

'But all this time the making of Barr Iron at Forges from Pit Coal pigs was not thought of. About 26 years ago my Husband conceived this Happy Thought that it might be possible to make bar iron from pit coal pigs. Upon this he sent some of our pigs to be tryed at the Forges, and that no prejudice might arise against them he did not discover from whence they came, or of what quality they were. And a good account being given of their working, he erected Blast Furnaces for Pig Iron for Forges. Edward Knight Esq., a capital Iron Master urged my Husband to get a patent, that he might reap the benefit for years of this happy discovery: but he said he would not deprive the public of Such an Acquisition which he was Satisfied it would be; and so it has proved, for it soon spread and many Furnaces both in this Neighbourhood and several other places have been erected for this purpose.

'Had not these discoveries been made the Iron trade of our

own produce could have dwindled away, for woods for charcoal became very scarce and landed Gentlemen rose the price of cord wood exceedingly high – indeed it would not have been to be got. But from pit coal being introduced in its stead the demand for wood charcoal is much lessen'd, and in a few years I apprehend will set the use of that article aside.'

Some 15 years later two foremen at the Coalbrookdale works, Thomas and George Cranage, improved on this. They discovered a means of converting pig iron into malleable wrought iron by using coal in a reverberatory furnace. In this the iron and the fuel were kept separate by a low partition wall called the firebridge, and the flame from the fuel was reflected down or reverberated on to the iron. The importance of these discoveries was stressed by the manager who succeeded Abraham II. This was Richard Reynolds and he wrote 'the nail trade would have been lost to this country had it not been found practicable to make nails with iron made with pit coal'.

Abraham II died on 6th June 1763, while his son Abraham III was only thirteen. Until he should be able to take over, the works was managed by Richard Reynolds, a member of another well-known Quaker family and the son-in-law of Abraham II. Many Quaker families were connected by marriage in this way since it was generally their rule that marriage should take place within the Society of Friends. Reynolds was first apprenticed to the Quaker William Fry, grocer of Bristol, among whose family was Joseph Fry, the founder of the chocolate industry.

Richard Reynolds was an able man of business who made a considerable fortune, much of which he gave away. He continued the Darbys' policy of building houses for the work people. At the works the main change he made was in the internal transport. This was a big problem where the ore, the fuel and the products had to be handled and carried over some distance between the mines, the furnaces and the wharves. Abraham II had met it by laying down wagon ways of wooden rails but Reynolds laid down iron rails in their place. This was the first time cast iron rails were ever used. Abraham's wife wrote:

'They used to carry their coal upon horses backs, but he got

20

roads made and laid with sleepers and rails, as they have them in the North of England. And one waggon with three horses will bring as much as 20 horses used to bring on horse's backs. But this laying the road with wood began a scarcity and raised the price of it, so that of late years the laying of the rails of Cast Iron was substituted; which although expensive, answers well for ware and duration. We have in the different works, nearly 20 miles of this road, which costs upward of £800 a mile. That of Iron Wheels and ashe-trees for these wagons was, I believe, my Husband's invention.'

There was another reason why Reynolds went in for iron rails. There was a slump in the iron trade but the Coalbrookdale policy was always to keep the furnaces going even if it meant piling up stocks. An obvious way to stock their iron was to lay it down on the wooden railway for it could always be taken up again if necessary.

Abraham III took over the management when he was only eighteen, though he always had advice from Reynolds. He continued to manage Coalbrookdale and other works nearby, at Horsehay and Ketley, for 21 years until his death in 1789, the year of the French Revolution. During this time he built two more furnaces, more houses and schools, and cast many Newcomen and Watt steam engines.

He is chiefly remembered for the building of the Iron Bridge over the river Severn at Coalbrookdale in 1779. This was the first bridge of iron ever built and it still stands today, scheduled as an ancient monument and used for foot traffic only. It was a bold scheme. Abraham III undertook the whole design, casting and erection of the bridge and he bore more than half the cost. The total weight of iron work was 378 tons. The bridge is nearly semi-circular, with a span of 100 feet, a rise of 45 feet above the river, and a width of 24 feet. There were numerous problems to be overcome. The first problem was the site. The banks were steep and of soft rock and the swiftly flowing river was known to flood its banks. Massive masonry supports had to be built. The casting was another difficulty. The five main ribs, curved and 70 feet long, each weighing more than 5 tons, were cast on an open sand floor and the furnace had to be enlarged and re-designed to deal with this size of casting. The great rib castings were brought into position by water, hoisted up and joined together at the crown. In the assembly of the bridge no bolts or rivets were used but all the parts were slotted or dovetailed together and secured by iron wedges or screws. These interlocking parts gave it great strength so that it remained a wonder for many years and a monument to Darby's boldness and faith. Robert Stephenson, the locomotive engineer, wrote years after: 'If we consider that the manipulation of cast iron was then completely in its infancy, a bridge of such dimensions was doubtless a bold as well as an original undertaking, and the efficiency of the details is worthy of the boldness of the conception.' (Plate I, facing p. 32)

This ends the great period of the Coalbrookdale Company, in which the basic advances in iron making were made. The company went on growing from about 1,000 employees in 1800 to between 3,000 and 4,000 in 1950. Other Darbys (including Abraham IV) managed it until that year but after that there were none left at the Coalbrookdale works.

By their inventions the three Abrahams laid the basis for the future development of England as an iron and steel making country. They did more than this for they made at Coalbrookdale a community of people working in friendship together. Some ironmasters merely made their pile and built themselves mansions, where they lived as country gentry, leaving the works to fall into decay. The Darbys stayed at Coalbrookdale living quietly and modestly, not amassing great fortunes but spending on experiments and social welfare. Their faith and principles helped them to success; they were active Quakers. They would not take any orders for guns and so they were bound to take a long view. They did not take advantage of war booms and therefore avoided the slumps at the end of the wars. One of the workmen at Coalbrookdale, Adam Luccock, said about the three Abrahams, 'They all liked a joke right well, and as for Kindness, it seemed as if they thought it a favour to be allowed to assist you.'

HENRY CORT (1740–1800)

Henry Cort was the successor to the Darbys in discovering how mineral fuel, coal or charcoal, instead of wood fuel, could be used in making iron. His inventions were equally, if not more, important to the iron industry.

So far it had been possible to use coal or coke in the furnaces for the smelting of ore into castings or into low grade pig iron which could be refined at the forges for the nail industry. However, all the hammering and refining of the pig iron into malleable or wrought iron at the forges had still to be carried out with charcoal fuel, and this was also needed for most of the production of high-grade pig iron in the furnaces. Cort's inventions made it possible to use coal for all this work.

How and why did these inventions come about? It was again true that necessity was the mother of invention. In the first place the charcoal was becoming more and more scarce as more was required for refining than for smelting. Secondly England became dependent on imports of wrought iron in bars from Sweden and Russia. These imports increased considerably, whereas England had great quantities of iron ore and coal if only the way to combine the two to produce wrought iron could be found. Henry Cort found this way with his discoveries of puddling and rolling in 1783 and 1784.

Cort was born in 1740 at Lancaster where his father was a builder and brickmaster. At the age of twenty-five he was carrying on a profitable business in Surrey Street off the Strand in London as an agent or contractor for the Navy. He found that the Navy would not accept British iron as it was so inferior to the imported iron. He therefore started experimenting and after a few years gave up his business to start iron making himself. He moved to Fontley near Fareham close to Portsmouth harbour and erected a forge and a slitting mill. There he did work for the Navy and continued his experiments. He visited James Watt at the Soho works, Birmingham, in 1782 to obtain one of their steam engines for his forge. When Watt wrote to his partner Matthew Boulton about this visit he gave a hint of Cort's discovery:

'We had a visit today, from a Mr. Cort of Gosport who says he has a forge there and has found out some grand secret in the making of iron, by which he can make double the quantity at the same expense and in the same time as normal. He says he wants some Kind of Engine but could not tell what, wants

23

some of us to call on him, and says he has had some correspondence with you on the subject. He seems a simple good natured man but not very Knowing. I think him a brother projector – and have therefore put him off until some of us can view the ground which he has readily agreed to as he has water for most of the year.'

The next year Cort had made successful trials of his invention and he gave definite views in a letter to James Watt:

'Sir, When I did myself the pleasure to call on you at Soho, we had some conversation on the Subject of Iron – I intimated I had solicited a Patent for my invention of manufacturing iron – an improved method – which I have obtained and you were Kind enough to say you would mention me to Mr. Wilkinson. I have therefore taken the liberty of enclosing a letter to that Gent and I will be obliged to you to forward him – amongst other things I profess to make ordinary Iron – Tough – by a short simple process.

When you can say anything of the forge to be worked with Steam – I will thank you to communicate the same to me – excuse this trouble – I will do as much or more for you.

I am, Sir,

Y Most Hble St.

Henry Cort.'

Cort's 'grand secret in the making of iron' as James Watt described it was basically a process of stirring molten pig iron heated by coal in a reverberatory furnace, then hammering it with a large forge hammer to expel the slag and finally passing it through grooved rollers which compressed it into bars of tough iron. The puddlers stirred and turned the molten iron through openings in the furnace door. The effect of the puddling or stirring was to remove the carbon from the pig iron by the action of the air circulating through the furnace. This made it purer and thus malleable, or workable, after it had been rolled. It was the combination of puddling and rolling which was the real discovery of Cort.

The result was startling. Whereas before Cort's invention the forge hammer could produce 1 ton of iron in 12 hours, now with the rolling mill 15 tons could be dealt with in the same

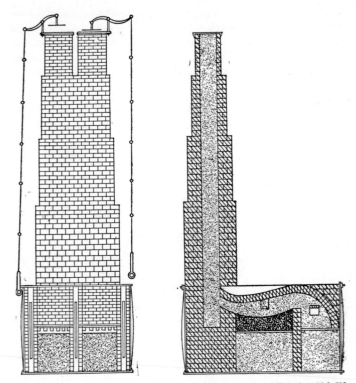

[From *A History of Technology*, Vol. IV

Puddling-furnace – (left) external view; (right) vertical section

time. There was an enormous increase in the output of pig iron
to be used for puddling and rolling into wrought iron. Fifty
years after Cort's discovery the output in England was 20
times bigger. At once the Navy found it to be satisfactory and
took many tons in the form of anchors and other iron work
on the wooden ships. The big ironmasters would not at first
believe that such an improvement was possible and James
Watt wrote to a friend:

'Mr. Cort has been treated most shamefully by the trade:
they are ignorant brutes; but he exposed himself to it by

showing them the process before it was perfect, and seeing his ignorance of the common operations of making iron, laughed at, and despised him; yet they will continue by some dirty evasion to use his process or such as they like, without acknowledging him in it. I shall be glad to be of any use to him.'

Soon, however, the ironmasters came to terms with Cort and he was to be paid a royalty of 10s. a ton. The big men like Richard Crawshay with his Cyfarthfa works in South Wales immediately seized the opportunity. At that time this works was producing 500 tons of bar iron a year; 25 years later it had

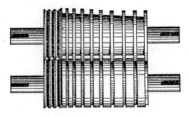

[From *A History of Technology*, Vol. IV

Grooved rollers for bar making

risen to 10,000 tons. This was happening all over the iron districts in Wales, the Midlands, Yorkshire and Derby. The price of iron also fell by half, since the new process was much cheaper.

Cort would have made a great deal of money from his patent if all had gone well. However, the connection with the Navy which had been such an advantage now brought about his ruin. He had entered into partnership with Samuel Jellicoe and large sums of money, amounting to £50,000, to finance the works had been lent by Jellicoe's father. In return Cort had handed over his patents as security for the loans. The father, Adam Jellicoe, was employed by the Admiralty as deputy paymaster of seamen's wages and he had used the public funds he controlled to make the loans to Cort. This misuse of public money was discovered, Cort was unable to repay the loans, and the Government confiscated the patents and seized all his property. Cort had no money left and he was ruined. The only people to benefit were the ironmasters from whom the Government did not collect the royalties due under the patents. Crawshay of Cyfarthfa alone saved £10,000 in this way.

Cort's subsequent history was an unhappy one. He asked the Government to restore his patent but without success. He had 12 children to support. Eventually, thanks to the Prime Minister, the young William Pitt, Parliament granted him a pension of £200 a year. This he received for six years until his death in 1800. Cort's discoveries had enriched many great families but when his widow appealed for help she was given a pension of £125 a year. Some few years later after Cort's death the iron industry agreed to collect a fund for his dependants but the sum raised from the whole of the country was only £871 16s.

According to a writer of the time:

'The advantages of the above discoveries give the command of the iron trade to Britain, and take it for ever, or at least, as long as the industry and liberty remains, from the Northern Kingdoms (i.e. Russia and Sweden) and America; because Britain is the only country hitherto known in which seams of coal, iron stone and iron ore and limestone (the three component parts or raw materials from which iron is made) are frequently found in the same field and in the near neighbourhood of the sea, or of short water carriage to the sea.'

THE IRONWORKERS

The great technical changes in the making of iron meant changes in the work and lives of the men working in the industry. Before the changes took place a furnace would employ about seven men. Two were skilled men, known as keepers; their job was to control the quantities of ore and fuel, regulate the blast and tap the molten metal from the furnace. Two or three fillers took the baskets laden with ore or fuel or limestone to the furnace, and two filled the baskets. Other casual labourers were employed. At a forge there were probably two skilled men, known as finers or hammermen, and a boy. Apprenticeship was necessary and the boy would serve for seven years. The master hammerman was a highly skilled craftsman and he was sometimes a small employer rather than a wage earner.

The inventions of the Darbys and of Cort changed all this. The new processes of puddling and rolling required new grades of worker. When the steam engine was introduced it required engineers to install and maintain. The scale of the operations increased and the firm became bigger. As these changes took place the new skilled workers needed more and more unskilled labourers to handle the raw material and its products and, as the firm grew in size, the foreman and works manager appeared in the place of the master hammerman.

The ironworkers needed to be strong men and they were healthier than those in some other occupations. They were 'men of athletic make and great bodily vigour, which was a consideration of no small consequence since it had been justly said that too many of our manufactures tended to deteriorate the physical constitution and produce a feeble and degenerate race of men, without spirit and ability to defend their rights'.

As might be expected the skilled men were scarce and so their wages were relatively good. But they were not as high as they would have been if people had been able to move more easily about the country from one job to another. One result of this was that a considerable number of workmen went abroad, attracted by good offers from countries such as Sweden and Russia which wanted to learn about the English techniques. This was taken so seriously by the masters that an Act of Parliament was passed, 'to prevent the inconveniences arising from seducing Artificers in the Iron and Steel Manufactures into foreign Parts'. The Act imposed a fine of up to £100 and imprisonment for three months on any persons found guilty of such 'seducing', and there were many prosecutions under the Act.

Another result of the scarcity of trained workmen was that the masters got the magistrates to protect their men from being forced into the Navy by the press gangs. This was done during the American War of Independence and the Napoleonic Wars.

Wages were often paid, even in those early days, on a basis of payment by results. This was either piece work or time wages with a bonus. A typical employer's view was, as written at the time:

'The only security and check an Iron-Master has over the workman, who is carrying on his business while he is asleep, and prevent him, by neglect, from suffering the metal to be burnt, or unduly wasted in the fire and spoiled is, by limiting him to, and frequently proving his yield, and paying him a bounty, in proportion to the degree of care and skill shown.'

We know, however, that when the bonus system was introduced at Coalbrookdale all kinds of equipment somehow disappeared into the furnace so as to boost the output, and the bonus.

We do know that the system known as truck was often used to exploit the workers and that it was greatly resented. Under this system of payment, part of the wages was paid in tickets which could be exchanged for food and other goods but the tickets could often only be exchanged at the stores run by the ironworks. The workers were so much defrauded under this system, which was widespread in other industries, that eventually Acts of Parliament were passed to forbid it. These Truck Acts still operate and it is illegal to pay wages in any other way than in cash, unless the employee agrees to be paid by cheque.

Trade unions did not yet exist among the ironworkers. This is remarkable because workers of all kinds have usually formed associations to protect their interests, provided there are no great obstacles. In allied occupations, in various branches of metal working, trade unions were founded by such men as the craftsmen in the Sheffield knife, scissors and saw industry at this time. The ironworkers had a few friendly societies, such as the Friendly Society of Ironfounders of Bolton in Lancashire, but with very few exceptions they did not take part in any trade union activity.

There were probably several reasons for this. The industry was scattered, often in isolated pockets, and there was no opportunity for the workers to get together in any great numbers. The skilled men would not be likely to combine with the unskilled and so it was unlikely that there would be enough men in any one place to support a powerful union. Above all, many of the ironmasters were good employers. There is no trace of grievances serious enough, or hardship severe enough, to drive the men to form unions against the opposition of the masters.

Additional Reading

A. Raistrick, *Dynasty of Iron Founders*, Longmans 1953.

T. S. Ashton, *Iron and Steel in the Industrial Revolution*, Manchester University Press 1951.

S. Smiles, *Industrial Biography: Iron Workers and Tool Makers*, Murray 1908.

CHAPTER TWO

The
Steam
Engine

THE origin of James Watt's great invention, and the world-wide use of steam engines, was the need to pump water. Pumps had to be used to drain mines, to give towns their water supply, to give water mills a constant supply of water, to fill canals. Many inventors had tried to make efficient pumps. One of these, and the forerunner of Newcomen, was Captain Thomas Savery.

Savery, a military engineer, invented the first practical steam pump in 1698. It used condensation of steam and atmospheric pressure as well as steam pressure to raise water to a higher level. His patent described it as a

'New invention of Raising of Water and occasioning Motion to all sorts of Mill Work by the Impellent Force of Fire, which will be of great Use and Advantage for Drayning Mines, Serveing Towns with Water, and for the working of all Sorts of Mills where they have not the benefit of Water nor Constant Windes.'

Steam engines were known for a long time as fire engines. Savery wrote a pamphlet called 'The Miner's Friend, or an Engine to raise Water by Fire described, and the Manner of fixing it in the Mines, with an Account of the several uses it is applicable unto, and an Answer to the objections against it'. In this pamphlet he explained how he came to invent the 'fire engine'.

'Though my thoughts have long been employed about waterworks, I should never have pretended to any invention of that kind had I not happily found out this new, but yet much stronger and cheaper cause of motion than any before made use of. But, finding this of rarefaction by fire, the consideration of the difficulties the miners and colliers labour under by the frequent disorders, and cumbersomeness in general of water engines encouraged me to invent engines to work by the new force.'

Savery's engine was used in Cornish and Staffordshire mines but the height to which it could raise water was very limited because it could not stand any considerable pressure of steam. It was used in a few big private houses, such as Sion House in London, and to pump London's water supply. In the following advertisement Savery invites the mine owners to visit his workshop.

'Captain Savery's engines which raise water by the use of Fire in any reasonable quantities and to any height, being now brought to perfection and ready for publick use; these are to give notice to all proprietors of Mines and Collieries which are encumbered with water, that they may be furnished with Engines to drain the same, at his workhouse in Salisbury Court, London, against the Old Playhouse, where it may be seen working on Wednesdays and Saturdays every week from 3 to six in the afternoons, when they may be satisfied of the performance thereof, with less expense than any other force of Horse or Hands, and less subject to repair.'

THOMAS NEWCOMEN (1663–1729)

There were scores of tin and copper mines in Cornwall (some of them very rich) where the water still had to be drained and lifted by horse power. Men were continually looking for a cheaper way of doing it. Thomas Newcomen frequently visited the tin mines as a dealer in iron tools, and he set about making a practical pump.

Newcomen was a skilled artisan; he carried on a small business as a blacksmith in Lower Street, Dartmouth. His partner in building the first engine was a John Calley, a man of his own kind, described sometimes as a plumber, sometimes as a glazier. Apparently Newcomen knew nothing of Savery's

Plate 1

Model of Coalbrookdale Iron Bridge, 1779

(Crown copyright, Science Museum, London)

Plate 2

Detailed view of cylinder, valves and governor (Front view)

Boulton and Watt's rotative beam ('Lap') engine, 1788

(Crown copyright, Science Museum, London)

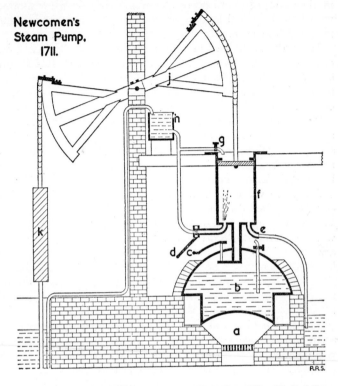

Newcomen's Steam Pump. 1711.

[From *A Survey of British History*, Book III, by C. P. Hill and R. R. Sellman

Newcomen's steam pump

(a) Furnace. (b) Boiler. (c) Steam cock, admitting steam to cylinder. (d) Injection cock, admitting cold water to cylinder to condense steam. (e) Escape valve through which water in cylinder is expelled by next blast of steam. (f) Cylinder. (g) Tap admitting water on to piston, to keep it airtight. (h) Cold water tank. (j) Balance beam. (k) Counterweight on pump gear, pulling piston up between strokes

Working: i (c) opened to admit steam to cylinder as counterweight raises piston, then closed. ii (d) opened to let cold water into cylinder, condensing steam and producing a vacuum, whereupon atmospheric pressure pushes piston down work; nor had he the education to understand the physics and mathematics of steam power. However, he and his assistant, with their practical know-how and perseverance, made their first engine in 1705, after a long period of trial and error.

His engine differed basically from Savery's in that it used only atmospheric pressure to work the pump. It used steam only, by condensing it, to form a vacuum in which atmospheric pressure would work. It was therefore really an atmospheric engine.

The water supply on top of the piston was used to exclude any air from the cylinder and maintain the vacuum. The water sealed a flexible leather disk on top of the piston. This was necessary because workshops could not make an accurately bored cylinder of that size.

A snifting valve enabled the air to escape from the cylinder. It required three men to work Newcomen's first engines. When the engine had stopped and was to be re-started the words were passed, 'Snift Benjy!' 'Blow the fire, Burley!' 'Work away, Joe!' The air outlet valve was named the snifting valve because when it was opened the air rushing through made a noise like a man snifting. The second man built up the fire under the boiler, and the third man let the condensing water into the cylinder through the injection water cock.

The first engine was very clumsy; two big improvements seem to have occurred purely by chance. At first the steam was condensed by throwing cold water at the outside of the cylinder. One day, Newcomen noticed that the engine made several strokes more quickly than usual, and found that cold water had got through a hole in the piston head as a jet into the cylinder. He therefore decided to inject water through a cock into the cylinder.

The other improvement may be a legend. The story goes that a boy called Humphrey Potter had the simple job of turning two cocks alternately, one of which admitted steam to the cylinder, the other injecting the cold water into it to condense the steam. Getting tired of this monotonous task he linked up the cocks with the movement of the main beam by a catch and pieces of string, and thus made it automatic. This also was incorporated in the engine and speeded it up.

The danger of explosion still remained. When this had been

34

removed by fitting a safety valve, the Newcomen engine was widely used, not only in Britain but also in France, Belgium and Germany.

Newcomen could not take out a patent because Savery's patent covered all 'fire engines' but the two came to an agreement and erected one of the first engines in Dudley Castle. The Thames Water Supply Company bought one in 1720 to replace a Savery engine. The boiler capacity was 450 cubic feet, the cylinder was $2\frac{1}{2}$ feet in diameter and 9 feet long, and the coal consumed cost £1,000 a year. Soon the Newcomen engine became essential for coal mining, particularly in the deep coalfields of the North where many pits had been abandoned because of flooding. Sometimes one pump emptied a mine and filled a canal alongside at the same time.

The size of the engine boiler and cylinder was increased by other men. At the Walker colliery near Newcastle upon Tyne where there were many Newcomen engines, the engine had a cylinder diameter of 6 feet 2 inches and a length of $10\frac{1}{2}$ feet. It was made at the Darby works at Coalbrookdale. John Smeaton, the great engineer, famous for the Eddystone lighthouse, improved the performance of the Newcomen engine as much as was possible within its limits.

There was nothing to compete with the Newcomen engine for sixty years. It had two main drawbacks. It used an enormous amount of coal in relation to the work done because of the continual cooling of the condensing cylinder. It was also impracticable to convert its single action to rotary motion. It needed the genius of James Watt to solve both these problems.

JAMES WATT (1736–1819)

James Watt was a mechanical genius who could have turned his mind to any problem. How was it that he tackled the steam engine in particular? There were two main reasons: because steam power had been used widely but inefficiently for 60 years and because scientists had for some time been enquiring into the nature and properties of steam. Some of these scientists were at Glasgow University; James Watt was employed there and came to be their friend.

Watt was fortunate in his grandparents, parents and his

35

upbringing. This was at Greenock, near Glasgow, where he was born on 19th January 1736. His grandfather, Thomas Watt, was a teacher of mathematics, who became a prominent citizen and an elder of the Kirk in the town. Two of his pictures hung on the wall of the house where Watt was born; they were portraits of Isaac Newton and John Napier, the mathematician. Later on Watt could remember, as a boy, studying these portraits.

His father, James Watt senior, was apprenticed to a shipwright and carpenter. He was a versatile man for he not only ran a prosperous business supplying ships with all kinds of equipment and repairing ships' instruments, but he was also a builder and something of an architect. At one stage he was prosperous enough to hold shares in several ships engaged in the tobacco trade with Virginia. Like his father, a highly respected citizen of Greenock, he was elected councillor and chief magistrate. Watt's mother, was related to the professor of Latin at Glasgow University. There were five children of whom only James Watt survived, and he was a delicate child, suffering badly from migraine.

His ill-health made him shy of the rough company of other boys. He never mixed with boys of his own age and he always had a quiet and retiring nature. As he could not attend school regularly, his parents taught him reading, writing and arithmetic. Later on he went to Greenock Grammar School where he shone at mathematics and learnt some Latin and Greek. He was a great reader of all kinds of books, but this was only part of his education. At home he had a thorough practical training and learnt through his fingertips instead of from books. While he was quite small he was given a specially small set of carpenter's tools. He had his own bench and small forge and as he spent more and more time helping in his father's workshop he acquired great skill with tools and machines. Without this early training it is doubtful if he would have become a famous inventor.

The kind of work which interested him most in his father's workshop was repairing ships' instruments and compasses, because of his knowledge of mathematics and mechanics. This made him decide that he wanted to be a mathematical instrument maker. At the age of eighteen he had to choose a trade to follow as his father's business had shrunk so much he could not look forward to taking it over.

He set off for Glasgow to learn the trade; in his bag was a quadrant, carpenter's tools and two Bibles. In Glasgow there was no instrument maker from whom to learn and so, through a professor at the University whom his mother's relatives knew, he went to London. This took a fortnight on horseback as there was no coach.

In London the delicate reserved young Scot had a hard time. It was difficult to find a master as he did not mean to spend seven years in apprenticeship. Eventually he was taken on for a year by an instrument maker in Cornhill on paying a fee of twenty guineas and without any wages. During this time his father kept him. He could not stir out of his lodgings because of the press-gangs recruiting for the Navy. He wrote home:

'They now press anybody they can get, landsmen as well as seamen, except it be in the liberties of the city, where they are obliged to carry them before the Lord Mayor; and unless one be either a prentice or a creditable tradesman, there is scarce any getting off again. And if I was carried before any Lord Mayor, I durst not avow that I wrought in the city, it being against their laws for any unfreeman to work even as a journeyman within the liberties.'

This, and unduly hard work made him ill, so that he had to return home. But by that time he had learnt to make all kinds of instruments, starting with brass scales and rules and going on to the more difficult compasses and theodolites, and he arrived in Glasgow as a skilled instrument maker. He had written to his parents: 'I think I shall be able to get my bread anywhere, as I am now able to work as well as most journeymen though I am not as quick as many.'

Back in Glasgow he was in difficulties. The local guild would not allow him to set up business as he had not served an apprenticeship nor was he a native of the city. Fortunately the University helped again. The same professor who had got him to London, gave him some instruments to repair, and then the University gave him a workshop, lodging and a shop to sell his instruments, all within the ancient college buildings and outside the power of the city guilds. He was now 'Mathematical Instrument Maker to the University'. There he could work in peace provided he could get enough business to make a living. He did not really succeed at this until he moved the shop out of the University to a busier neighbourhood. It did well, and he got married.

It was in his shop that he met the professors and students who came in to see his instruments and stayed to admire them. They found him an interesting man to talk to and they exchanged ideas as equals. They told him about their research into steam power, explained the recent discovery of the theory of latent heat, suggested steam might even be used to drive wheeled carriages. Watt studied these problems, experimented with steam, and read widely.

One day in the winter of 1763–64 a professor asked Watt to repair a model of Newcomen's atmospheric engine which was used for lecture demonstrations. It was a small-scale model with a cylinder of 2 inches diameter. This was the crucial moment in Watt's life and work. When the boiler was going he found that the engine would perform only four or five strokes. He repaired the engine, but unlike the ordinary mechanic he did not stop there. He went on to analyse it so as to improve it.

The boiler of the model had been reduced in size in proportion to the engine. He asked himself why the model needed so much more steam than a full sized engine. He saw that it was because the interior surface area of the small cylinder was larger than that of the full-size one in relation to the volume of steam in it. As the cylinder was cooled by the water jet, the loss of heat through the cylinder surface area was correspondingly greater.

This led him to think about the loss of heat. He saw that the cylinder must be kept hot, not alternately heated and cooled as in the Newcomen engine. To satisfy himself on this point he carried out many experiments to find why the loss of heat occurred. With the help of Professor Joseph Black, the famous chemist, he discovered the scientific reason why so much steam was required in the cold cylinder to produce a vacuum after it had been condensed. He was now doubly sure that the great loss of heat could only be avoided if the condenser could be kept at steam-heat. Yet apparently the condenser had to be cooled to get condensation of the steam in it.

Watt wrestled with this problem for a long time. One day the solution flashed into his mind:

'It was in the Green of Glasgow. I had gone to take a walk on a fine Sabbath afternoon. I had entered the Green by the gate at the foot of Charlotte Street – had passed the old washing house. I was thinking upon the engine at the time, and had gone as far as the herd's house, when the idea come into my mind that as steam was an elastic body it could rush into a vacuum, and if a communication was made between the cylinder and an exhausted vessel, it would rush into it, and might then be condensed without cooling the cylinder. I then saw that I must get rid of the condensed steam and injection water if I used a jet, as in Newcomen engine. Two ways of doing this occurred to me . . . I had not walked further than the Golf-house, when the whole thing was arranged in my mind.'

This was the brilliant invention of the separate condenser. Today it may seem a simple enough idea, but it was a revolutionary one which broke through a hundred years of tradition. Watt immediately made a model which proved the idea was correct.

This led him to an equally important change which in fact converted the Newcomen atmospheric engine into a real steam engine. On the Newcomen engine the piston top was sealed by a leather disk and a layer of cold water. 'He realized that Newcomen's method of sealing the piston with cold water would have to be abandoned, because it conflicted with the principle of keeping the cylinders as hot as possible, and that the atmosphere should not act directly on the piston for the same reason. He therefore decided to provide a cylinder-cover with a hole and stuffing-box for the piston-rod to pass through, and to use steam instead of atmospheric pressure to force the piston down.' This first model is in the Science Museum where it can be seen that Watt used a thimble to close a pipe.

The next step of making a larger working engine was too much for him to carry out alone. As an instrument maker he was not used to larger scale engineering, which in any case was primitive. It was not possible to get a cylinder bored and so he had to hammer it out himself. He had no money to spare and incurred debts of £1,000. He still suffered from attacks of migraine and severe headaches which he was to have throughout his life.

Then he met Dr. John Roebuck, a man of parts, doctor, chemist and industrialist who had built the big Carron ironworks in Scotland. Roebuck was interested in any new pumping device for his mines and agreed to finance Watt so that his engine could be made at the works. In the meantime Watt found that his shop had gone down hill. To earn enough to live on he turned to surveying and he was appointed as surveyor for a canal between the Clyde and the Forth. Hence the engine made slow progress but eventually it seemed worth while to apply for a patent. In 1769 the famous patent was granted for 'A new Method of Lessening the Consumption of Steam and Fuel in Fire Engines'. This title gives us the purpose of his work.

The next few years were years of frustration for Watt. The engine could not be completed satisfactorily partly because the workmen could not make to the accuracy required, partly because Roebuck was losing money. After one unsuccessful trial Watt wrote: 'Of all things in life there is nothing more foolish than inventing. Today I enter the thirty-fifth year of my life, and I think I have hardly yet done thirty-five pence worth of good in the world; but I cannot help it.'

His ill-health continued and the surveying he was obliged to keep on with meant working outside in severe weather. Worst of all his wife died and she had been his greatest help.

Then Watt met the man without whom he might never have seen his steam engine used in factories throughout the country. This was Matthew Boulton, wealthy owner and manager of the Soho factory near Birmingham. The partnership of Boulton and Watt, makers of steam engines, became world famous.

Before the two met, Boulton's factory was already famous for the quality of its products – metal ware of all sorts, buckles, buttons, clocks and plate – for his machinery and his skilled workmen. Watt was greatly impressed by the production facilities. The two men liked each other, Watt the crotchety thinker, Boulton the confident, vigorous, genial business leader. Roebuck had become bankrupt and his two-thirds interest in Watt's patent (which was considered valueless) was transferred to Boulton. Watt left Scotland and its climate for good and he was glad to go. He wrote:

'I am still monstrously plagued with headaches, and not a little with unprofitable business. I don't mean my own whims: these I never work at when I can do any other thing: but I have got too many acquaintances; and there are too many beggars in this country, which I am afraid is going to the devil altogether.'

At Soho a new life opened. Boulton later described the arrangement made:

'The first engine that was erected at Soho I purchased of Mr. Watt and Dr. Roebuck. The cylinder was cast of solid grain tin, which engine with the boiler, the valves, the condenser, and the pumps were all sent from Scotland to Soho. The engine was erected for the use of the Soho manufactury, and for the purpose of making experiments upon by Mr. Watt, who occupied two years of his time at Soho with that object, and lived there at Mr. Boulton's expense.'

The cylinder made of block tin soon collapsed. Fortunately a machine by which cylinders could be fairly accurately bored was made in the same year by John Wilkinson, the famous ironmaster. With a new cylinder the engine was a success and Watt wrote home to his father: 'The business I am now about has turned out rather successful; that is to say the fire engine I have invented is now going, and answers much better than any other that has yet been made; and I expect that the invention will be very beneficial to me.'

Before production could go ahead one more thing was necessary. Boulton would have to spend many thousands of pounds; it would take some years to get any return on it, and Watt's patent had only eight years more to run. They petitioned Parliament for an extension of the patent which, in spite of strong opposition to the monopoly being continued, was granted for 25 years, up to 1800.

At Soho Boulton went ahead as fast as possible. Directly it was known that he was interested in a steam engine

41

enquiries began to come in, particularly from Cornwall where many engines had stopped working because of the cost of coal. A great deal depended on Wilkinson's ability to turn out cylinders. Boulton wrote to Watt:

'The new forging shop looks very formidable: the roof is nearly on, and the hearths are both built.

'Pray tell Mr. Wilkinson to get a dozen cylinders cast and bored, from 12 to 50 inches in diameter, and as many condensers of suitable sizes. The latter must be sent here, as we will keep them ready fitted up, and then an engine can be turned out of hand in two or three weeks. I have fixed my mind upon making from twelve to fifteen reciprocating and fifty rotative engines per annum. I assure you that of all the toys and trinkets which are manufactured at Soho, none shall take the place of fire engines in respect of my attention.'

Ten years of intense activity followed. The first engine built was sold to John Wilkinson to operate the blast for his furnace at Broseley Ironworks in Shropshire. Its success with such a well-known firm meant that orders came in fast. The first engines were supplied to Bloomfield colliery, near Birmingham, Bedworth Colliery, near Coventry, a distillery at Stratford-le-Bow. Boulton usually looked after the business side; Watt disliked it but sometimes he had to negotiate an order. The Shadwell Waterworks Company had enquired about a pumping engine, and he wrote to Boulton:

'Yesterday I went again to Shadwell to meet the deputies of the Committee, and to examine their engines when going. We came to no terms further than what we wrote them before, which I confirmed and offered moreover to keep the engine in order for one year. They modestly insisted that we should do so for the whole twenty-five years, which I firmly refused. They seemed to doubt the reality of the performance of the Bow engine; so I told them we did not solicit their orders, and would wait patiently until they were convinced – moreover while they had any doubts remaining, we would not undertake their business on any terms. I should not have been so sharp with them had they not begun with bullying me, *selon la mode de Londres*. But the course I took was not

42

without its effect, for in proportion as they found I despised their job, they grew more civil. After parting with these heroes I went down to Stratford-le-Bow, where I found that the engine had gone very well. I caused it to be kept going all the afternoon, and this morning I new-heated the piston and kept it going till dinner time at about fifteen strokes per minute with a steam of about one inch or at most two inches strong, and the longer it went the better it grew. A relapse of the engine would ruin our reputation here, and indeed elsewhere.'

Most of his time, however, Watt spent with drawings, calculations and correspondence, at his new home, Regent's Place, near Soho. He had married again. His second wife was Ann Macgregor, daughter of a well-to-do dyer of Glasgow. She insisted on a substantial house. She looked after Watt and his three children and his health began to improve.

The first important market for the steam engine was the Cornish copper and tin mines. They had had Newcomen engines for many years, with their heavy consumption of fuel, but coal was so expensive in Cornwall that it was doubtful if the mines could keep on.

During the next few years Watt spent long periods at Chacewater and Truro installing and supervising the engines. These were weary months for him; it was not work he liked. The miners were tough characters. 'Certainly they have the most ungracious manners of any people I have ever yet been amongst', he wrote, 'the bulk of them would not be disgraced by being classed with Wednesbury colliers.' They did not like his new method of fixing the royalty to be paid. This was based on one-third of the saving of fuel compared with the consumption of an ordinary Newcomen engine; there were endless disputes about it. Watt felt that he was incapable of dealing with these matters and appealed to Boulton to come down. 'If you had been here,' he wrote to Boulton after a disagreeable meeting, 'and gone to that meeting with your cheerful countenance and brave heart, perhaps they would not have been so obstinate.'

Watt varied between extreme anxiety and extreme confidence. He was continually in despair about the bad workmanship of his men. He asked too much of them to expect that they could remedy all the faults which might develop in a new and, for those days, complicated engine. His usual action was to ask Boulton to dismiss them. His anxiety was increased by the difficulty of getting money out of the Cornishmen. Then when an order came in he could be cock-a-hoop as the following unusual letter shows:

> 'Hallelujah! Hallelujah!
> We have concluded with Hawksbury,
> 217 l. per annum from Lady-day last:
> 275 l. 5s. for time past; 157 l. on account,
> We make them a present of 100 guineas,
> Peace and good fellowship on earth –
> Perrins and Evans to be dismissed –
> 3 more engines wanted in Cornwall –
> Dudley repentant and amendant.'

Perrins, Evans and Dudley were erring workmen. Boulton, however, was wiser and kept them on because he knew better could not be found.

By 1780, five years after the partnership was founded, forty pumping engines had been made and sold. The diagram shows the single-acting engine after numerous improvements.

The time had come to think of other uses for the steam engine. Watt was still at the height of his inventive powers and Boulton saw the opportunities for expanding the business. He wrote to Watt in the summer of 1781:

'There is no other Cornwall to be found, and the most likely line for the consumption of our engines is the application of them to mills which is certainly an extensive field. The people in London, Manchester and Birmingham are *steam mill mad*. I don't mean to hurry you but I think in the course of a month or two we should determine to take out a patent for certain methods of producing rotative motion of the fire-engine.'

This was the turning point. If Watt was successful it meant that for the next 20 years, until the patent expired, the firm would have the monopoly of supplying engines to the cotton mills and other mills throughout the country. He set to work. In those days an inventor had to declare his invention before

44

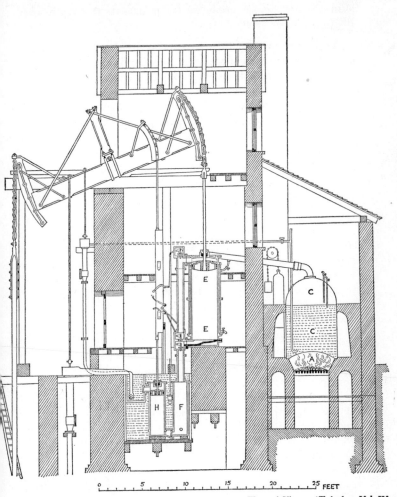

0   5   10   15   20   25 FEET

[From *A History of Technology*, Vol. **IV**

Watt's single-acting engine for pumping water for draining mines, 1788. The boiler C is placed in an outhouse, and the steam passes to the cylinder E, which is kept hot all the time by a separate steam jacket. F is the separate condenser and H an air-pump a magistrate before applying for a patent. A month after Boulton's letter he replied:

'Yesterday I went to Penrhyn and swore that I had invented certain new methods of applying the vibrating or reciprocating motion of steam or fire engines to produce a continued rotation or circular motion round an axis or centre, and thereby to give motion to the wheels of mills or other machines.'

There were difficulties. The main one was that the obvious method of converting the engine to rotary motion, the crank and connecting rod as used on the foot-lathe for centuries, was already covered by patent. Anxiety over the problem brought back his headaches. He wrote to Boulton:

'I tremble at the thought of making a complete set of drawings. I wish you could find me out a draughtsman of abilities; as I cannot stand it much longer. I am not philosopher enough to despise the ills of life; and when I suffer myself to get into a passion, I observe it hurts me more than it does anybody else. I never was cut out for business, and wish nothing so much as not to be obliged to do any; which perhaps will never fall to my lot; therefore I must drag on a miserable existence the best way I can.'

However, the specification was ready on time. The main invention was the epicyclic or sun-and-planet gear by which the shaft made two revolutions for each double stroke of the engine.

The second essential step was to make the engine double-acting, i.e. so that it could push as well as pull. In the pumping engine the piston rod was connected to the beam by a chain which could only transmit a pull. But for rotary action the force had to be transmitted in either direction. Watt invented a system of linked rods, known as the parallel motion. He was more proud of this invention than of any other. As soon as he had the idea he wrote to Boulton about it:

'I have started a new hare. I have got a glimpse of a method of causing a piston rod to move up and down perpendicularly by only fixing it to a piece of iron upon the beam, without chains or perpendicular guides or untowardly friction, arch heads, or other pieces of clumsiness; by which contrivance it

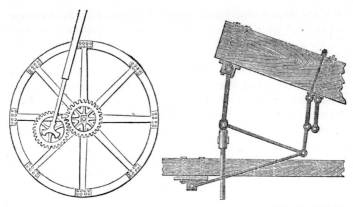

[From *Boulton and Watt*, by S. Smiles

Sun and planet motion   The parallel motion

answers fully to expectation. I have only tried it in a slight
model yet, so cannot build upon it, though I think it is a very
probable thing to succeed. It is one of the most ingenious
simple pieces of mechanism I have ever contrived, but I beg
nothing may be said on it till I specify.'

The parallel motion was first used on an engine supplied to
Whitbread's brewery; Watt informed Boulton that 'the
parallel motion of Whitbread's answers admirably'.

Orders for the new engine began to come in from all kinds of
mill, flour mills, malt mills, cotton mills, sugar cane mills, flint
mills. This use of the engine in manufacture necessitated
another invention. Some mechanism was required to maintain
constant engine speed when the load varied. Watt's solution
was the centrifugal governor, an old idea now first applied to
the steam engine. The governors controlled automatically a
valve in the steam inlet pipe. When the engine speed increased
the governors moved outwards and closed the valve, thus reducing the engine speed.

Watt's steam engine had now reached its final form. The
engine shown in Plate II was made in 1788 and was the first to

47

be fitted with a centrifugal governor. It was used in the Soho works to drive machinery for lapping or polishing steel and silver ornaments and it worked for 70 years. It developed about 12 horse power.

For the first time the partnership now began to make substantial profits, and Watt was relieved of his continual anxiety about money. Until 1800 all the world had to get its steam engines from Soho. By that date the firm had supplied 84 engines to cotton mills alone, and had made 321 engines altogether. Watt often said he wished to retire; he grew tired of the steam engine. But the works was too busy to let him go. He stayed on until the firm had to be reorganized. That was in 1800 when the condenser patent expired. Boulton and Watt no longer had a monopoly. Watt's son, James, and Boulton's son, Matthew, were ready to take over and so the fathers decided to build a new works at Smethwick, called the Soho Foundry, where the sons would make engines in competition with the rest of Britain, under the names of Boulton & Watt & Sons. The Soho Foundry became, and remained famous for many years.

Watt was now sixty-four and he had 19 years of retirement. These he enjoyed, probably more than his working life. He now had no business worries, he no longer suffered from headaches, and he had plenty to occupy his time. He was a great reader on all subjects and he travelled widely. He had a new house built at Handsworth, 20 minutes walk from the Soho Foundry, and he spent much of his time arranging the grounds. In a garret of the new house, Heathfield House, he had a workshop containing his work bench, foot-lathe and stove. There he continued inventing, as a hobby. Six years before his death he was busy on a machine for copying statuary; he wrote to William Murdoch, his chief assistant in the old days:

'I have done a little figure of a boy lying down and holding out one arm, very successfully; and another about six inches high and holding out both his hands, the legs also being separate. But I have been principally employed in making drawings for a complete machine, all iron, which has been a very serious job, as invention goes on very slowly with me now.'

He was now able to enjoy the honours he received. He was

elected a Fellow of the Royal Society, received a doctorate of laws from Glasgow University where he started as instrument maker: he was offered a baronetcy but, with typical modesty, refused it. He outlived all his friends. All he now wanted was a quiet life and finally to be buried 'in the most private manner without show or parade' beside Matthew Boulton. When he was asked to accept the honour and duties of sheriff for Staffordshire he declined saying:

'My inventions are giving employment to the best part of a million people, and having added many millions to the natural riches, I have a natural right to rest in my extreme age.'

THE ENGINEERING WORKERS

The men who were most directly affected by the coming of the steam engine were the millwrights. They were the men who, together with the blacksmiths and carpenters, erected the engines. There were only these three main trades in the early engineering work, and so the men had to be very versatile.

As their name suggests they were originally the men who constructed mills, mostly corn mills, throughout the country. They had done this for centuries; there were millwrights before the Norman conquest. Then they became skilled at other engineering work. A picture of them, as the all round skilled engineers of the eighteenth century, was given many years later by Sir James Fairbairn, a famous engineer who was himself apprenticed as a millwright.

'The millwright of former days was an intinerant engineer and mechanic of high reputation. He could handle the axe, the hammer and the plane with equal skill and precision; he could turn, bore or forge with the despatch of one brought up to these trades. Generally he was a fair mathematician, knew something of geometry, levelling and mensuration, and in some cases possessed a very competent knowledge of practical mathematics. He could calculate the velocities, strength and power of machines, and could draw in plan and section, and could construct buildings, conduits or water courses in all forms and under all conditions, required in his professional practice. He could build bridges, cut canals and perform a variety of

49

work now done by civil engineers. . . . This was the class of men with whom I associated in early life – proud of their calling, fertile in resource, and aware of their value in a country where the industrial arts were rapidly developing.'

The steam engine throve 'where the industrial arts were rapidly developing'. James Watt's chief assistant at Soho, William Murdock, was a millwright by trade. Murdock's father was a millwright and also a miller, and he invented some bevelled cast iron gear for mills. In the construction of the new engines the millwrights 'made the patterns, cast the iron, produced the plane surfaces with hammer, chisel and file, the cylindrical surfaces and bores with hand-tools in hand or foot-driven lathes'. The work was changing and developing all the time. Their skill was scarce. Boulton and Watt, for instance, could never get enough of it, and there were continual arguments about wages.

For a long time the millwrights had had their trade clubs which provided friendly benefits in times of sickness and death. These clubs or friendly societies began to negotiate wages with the masters. This was only possible where a considerable number of men were gathered together as, for instance, in engine construction or bridge building. When this happened they began to stand together against the masters, whereas previously they had stood together with the masters on behalf of the trade against the general public. They refused to work with men outside the societies. If men outside the society were taken on they would all leave the workshop in a body.

London was one of the main centres of the societies of mill-wrights, some of which were strong and more like trade unions than friendly societies. The chief of them, called the London Fellowship, met at the Bell Inn, Old Bailey. It was in London that Boulton and Watt established the big Albion Flour Mills at Southwark which, after they were equipped with a steam engine, became one of the sights of London. A few years after that the masters of London had become so alarmed at the organization among the millwrights that they petitioned Parliament to suppress it:

'A dangerous combination has for some time existed among the Journeymen Millwrights, within the metropolis, and the limits of 25 miles round the same, for enforcing a general increase in their wages, preventing the employment of such journeymen as refuse to join in their confederacy, and for other illegal purposes. Frequent conspiracies of this sort have been set on foot by the journeymen, and the masters have been so often obliged to submit, and that a demand for a further increase in wages has recently been made, which, not being complied with, the men, within the limits aforesaid, have refused to work; and a compliance with such a demand for an advance of wages hath generally been followed by further claims, with which it is impossible for the masters to comply, without occasioning so considerable advance in the price of mill work as most materially to affect the said business; and that in support of the said combination, the journeymen have established a general fund and raised subscriptions, and so regular and connected is their system that their demands are sometimes made regularly by all the journeymen at the same time, and at other times at some particular shop, and, in the case of non-compliance, the different workshops are wholly deserted by the men, and the journeymen are prohibited from applying for work until the master millwrights are brought to compliance, and the journeymen who have thus thrown themselves out of employ receive support meanwhile from their general fund.

'And therefore praying that leave may be given to exhibit a petition for leave to bring in a Bill, for the better preventing the unlawful combinations of workmen employed in the millwright business, and for regulating the wages of such workmen, in such a manner as the House shall deem meet.'

The millwrights were not, of course, the only trade to combine together in Societies – there were many others, tailors weavers, hatters, papermakers – but they were leading men, and therefore the rules of the House of Commons were waived to allow the petition to be heard immediately. A Bill to satisfy the masters was drawn up. Then on the suggestion of William Wilberforce a Bill to apply to all trades, not only to the millwrights, was substituted for it. The young William Pitt introduced the Bill and it was passed in great haste. The petition had been received on 25th April 1799 and by 2nd July in the same year the Bill received the royal assent. The Government was nervous of any unrest because the country was at war with France.

In this way the Combination Acts made all trade unions illegal and so they remained until the Acts were repealed 25 years later.

THE ILLEGAL TRADE UNIONS, 1800–1825

In spite of the fact that they were banned by law, the very early trade unions did not disappear because many trades felt a strong need to continue so as to negotiate with the masters, or if necessary strike against them. The law was not enforced against them everywhere but many were prosecuted and their members sent to prison.

Prosecutions took place mostly against the workers in the new power-driven factories, particularly in Lancashire and Yorkshire where the Government felt there was danger to law and order. Thus the president and secretary of the Bolton weavers were imprisoned for one and two years respectively. Cotton spinners of Manchester were arrested in 1819, and most of them sentenced to prison. In Scotland also, in 1812, after a strike of thousands of weavers over wages, the central committee of five were all sent to prison for periods ranging from four to eighteen months. There were many other examples. The strength of their organization was shown in the Manchester strike of spinners in 1810, in which several thousands took part and strike pay of £1,500 per week was distributed. Many unions disguised themselves as friendly societies and clubs.

Among the old skilled trades, such as millwrights, there was less prosecution. There were exceptions, such as the case of the compositors of *The Times* in 1810 who were sentenced to prison for being in a trade union by the Common Sergeant of London, Mr. John Sylvester, popularly known as Bloody Black Jack. Many skilled trades, some of them being old, had their societies which negotiated with the masters. For instance the Liverpool Ropemakers withdrew all their men when a firm tried to employ labourers. The firm tried to get men from Hull and Newcastle, but failed because the local societies had been informed. When it imported men from Glasgow, the rope-makers 'persuaded' them not to join the firm. Even the London workmen refused to supply the firm with yarn. The rope-makers' leaders were arrested for combination but this time they were acquitted by a Liverpool jury.

In these disputes there was widespread solidarity and mutual help among the societies in different trades. We find the small but strong society of London Goldbeaters lending considerable sums to the societies. Their cash book read:

May 29 1810	Paid ye Brushmakers	£15	0s.	0d.
	Lent ye Brushmakers	£10	0s.	0d.
June 26 1810	Paid ye Silversmiths	£10	0s.	0d.
July 24 1810	Paid ye Braziers	£10	10s.	0d.
	Paid ye Bookbinders	£10	0s.	0d.
	Paid ye Curriers	£10	0s.	0d.
August 21 1810	Lent ye Bit and Spurmakers	£5	0s.	0d.
	Lent ye Scalemakers	£5	0s.	0d.
December 11 1810	Lent ye Ropemakers	£10	0s.	0d.
July 20 1812	Lent ye Sadlers	£10	0s.	0d.
October 12 1812	Paid to Millwrights	£50	0s.	0d.

The Millwrights certainly continued to organize in spite of the law. They had three separate societies in London which were strong enough to fix a minimum wage and hours of work (6.0 a.m. to 6.0 p.m. in summer and from light until dark in winter).

Their power is illustrated by their reception of a young engineer from Newcastle upon Tyne who came up to London in 1810 to try his fortune. He was later the famous engineer, Sir William Fairbairn. He and a friend were taken on by William Rennie, the builder of Waterloo Bridge, but the foreman, Walker, told him he would have to join the Mill-wright's Society.

'Mr. Walker directed us to the Secretary of the Society, as they had none but Society men in the shop. On application to the Secretary we were informed that our claims could not be investigated until the next monthly meeting, and we had there-fore nearly four weeks to wait until the time of trial arrived. We manufactured two seven years' indentures and waited for the day on which we should appear before the arbitrators of our future destinies in London. Before the time arrived, we found, to our mortification, that the water mark on the stamped paper of the new indentures was three years later than the date of the indentures themselves. We had, therefore, to set to work, and erase the date, which no doubt awakened suspicion in the minds of the Committee when the indentures were presented . . . When the day of trial arrived we were at once declared illegitimate, and sent adrift to seek our fortunes elsewhere.'

No wonder that in the opinion of the employers the Combination Acts had no effect in preventing trade unions among engineers and millwrights.

While the millwrights' societies were strong they were doomed to be replaced by others. As new tools and machines, such as the slide rest on the lathe and the planer, were invented so new skills to operate them and new trades arose. The men in them formed new separate societies; in the eighteen twenties there had appeared the Friendly and Benevolent Society of Vicemen and Turners, the Friendly Society of Ironmoulders, the Mechanic's Friendly Union, and the Steam Engine Makers' Society. Eventually some of these new societies came together again with the old millwrights to form the Amalgamated Society of Engineers, which was the forerunner of the present Amalgamated Engineering Union.

Additional Reading

The Science Museum, *The First 100 Years*, H.M.S.O. 1957.
S. Smiles, *Boulton & Watt*, Murray 1904.
H. W. Dickinson and H. P. Vowles, *James Watt and the Industrial Revolution*, Longmans 1948.
J. B. Jefferys, *The Story of the Engineers*, Lawrence & Wishart 1945.

CHAPTER THREE

Road and Bridge Builders

TODAY Britain has a difficult road problem. Two hundred years ago also, there was a serious road problem but it was of a different kind. Whereas now it is caused by the great number of cars on the roads then it was due to the disrepair of the roads. This was because the old system of road maintenance since Queen Mary's reign had broken down. Each parish was responsible for its own roads and no money or labour could be found for them. People were concerned only with local roads and no one had the responsibility for through roads.

A new system of road maintenance came in with the turn-pike trusts. These trusts were local bodies of landowners and other well-to-do people which repaired roads and levied tolls at the gates to pay for them. They made some improvement but the knowledge and skill required to make good roads was lacking. No one knew how to make them or keep them up. What was required was new techniques of road making.

How badly new methods were needed is shown by the flood of complaints at the time. Loaded wagons and carts took so long that merchants preferred trains of pack-horses to carry their goods.

A famous traveller and journalist, Arthur Young reported on the state of the roads all over the country. The road in Lancashire between Preston and Wigan:

'I know not in the whole range of language terms sufficiently expressive to describe this infernal road. Let me seriously caution all travellers who may propose to travel this terrible country, to avoid it as they would the devils; for a thousand to one they break their necks or their limbs by overthrows or breakings-down – they will here meet with ruts, which I actually measured, *four feet deep*, and floating with mud only from a wet summer. What therefore must it be after a winter? The only mending it receives is tumbling in some loose stones which serve no other purpose than jolting a carriage in the most intolerable manner. These are not merely opinions, but facts; for I actually passed *three carts broken down* in those eighteen miles of execrable memory.'

Of the road in Essex between Billericay and Tilbury:
'Of all the cursed roads that ever disgraced this Kingdom in the very ages of barbarism none ever equalled that from Billericay to the King's Head at Tilbury. It is for near twelve miles so narrow that a mouse cannot pass by any carriage. I saw a fellow creep under his waggon to assist me to lift, if possible, my chaise over a hedge.'

In Suffolk, the road between Bury and Sudbury:
'I was forced to move as slow in it as in our unmended lane in Wales. For, ponds of liquid dirt, and a scattering of loose flints just sufficient to lame every horse that moves near them, with the addition of cutting vile grips across the road with the pretence of letting the water off, but without effect, altogether render at least twelve out of these sixteen miles as infamous a turnpike as ever was beheld.'

From Chepstow to Newport and Cardiff:
'What am I to say of the roads in this country! the turnpikes! as they have the assurance to call them and the hardiness to make one pay for? From Chepstow to the half-way house between Newport and Cardiff they continue mere rocky lanes, full of hugeous stones as big as one's horse, and abominable holes. The first six miles from Newport they were so detestable and without either direction posts or milestones that I could not well persuade myself I was on the turnpike . . . Whatever business carries you into in this country, avoid it, at least till they have good roads.'

Business was indeed increasing. The growth of iron machines, the manufacture of cotton goods and of steam engines meant that more and more heavy goods had to be carried somehow.

The new knowledge of road making came because it was so badly needed and it came in Britain mainly from three extraordinary men – John Metcalfe, Thomas Telford and John Loudon McAdam.

This man was known as Blind Jack of Knaresborough because as a boy of that village he lost his sight through smallpox. He had no training as a road builder or engineer. His only qualifications were a very thorough knowledge of the countryside gained through his travels, an extraordinary development of the other senses which some blind people have, and great energy and enterprise.

As a boy he learned to play the violin and earned money by playing at dances and assemblies. He bought a horse and rode all over Yorkshire. He visited London and walked back to Harrogate in six days in order to play the violin in the season there. He married the daughter of the local innkeeper. When he had settled down with his wife he tried various ways of supplementing his income as a violinist. One was fish-dealing which involved him in a great deal of travelling along the roads between the coast and the towns.

When Metcalfe was twenty-eight there occurred the Jacobite rising of 1745, in which the Scottish highlanders under the Young Pretender, Charles Edward, invaded England, and marched south as far as Derby before being turned back and eventually overwhelmed at the battle of Culloden Moor. With his violin, dressed in uniform, Blind Jack played marches at the head of a company of Yorkshire Volunteers in the English army as it pursued the Scots back to the north.

After this remarkable adventure of a blind man he really settled down at last. He bought a wagon and set up as a carrier, particularly between York and Knaresborough. This journey of 15 miles he made twice a week in summer and once a week in winter, often carrying soldiers' baggage. Knowing the roads like the back of his hand, where they were bad and where good and what traffic was passing, he soon made a very comfortable living.

This was his way of life until he was forty-seven or eight. By that time he had been musician, soldier, fish-dealer, wagoner, and thereby had come to know very well the roads of the north, particularly between the Humber and the Mersey. His blindness had taught him to know them better than most men with sight.

Until he was nearly fifty, therefore, he had not begun his great road making work. He had overcome his handicap through great strength of mind and enterprise and a very alert brain; he often surprised people with the speed of his mental calculations.

No one knew better than he the need for new roads. Many new turnpike trusts were beginning and Metcalfe thought that there would be a future for him in road construction. When therefore it was known that a turnpike road was to be made between Harrogate and Boroughbridge he proposed to the surveyor that he should build three miles of it. At that time there was no such thing as a road-contracting business or industry. Metcalf's reputation secured him the contract. He sold his carrier's business and began thirty years of road making. Many of these roads crossed the marshy moors of the Pennines and Metcalfe devised his own method of laying a road across a bog, which had been thought impossible. This was by putting down layers of small bundles of heather and ling, each layer across the other, and covering them with gravel and stone. In the next century George Stephenson used the same method of a floating road when he built the railway across Chat Moss.

During the following years Metcalfe made roads all over his own county of Yorkshire, for example from Wakefield to Doncaster, from Wakefield to Huddersfield, from Huddersfield to Halifax; then going into Lancashire, between Bury and Blackburn and between Ashton-under-Lyme and Stockport, and other important roads connecting Yorkshire with Lancashire. After this, going farther afield to Derbyshire and Cheshire and in the rocky Peak district, he built roads such as those between Macclesfield and Chapel-en-le-Frith and between Buxton and Whaley Bridge. In all about 180 miles of turnpike road, including many bridges, stand to his name.

The particular value of Metcalfe's roads was that many of them were made in the district where the first factories were appearing. In fact he himself invested his money in half a dozen jennies, and for a short time ran a small spinning business. Whereas the pack-horse had often been the only means of carriage, now wagons, carts and coaches could carry the materials, products and people. If it had not been for Metcalfe's work the factory system, with all the good and evil following it, would have developed more slowly.

Metcalfe was not only a contractor but, versatile as he was, he also personally surveyed and laid out the roads, often in difficult and hilly country. There is a contemporary account of this:

'I have several times met this man traversing the roads, ascending steep and rugged heights, with the assistance only of a long staff, exploring valleys and investigating their several extents, forms and situations, so as to answer his designs in the best manner. The plans which he makes, and the estimates he prepares, are done in a method peculiar to himself, and of which he cannot well convey the meaning to others. His abilities in this respect are, nevertheless, so great, that he finds constant employment. Most of the roads over the Peak in Derbyshire have been altered by his directions, particularly those in the vicinity of Buxton; and he is at this time constructing a new one betwixt Wilmslow and Congleton to open a communication with the great London road, without being obliged to pass over the mountains. I have met this blind projector while engaged in making his survey. He was alone as usual, and, amongst other conversation, I made some inquiries respecting this new road. It was really astonishing to hear with what accuracy he described its course and the nature of the different soils through which it was conducted. Having mentioned to him a boggy piece of ground it passed through, he observed that "that was the only place he had doubts concerning, and that he was apprehensive they had, contrary to his directions, been too sparing of their materials".'

Metcalfe continued road making until he was well over seventy. Although he was well-to-do by that time, not all his contracts were profitable. This depended on whether unforeseen difficulties in building occurred and whether he could get labour easily, for this was also the period of canal making which employed vast number of labourers. The very last road Metcalfe made in 1790, between Accrington and Hasleden, met with the difficulty that the demand for labour on the canals increased the wages he had to pay, so that after two years the result of the contract was a loss of £40.

When he was seventy-five he retired to a small farm he had bought. There he spent his last years, supervising the farm and dealing in hay and wood. He died at the age of ninety-two and left four surviving children, 20 grandchildren, and 90 great-grandchildren.

THOMAS TELFORD (1757–1834)

Very few districts of England had a Blind Jack and good methods of road making needed to be spread throughout the country. Thomas Telford spent much of his life doing this. He was nicknamed the Colossus of Roads but he was not only a road maker. He was also a great bridge builder and he is still famous for his bridge over the Menai Straights on the London-Holyhead road to Ireland. Scores of other bridges, of stone and of iron, stand to his name, and he built many canals. He was first a stonemason, then architect, then engineer and finally he founded the profession of civil engineer.

Telford was a pioneer in two ways. He used a technique of road making which was new to Britain. Although he was a stonemason by training, he developed new ways of using iron for bridge building.

He began his life of great achievements as the son of a shepherd in a remote hilly corner of Eskdale in the county of Dumfries. The little shepherd's shieling of mud walls and thatch on the Megget Water, a tributary of the river Esk, was the starting point of the Menai bridge. Telford was an orphan before he was a year old and his mother had to move into one room of a cottage lower down the valley. Here he grew up, helping the farmers as soon as he was big enough and until his uncle paid the fees for him to attend the parish school.

As soon as he left school Telford was apprenticed to a stonemason in Langholm. This was very valuable later on when engineers and contractors respected him because he knew the work so well. His training was very thorough; the local landowner was building many farmhouses and bridges and today Telford's mark can be seen in the masonry blocks of a bridge over the Esk. 'Laughing Tom', as he was called, remained in Langholm as a journeyman for some years and became a first-class craftsman in stone.

During this time he gained another qualification which gave enjoyment for the rest of his life. At school he had been good at reading and writing and now he was introduced to the whole range of English literature by an elderly spinster who lent him all her books to read on the hillside or by the cottage fire. Among these was Milton's *Paradise Lost*. Telford could hardly express his feelings: he said, 'I read and read, and glowred; then read and read again.' Throughout his life he wrote verse at various times to express his feelings. At about this time he wrote the following lines about himself:

> 'Nor pass the tentie curious lad,
> Who o'er the ingle hangs his head,
> And begs of neighbours books to read,
> For hence arise
> Thy country's sons, who far are spread,
> Baith bold and wise.'

Before he left home for good Telford worked for a year in Edinburgh on the building of the New Town but at the age of twenty-four he went to London like so many other Scots. There he quickly found work on the new Somerset House and he was soon promoted to first-class mason. But he was ambitious and planned to start his own business in partnership with a fellow mason. He wrote home:

'Tis impossible to inform you of much concerning myself at present. I am laying schemes of a pretty extensive kind if they succeed, for you know my disposition is not to be satisfied unless when plac'd in some conspicuous Point of view. My innate vanity is too apt to say when looking on the Common drudges, here as well as other places, "I am born to command ten thousand slaves like you" – This is too much, but at the same time it is too true, for I find the workmen here more ignorant than they are in Eskdale Shores.'

The partnership came to nothing because of lack of capital but something better happened. Telford went up into the foreman class for he obtained the job of superintending the construction of various buildings in Portsmouth Dockyard.

At the age of twenty-six he had already made a big step forward in his ambition. Yet although he now had a responsible job he still used every hour of the day to educate himself for the future. A letter written in 1786 shows how he occupied his day in doing this.

'You ask me what I do all winter – I rise in the morning at 7 o'clock and will continue to get up earlier till it comes to 5. I then set seriously to work to make out Accounts, write on business, or draw till breakfast which is at 9 – next go to breakfast and get into the Yard about 10. Then all the officers are in their offices and if they have anything to say to me or me to them, we do it. This and going around amongst the several works brings my dinner time, which is about 2 o'clock; and an hour-and-a-half serves this and at half after 3 I again make my appearance when there's generally something wanted and I again go round and see what is going on – and draw until 5 then go to tea till 6 – then I come back to my room and write, draw or read until half after 9 – then comes supper and bedtime . . . my business requires a great deal of drawing and writing – and this I always take care to keep under by having everything ready. Then as knowledge is my most ardent pursuit, a thousand things occur that would pass unnoticed by good easy people who are contented with trudging on in the beaten Path, but I am not contented until I can reason on every particular.

'I am now very deep in Chemistry . . . I have plenty of fire and candle allowed me and often my dear Andrew do I wish to have you along with me . . . You would find Andrew that I am not idle but much in the old way of stirring the Lake about one to prevent it stagnating . . . I am powdered every day, and have a clean shirt three times a week; Portsmouth is what you have said of it, but what's that to me. The man that will neglect the Business and suffer himself to be led by the Nose deserves to be P-x'd! . . . I wish Andrew that you saw me at the present instant surrounded by Books, Drawings, Compasses, Pencils and Pens; great is the confusion but it pleases my taste and *that's enough.*'

When the Portsmouth Dockyard work was finished Telford had a stroke of good luck which launched him well on the way to great achievement. He had advised a wealthy landowner about alterations to one of his houses near Langholm and this man's influence now obtained him the post of Surveyor of Public Works for the County of Salop in 1787 when he was thirty years old.

Engineering was not yet a recognized profession. Telford's ambition was to make a name as an architect and he studied hard to do so. Much of his work was architectural. He was responsible for renovations to Shrewsbury Castle, rebuilding the High Street, making plans for houses and squares, for a gaol and infirmary and for churches. He became better off and began to send money to Eskdale to his mother. He wrote to his closest friend there:

'I have at present the opportunity of earning money. You have not and I therefore insist on the privilege of sharing a little . . . This is not ostentation because I don't wish anybody to know of it besides yourself . . . To set my mother and you above the fear of want has always been my first object altho' I have never told you so before – and next to that to be that somebody that you have always told me I had the right to be. And I humbly presume that there is something in it – it may be self-confidence but I think I have observed that there has always been a bustle where I was.'

Busy as he was, living in Shrewsbury gave him the opportunity to continue reading and writing poetry, to visit the theatre and even to go to concerts, though he confessed he could not enjoy music. Indeed he asked himself whether this was because of a defect in him or lack of training when young.

However, it was the bridge building he had to undertake which in the end led him away from architecture to engineering. Between 1790 and 1796 he built forty bridges of very different sizes, some of stone and some of iron. The most remarkable were those over the river Severn. These were at Buildwas, Bridgnorth and Bewdley, the first of which had been carried away and the others damaged by the Severn floods which Telford knew well.

The Buildwas bridge was a little way above the famous Iron Bridge cast by Abraham Darby III and Telford seized his first opportunity to use iron. The bridge was a single span of 130 feet, was longer than Darby's bridge but only half its weight. Such was the improvement in only 20 years. The Bewdley bridge was of local stone and Telford was very pleased with it and with John Simpson, a mason from Shrewsbury:

'The dry season . . . has enabled us to raise Bewdley Bridge as by enchantment. We have thus raised a magnificent Bridge over the River Severn in one Season. Which is no contemptible work for John Simpson and your humble servant . . . John Simpson is a treasure of talents and integrity . . . and he has now all the works of any magnitude in this great and rich district.'

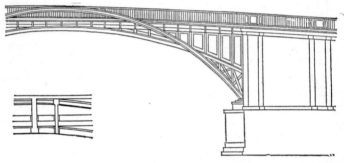

[From *A History of Technology*, Vol. IV

Telford's iron bridge at Buildwas, 1795

Now there was a turning point in Telford's life which set him on the path to becoming a famous engineer, rather than an architect. He was thirty-six. In 1793 he was appointed 'General Agent, Surveyor, Engineer, Architect and Overlooker' of the new Ellesmere Canal. This canal was to link the Mersey with the Dee at Chester and then with the Severn at Shrewsbury. It was to carry chiefly iron and coal and it was backed by the Shropshire ironmasters. Telford held this post for 12 years and by the end he had a national reputation as an engineer. He wrote:

'It is the greatest Work, I believe, that is now in hand in this

Kingdom and will not be completed for many years to come . . . this is a great and laborious undertaking, but the line which it opens is vast and noble and coming in this honourable way I thought it too great an opportunity to be neglected, especially as I have stipulated my right to carry on my Architectural profession . . . It will require great exertions but it is worthy of them all. There is a very great Aqueduct over the Dee, besides Bridges over several Rivers which cross the Line of March.'

Part of the canal crossed difficult hilly country and there were in fact three aqueducts, at Chirk over the river Ceiriog, at Longdon over the river Tern, and – the greatest – Pont Cysyllte over the river Dee. The first two were a preparation for the third. He tried out successfully what he called 'a principle entirely new'; this was to carry the water in a long cast-iron trough along the aqueducts.

The great aqueduct of Pont Cysyllte took ten years to build, partly because of a financial slump. In all that time under Telford's supervision only one life was lost. This was typical of his great care with men's lives. Pont Cysyllte had nineteen spans and a total length of 1,007 feet. The stone piers carried the cast-iron trough at a height of 127 feet above the river. The trough was 11 feet 10 inches wide. The problem of carrying a canal at such a height had never been tackled before and it called for new methods of construction. One of these was to have the stone piers hollow above a certain height but strengthened by internal cross walls.

It was marvellous for people far beneath in the valley to look up and see the boats gliding over their heads. No wonder it was called 'the stream in the sky'.

Telford now returned to work in his native country, but far in the Highlands, not in the Lowlands where he was born; for nearly 20 years he was in charge of a great road, bridge and canal building project.

The Highlands had never recovered from the Stuart rising of 1745 when the clans were suppressed by General 'Butcher' Cumberland, and the result was poverty, emigration and despair. Communications were so bad that large parts of the Highlands were cut off, and the Government at last decided

65

to do something. Two commissions were therefore set up, one for Highland roads and bridges and the other for the Caledonian Canal through the Great Glen from Fort William to Moray Firth on the east coast. Telford was made Engineer for both in 1803.

First he carried out a great survey, travelling over the whole area:

'I have carried regular surveys along the Rainy West through the middle of the tempestuous wilds of Lochaber, on each side of the habitation of the far-famed Johnny Groats, around the shores of Cromarty, Inverness and Fort George, and likewise the coast of Murray. The apprehension of the weather changing for the worse has prompted me to incessant and hard labour so that I am now almost lame and blind.'

A few months later he wrote:

'I have been kept in continual motion from the Country to the Town, and from the Town to the Country . . . Never when awake – and perhaps not always when asleep – have my Scotch Surveys been absent. My plans are completed, the Draft of my Report has been made out . . . and I hope to deliver in the whole in the course of a few days. I shall then be fully committed, and then the L . . D have mercy upon me – or rather, may they be productive of good and that good benefit Scotland.'

When the new road system was finished some 18 years later it stretched from Fort William to Thurso in the extreme north and across to Skye in the extreme west, as well as from Carlisle to Glasgow in the south. Some 920 miles of new road and over 1,000 bridges of all sizes had been built. The work was pushed on relentlessly in all weathers with great physical hardship and enormous labour. It was Telford's greatest achievement. He organized the whole work in six Highland districts – Argyll, Badenoch, Lochaber, Skye, Ross-shire, Caithness and Sutherland.

At the same time Telford had surveyed and planned the Caledonian Canal which took 18 years to complete and cost £900,000. It was to save ships going round the North of Scotland through the Pentland Firth, and also so that they could avoid French privateers. The work was tremendous. Scores of locks and cuttings had to be made, often in the rock. At one of these cuttings, the great summit cutting at Laggan, Robert Southey, the poet-laureate and a friend of Telford, described the scene:

'Here the excavations are what they call "at deep cutting", this being the highest ground in the line, the Oich flowing to the East, the Lochy to the Western sea ... The earth is removed by horses walking along the bench of the Canal, and drawing the laden cartlets up one incline plane, while the emptied ones, which are connected with them by a chain passing over pullies, are let down another. This was going on in numberless places, and such a mass of earth had been thrown up on both sides along the whole line, that the men appeared in the proportion of emmets to an ant-hill amid their own work. The hour of rest for men and horses is announced by blowing a horn; and so well have the horses learnt to measure time by their own exertions and sense of fatigue, that if the signal be delayed five minutes, they stop of their own accord without it ...'

Though the canal was a great engineering achievement it never paid for itself.

Telford is best known today for the Menai Bridge, which came as the last link in making a new road system to Holyhead for Ireland. Irish members of Parliament had demanded improved communication between London and Dublin, and the Post Office could not operate mail coaches west of Shrewsbury because of the bad road. In 1815, when Telford was fifty-eight, he was asked by the Government to survey the route. It took his three assistants eighteen months to do this. For the Shrewsbury–Holyhead section he chose the route Llangollen–Bettwys-y-Coed–Capel Curig–Lake Ogwen and the Nant Ffrancon pass through the heart of the mountains. Within two years coaches could get through to Bangor.

For this road Telford used the famous technique which he had developed in the Highlands. His instructions in his own words were:

'Upon the level bed prepared for the road materials the bottom course, or layer of stone, is to be set by hand in the

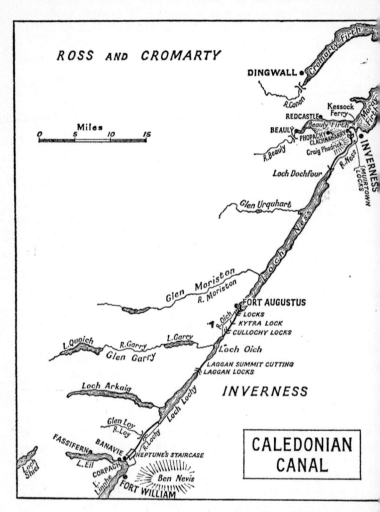

ROSS AND CROMARTY

DINGWALL

Miles
0   5   10   15

Cromarty Firth

R.Conan

Kessock
Ferry

REDCASTLE

BEAULY

R.Beauly

PHOPACHY
CLACHNAHARRY

Beauly Firth

Moray Firth

INVERNESS

Craig Phadrick

R.Ness

INVERNESS
(MUIRTOWN
LOCKS)

Loch Dochfour

Glen Urquhart

Loch Ness

Glen Moriston

R. Moriston

FORT AUGUSTUS

LOCKS

KYTRA LOCK

CULLOCHY LOCKS

R. Oich

L.Quoich

R.Garry

L.Garry

Glen Garry

Loch Oich

LAGGAN SUMMIT CUTTING

LAGGAN LOCKS

Loch Arkaig

INVERNESS

Glen Loy

R.Loy

Loch Lochy

R.Lochy

FASSIFERN

BANAVIE

NEPTUNE'S STAIRCASE

Loch
Shiel

L. Eil

CORPACH

Ben Nevis

L.
Linnhe

FORT WILLIAM

CALEDONIAN
CANAL

[From *Thomas Telford*, by L. T. C· Rol

form of a close firm pavement. They are to be set in the broadest edges lengthwise across the road, and the breadth of the upper beds is not to exceed four inches in any case. All the irregularities of the upper part of the said pavement are to be broken off by a hammer, and all the interstices to be filled with stone chips, firmly wedged together by hand with a light hammer. The middle eighteen feet of pavement is to be coated with hard stone as nearly cubical as possible, broken to go through a $2\frac{1}{2}$ inch ring, to a depth of six inches, four of these six inches to be first put on and worked by traffic, after which the remaining two inches can be put on. The work of setting the paving stones must be executed with the greatest care and strictly according to the foregoing directions, or otherwise the stones will become loose and in time may work up to the surface of the road. When the work is properly executed, no stone can move; the whole of the material to be covered with $1\frac{1}{2}$ inches of good gravel, free from clay or earth.'

He insisted on accurate grading of stones and kept bins for them along the route. A road made by hand with such care was bound to be expensive. Telford's skill was shown in the moderate gradients employed. He determined to have no gradient more than one in twenty and the maximum gradient, which was over the summit of the Nant Ffrancon pass, is one in twenty-two. The road was made to last and it has lasted.

Now remained the problem of crossing the Menai Straits, a problem which many people had thought about for many years. The Admiralty said that all ships (with the lofty masts of those days) must pass under any bridge. Telford therefore designed a suspension bridge, although only one large one had so far been built in Britain.

There was a single span of 579 feet suspended 100 feet above water at high tide, the total length of the bridge being 1,710 feet. The bridge platform was held by 16 massive chains, each weighing about 20 tons, composed of iron links each five feet long slung from the top of the two great masonry piers. Telford was extremely careful to test all calculations by experiments. The strength of each link was tested, as well as the first chain and the power required to raise it into position.

After many months the day arrived for raising into position

the first chain. The method was to float the central part of the chain on a raft into position under the bridge, connect it with one end of the chain fastened to one of the piers, then haul up the chain by capstan to the other pier. Telford was so anxious that he could not sleep. Here is the scene:

'An immense assemblage collected to witness the sight; the day – the 26th of April – being bright, calm and in every way propitious. At half-past two, about an hour before high water, the raft bearing the main chain was cast off from near Treborth Mill, in the Caernarvon side. Towed by four boats, it began to move gradually from the shore, and with the assistance of the tide, which caught it at its further end, it swung slowly and majestically round to its position between the main piers, where it was moored. One end of the chain was then bolted to that which hung down the face of the Caernarvon pier; whilst the other was attached to ropes connected with strong capstans fixed on the Anglesea side, the ropes passing by means of blocks over the top of the pyramid of the Anglesea pier. The capstans for hauling in the ropes bearing the main chain, were two in number, manned by about 150 labourers. When all was ready, the signal was given to "Go along!" A band of fifers struck up a lively tune; the capstans were instantly in motion, and the men stepped round in a steady trot. All went well. The ropes gradually coiled in. As the strain increased, the pace slackened a little; but "Heave away, now she comes!" was sung out. Round went the men, and steadily and safely rose the ponderous chain.

'The tide had by this time turned, and bearing upon the side of the raft, now getting free of its load, the current floated it away from under the middle of the chain still resting on it, and it swung easily off the water. Until this moment a breathless silence pervaded the watching multitude; and nothing was heard among the working party on the Anglesea side but the steady tramp of the men at the capstans, the shrill music of the fife and the occasional order to "Hold on!" or "Go along!" But no sooner was the raft seen floating away, and the great chain safely swinging in the air, than a tremendous cheer burst forth along both sides of the Straits.'

In the following months the other chains were raised in the

same way and on a cold dark night of January 1826 the bridge was opened when the down Royal London and Holyhead mail coach passed over it for the first time.

While this work was going on Telford had designed the Conway bridge. This was of similar design except that the towers were castellated to harmonize with Conway Castle. The tidal sands made a great approach embankment necessary. This bridge was opened only six months after Menai.

Telford was now sixty-nine and he had eight more years to live. He carried out drainage in the Fens. He was made a Fellow of the Royal Society and received a knighthood from Sweden in recognition of his work on the Gotha Canal, although he refused to have it recognized in England as he

[From *A History of Technology*, Vol. IV

Telford's Menai bridge, 1826

preferred to be known only by his works. At the age of seventy-four he went on a trip by road steam carriage from London to Stony Stratford because he believed these carriages had a future. In his retirement it gave him great satisfaction that the young Institution of Civil Engineers received a Royal Charter and thus official recognition. He was the first president of the Institution, founded in 1818; he made sure it had come to stay, and thus put civil engineering on its feet as a profession.

JOHN LOUDON MCADAM (1756–1836)

McAdam was so famous as a road builder that his name became a part of the English language. Roads were 'macadamized', and people in the nineteenth century spoke of 'water-bound macadam' and in the twentieth century of 'tar macadam'. Macadam roads spread throughout Europe and the United States.

Telford's method of construction was to ensure proper

drainage of the road, but the very thorough foundations made it expensive. McAdam's method was to get proper drainage but at low cost.

Although he was a Scot, like Telford, his birth and upbringing were quite different. He had money or made it in business in New York as a young man. On his return to Britain he became deputy-lieutenant of Ayrshire and a trustee of a turnpike trust. This aroused his interest in road construction. He spent thousands of pounds of his own on experiments in different ways of making roads, road repairs, and inspecting thousands of miles. After some years of this he became surveyor-general of the Bristol road trusts and, using his own system, set about rebuilding their 180 miles of road. This was when he was fifty-nine.

McAdam believed that the expensive stone foundation laid by hand, as in the Telford road, was unnecessary. Provided the earth was made dry and kept dry, the road surface could be laid directly on it and it would carry the weight of the traffic. Thus the road kept some resilience, which was better for the horses. However, it was essential that the earth should be properly drained and kept dry by spreading on it a layer ten inches deep of very carefully graded stone chips. After this was well pressed down by the traffic two additional layers were put down. No stone was to weigh more than six ounces.

Here is what he wrote:

'As no artificial road can be made so good as the natural soil in a *dry state*, it is necessary to preserve this state. The first operation should be the reverse of digging a trench. The road should not be sunk below, but raised above, the adjacent ground; that there be a sufficient fall to take off the water, so that it should be some inches below the level of the ground upon which the road is, either by making the drains to lower ground or, if that be not practicable from the nature of the country, then the soil upon which the road is to be laid, must be raised some inches above the level of the water.

'Having secured the soil from *under* water, the road-maker is next to secure it from rain-water, by a solid road, of clean, dry stone, or flint, so selected, prepared and laid, as to be impervious to water; and this cannot be effected, unless the greatest care be taken, that no earth, clay, chalks, or other matter, that will hold water, be used with the broken stone; which must be so laid, as to unite by its own angles into a firm, compact, impenetrable body.'

This system was so new that before any large amounts of money could be spent Parliament had a special investigation and report made. However the methods were efficient and the roads were much easier and cheaper to make. Parliament repaid McAdam the money he had spent and made him a grant of two thousand pounds. In 1827, at the age of seventy-one, he became surveyor-general of the Metropolitan roads.

The roads by Metcalfe, Telford and McAdam made possible in Britain fast coach services, the best in Europe. An average of between 9 and 10 m.p.h. was common; the mail was carried from London to Birmingham in twelve hours. But very soon people began to talk about railways.

THE STONEMASONS

We know little about the lives and working conditions of the masons and other craftsmen and the army of labourers who worked for Telford and McAdam. There were undoubtedly societies of the men who worked with the materials used, stone and iron. In the same year that the Menai bridge, with its great iron suspension chains, was begun ironfounders were prosecuted under the Combination Laws for having trade unions.

The stonemasons were a very old craft. As they wandered all over the country from one job to another they were unlikely to have local guilds. In the Middle Ages an Act of Parliament prohibited their 'yearly congregations and confederacies'. However, these societies of master craftsmen continued for hundreds of years. Their aim was to maintain their standard of living. A few years before the birth of Telford one of these societies, the masons' lodge of Atchisons Haven, in Scotland passed the following resolution:

'The Company of Atchisons Haven being mett together, have found Andrew Kinghorn guilty of a most atrocious crime against the whole trade of masonry, and he not submitting

73

himself to the Company for taking his work so cheap that no man could have his bread of it. Therefore in not submitting himself he has excluded himself from the said Company; and therefore the said Company doth hereby enact that no man, neither fellow craft nor enter'd apprentice after this shall work as journeyman under the said Andrew Kinghorn, under the penalty of being cut off as well as he. Likewise if any man shall follow the example of the said Andrew Kinghorn in taking work at eight pounds Scots per rood the walls being twenty feet high, and rebates at eighteen pennies Scots per foot, that they shall be cut off in the same manner.'

Later, as the great schemes of Telford and McAdam developed, there appeared big contractors who could undertake work far beyond the power of the small master. As these contractors began to employ large numbers of masons so the masons began to form themselves into friendly societies and trade unions. This happened during Telford's lifetime. A few years before his death in 1834 the masons were foremost in forming the National Operative Builders' Union. A little later they formed their own Operative Stonemasons' Friendly Society.

The Operative Builders' Union, which had 6,000 members, had ambitious plans for taking over the whole industry and running it as a co-operative, but it was not strong enough to deal with the lock-outs and strikes which broke out. In London a strike against Cubitt, the big contractor, caused the Union to collapse. However, the Stonemasons' Society remained and continued to be a strong union throughout the century.

Additional Reading

L. T. C. Rolt, *Thomas Telford*, Longmans 1958.
S. Smiles, *Lives of the Engineers: Metcalfe and Telford*, Murray 1904.
S. and B. Webb, *History of Trade Unionism*, Longmans 1920.

CHAPTER FOUR

The Toolmakers

THIS chapter is about the invention of the first machine tools. Without these the steam engines of Watt and the jennies, mules and looms could not be made accurately and only a few of them could be made at a time.

Before the three toolmakers named below came on the scene, a very early machine tool was invented by John Wilkinson, the great ironmaster who was so mad on iron that he made himself an iron coffin. This was his boring-mill, first made to improve the boring of big gun-barrels. It was more successful than any before because the long rod with the cutting tool at its head was held rigid with the cylinder and thus a true cut was obtained.

This boring-mill was very important because all the cylinders for Watt's steam engines were made with it for twenty years. It gave the accuracy required then, as a letter from Watt's partner, Matthew Boulton shows:

'Wilkinson hath bored us several cylinders almost without Error; that of 50 inches diameter for Bentley and Company doth err the thickness of an old shilling in no part . . .'

JOSEPH BRAMAH (1748–1814)

Bramah was born in Yorkshire where his father was tenant of a small farm. After going to the village school he started work on his father's farm. As a boy he showed a marked ability with tools. Then an injury to his leg made him unable to do farm work. This was a blessing in disguise for it resulted in his being apprenticed to the village carpenter. Thus he became a craftsman and gained the skill he was to use as an inventor.

As soon as his apprenticeship was finished he decided to go to London, like many others. There he found work with a cabinet maker and soon after set up his own small business. This led him to make his first patented invention which had nothing to do with tool making. It was his improved water closet, made in 1778 when he was thirty. The water closet was usually placed in a built-in cupboard and, as this was part of his business, Bramah had decided to improve on the unsatisfactory apparatus of the time. Improvements in house drainage were now becoming essential as the population of towns increased.

It was as a lock maker that Bramah became famous in his day. He moved to a bigger workshop in Pimlico and spent some years on inventing an improved lock which could not be picked, for which there was a great demand. At length, in 1784 he patented a completely fool-proof lock. So confident was he that he put a notice in his window in Piccadilly – 'The artist who can make an instrument that will pick or open this lock shall receive two hundred guineas the moment it is produced.' This was a large sum to be offered by a cabinet maker, or engine maker as Bramah now described himself. However it was quite safe. The money was not won until 1851, sixty-seven years later, when an American mechanic succeeded in opening the lock after working at it for fifty hours.

Because this lock was so complicated Bramah had to make a number of machine tools so that it could be made at reasonable cost. He employed young Henry Maudslay to help him with this and Maudslay made many of the tools before he left Bramah and became an independent inventor.

'Bramah used milling cutters mounted on the spindle of a lathe while the part to be machined was held in an indexing-bush in a quick-vice grip mounted on a lathe bed. These tools have been preserved in the Science Museum, London, together with a machine for sawing slots in the lock-barrels, and a spring-winding machine. This latter machine is made on the lines of a screw-cutting lathe, having a saddle that traverses the whole length of the bed and is drawn along by a lead-screw. The lead-screw is driven from the head-stock by change-gears which permit the relative speed of headstock-rotation and saddle-travel to be varied, so that springs of different pitch can be made. Instead of a cutting tool, however, the saddle carries

76

a reel of wire which is wound on to an arbor held between centres. This machine is a forerunner of Maudslay's screw-cutting lathe.'

Bramah's next achievement, in 1795, was a hydraulic press and he followed this two years later with the beer-pump used to pump up beer from the casks below. He next showed his versatility by inventing in 1802 a wood-planing machine which was used for many years in Woolwich Arsenal.

Bramah went on making many inventions, the most notable of which was a machine for numbering bank notes, made for the Bank of England. In 1814 he was supervising the use of his hydraulic press in uprooting forest trees when he caught cold and died from pneumonia. So died the man who might be called the father of machine tools. His influence was very great because he trained many other inventors and mechanics in his workshops.

HENRY MAUDSLAY (1771–1831)

Maudslay was an even more remarkable inventor. His inventions covered the basic essentials of mechanical engineering – the production of accurate plane surfaces; the use of a slide rest on the lathe; the production of accurate screws; and all-metal construction of machines.

Maudslay's father must have had a big influence on his career. The father, William Maudslay, was a joiner by trade and he worked at making textile machinery which was then still made of wood. He enlisted in the Royal Artillery and, being wounded overseas, was sent home for discharge to Woolwich, the headquarters of the corps. There he got work as a storekeeper and settled down. Maudslay's birthplace was near to the Arsenal and he naturally started work there.

This was at the age of twelve and at that tender age he was employed in making and filling cartridges. After two years he was put in the carpenters' shop but after another year he found the work he liked doing more than anything else when he was moved to the blacksmith's shop. There he became a first-rate smith and metal worker and his skill became well known in the London workshops.

77

When, therefore, Joseph Bramah was in difficulties with his patent lock and he heard of Maudslay's skill he sent for him, although Maudslay was then only eighteen. Since he had not served an apprenticeship and was such a youngster, Bramah and the foreman were doubtful if he could do the work in that famous workshop. How Maudslay proved his ability is described by Samuel Smiles:

'Pointing to a worn-out vice-bench, he said to Bramah, "perhaps if I can make that as good as new by six o'clock tonight, it will satisfy your foreman that I am entitled to rank as a tradesman and take my place among your men, even though I have not served a seven years' apprenticeship." Off went Maudslay's coat, up went his shirt sleeves, and to work he set with a will upon the old bench. The vice jaws were re-steeled, filed up, re-cut, all the parts cleaned and made trim, and set into form again. By six o'clock the old vice was screwed up to its place, its jaws were hardened and let down to proper temper and the old bench was made to look so smart and neat that it threw all the neighbouring benches into the shade. It was examined and pronounced a first rate job . . . and next Monday morning he came on as one of the regular hands.'

Maudslay stayed with Bramah for ten years until he was twenty-eight and had become head foreman. It was a great opportunity to develop his inventive power. From being a highly skilled craftsman (he actually made the first Bramah patent lock which was exhibited in the Piccadilly shop window) he invented, designed and made machine tools to make the locks. He was successful in another way too, for he courted and won Bramah's housemaid, Sarah Tindel.

His wage was still 30s. a week but he knew he was worth more and he needed more as he had started a family. When he was refused an increase in wages he left and set up his own business in 1797. This was a small workshop and smithy in Wells Street off Oxford Street. His reputation followed him, he took on a journeyman to help and after five years, finding the place too small, he moved to a bigger workshop in Margaret Street, Cavendish Square, where he could employ more men.

His first important order was for a whole plant of machine tools to be used for making ships' blocks in Portsmouth dockyard. But before this occurred he made his two most important inventions -- the slide rest, and the screw-cutting lathe.

The slide rest was called 'Maudslay's Go-cart' and it is not difficult to see why. The lathe had been known for centuries, but the operator had to hold very firmly under his arm a heavy turning tool on a rest against the revolving metal. On a big job it was tiring work and accuracy depended on the operator being able to maintain the same pressure on the tool all the time. This led Maudslay in 1794, while he was still with Bramah, to invent the slide rest in which the cutting tool was fixed in the rest.

[From *One hundred and fifty years progress, 1811–1961*, Amalgamated Engineering Union

The early lathe, a mainly wooden construction, with the tool held manually

The screw-cutting lathe was produced a few years later in about 1800 in Maudslay's first small workshop. It depended on the use of a lead-screw and change-gears. The idea was not new. Indeed Leonardo da Vinci had designed a screw-cutting machine with lead-screws and change-wheels as early as the fifteenth century but it was never made. Maudslay, however, was the first to combine slide rest, lead-screw and change-gears in a practical screw-cutting lathe. Before this every screw thread had to be made by hand and each nut was different from another. After this the way was open to the standardization of screw threads as carried out by Joseph Whitworth in the next generation.

'Maudslay's original screw-cutting lathe no longer possesses its gear wheels; they would have been fixed on the three spindles on the right, thus linking the lead-screw with the head-stock. The slide rest, driven by the lead-screw, travels on two triangular bars. This lathe is notable from being made entirely of metal and marks the abandonment of wood in the construction of metal-working machines.' (Plate III.)

It was Maudslay's contract for the Portsmouth Dockyard block-making machinery which really made his name widely known. Pulley blocks were an essential part of all sailing vessels for raising and lowering the sails, yards and masts. Tens of thousands were made every year. One 74-gun man-of-war alone required 1,400 blocks of different sizes; the Admiralty needed 100,000 a year, and England was in the middle of a long war with France.

The Admiralty decided to introduce labour-saving machinery for the blocks at Portsmouth. It was designed by Marc Isambard Brunel (father of Brunel the railway engineer) who had been a royalist refugee from revolutionary France. When Brunel was searching for someone who could make the complicated machines he was put in touch with Maudslay.

It was not a simple job. Each pulley block consisted of the shell, the sheaves which turned inside the shell, and the pins to fasten them together. The blocks had to be completely reliable and easy running. The whole of the block-making machinery was completed by Maudslay in 1808 after six years' work. There were no less than 43 machines: these carried out all the operations necessary to convert the elm logs used into pulley blocks, except for fitting and polishing. They included sawing-, boring-, mortising-, shaping-, rounding-, and milling-machines. They were worked by a 32-h.p. steam engine.

The plant was a complete success. Its output was 130,000 blocks per year. Much labour was saved and the Admiralty expenditure greatly reduced. Some of the machines were still being used until recent years. This was one of the first examples of mass-production by the use of machine tools, 150 years ago.

'The machine illustrated could cut mortises in two blocks at a time. The shaft rotating at 400 r.p.m. imparted a reciprocating motion to the chisels, which carried projecting tongues to clear the chips of wood. A ratchet actuated by a cam on a shaft, engaged a toothed wheel on the lead-screw which caused the block-holder to advance after each cut. At a predetermined point the process was finished by automatically disengaging the ratchet. This machine is the earliest mortising machine and the ancestor of the slotter or vertical shaper.' (Plate III, facing p. 96.)

'A cutter, guided by a former, was moved across the face of the blocks as they revolved in the drum in which they were mounted. The simultaneous indexing of all the blocks about their centres was effected through bevel-and-worm gearing mounted on radial shafts actuated by a central crown wheel. The blocks were turned through 90°, the other former was selected and the blocks were faced in their new position. The procedure was continued until the four sides had been shaped.'

As Maudslay's business grew, he found he needed more room. He bought a piece of ground in Westminster Road, Lambeth, where there was an empty building which had been used as a riding school. There he built up the firm which became well known as Maudslay, Sons and Field. His eldest son carried it on when Maudslay died in 1831 after catching a chill on a channel crossing.

Maudslay insisted above all on strict accuracy. This applied particularly to the making and use of perfectly flat or true plane surfaces. This aspect was described by James Nasmyth, inventor of the steam hammer, who worked for Maudslay:

'No one that I ever met with could go beyond Henry Maudslay himself in his dexterous use of the file. By a few masterly strokes he could produce plane surfaces so true that when their accuracy was tested by a standard plane surface of absolute truth, they were never found defective.

'The importance of having such standard planes caused him to have many of them placed on the benches beside his workmen, by means of which they might at once conveniently test their work. Three of them were made at a time, so that by the mutual rubbing of each on each the projecting surfaces were effaced. When the surfaces approached very near to the true plane, the still projecting minute points were carefully reduced by hard steel scrapers, until at last the standard plane surface was secured. When placed over each other they would float upon the thin stratum of air between them until dislodged by time and pressure. When they adhered closely to each other, they could only be separated by sliding each off each. This art of producing absolutely plane surfaces is, I believe, a very old mechanical "dodge". But as employed by Maudslay's men, it greatly contributed to the improvement of the work turned out.'

Maudslay was a shrewd self-made man. He was fully of pithy sayings, which he stored up in his mind, like proverbs, and produced at the right moment. He would say, 'First, *get a clear notion* of what you desire to accomplish, and then in all probability you will succeed in doing it.' Or, 'Keep a sharp look-out upon your materials; get rid of every pound of material you can *do without*; put to yourself the question, "What business has it to be there?", avoid complexities, and make everything as simple as possible.'

Inventors frequently called to see him about their projects. He had his own method of weighing them up. He gave them marks on a scale up to 100 so that a very good man was given 95, others 90, 80, etc. After someone had been to him for advice he would say to his assistant, 'Jem, I think that man may be set down at 45, but he might be *worked up* to 60,' using the terms applied to a steam engine.

Like Bramah, Maudslay had great influence on following generations of engineers. Among those who were employed in his workshops were four other inventors – Joseph Clement, Joseph Whitworth, Richard Roberts and James Nasmyth.

JOSEPH CLEMENT (1779–1844)

Clement was another of the Bramah engineering family. He was employed by and learnt from Maudslay who in turn was employed by Bramah.

His parents, like those of many others of these inventors, were ordinary working people. He always spoke with the strong accent of Westmorland where he was born. His father worked at the trade of hand loom weaving which was dying in the face of machinery.

Clement was at the village school for only a short time and he learnt only elementary reading and writing. His father needed him to help on the loom. But as the work for the hand loom soon began to disappear Clement turned to being a thatcher and slater. This was his work between eighteen and twenty-three. However, at the same time he showed a great interest in mechanics, like his father before him. He made friends with the village blacksmith and was soon able to use his tools skilfully. A friend lent him books on mechanics.

Having made himself into a useful smith he decided to give up slating and left the village to get a job in a factory at Kirkby Stephen, making power looms. In a year or two he went to the bigger town of Carlisle, working at the same trade. Still restless and looking for more scope for his abilities, he moved on again, still northwards to the city of Glasgow. There he worked as a turner. This was in 1807, when he was twenty-eight. His employers at Carlisle gave him the usual leaving certificate which stated he had worked 'with great sobriety and industry, entirely to their satisfaction'.

The turning point in Clement's life took place at Glasgow. He determined to make himself into a draughtsman. This was an unusual qualification; draughtsmen were wanted everywhere and were more rare than even skilled mechanics. After taking drawing lessons and working late at night by candlelight he got a job, designing and making power looms with a firm, still farther north at Aberdeen. His wages now rose to as much as three guineas a week, a high wage for that time.

At last, in 1813 when he was thirty-four he decided to turn south and look for new opportunities in London. When he got off the coach in Holborn the guard directed him to the well-known firm of Galloway for a job. 'What can you do?' asked Galloway. 'I can work at the forge,' said Clement. 'Anything else?' 'I can draw.' 'What?' said Galloway, 'can you draw? Then I will engage you.'

Clement afterwards described Galloway as 'only a mouthing common-council man, the height of whose ambition was to be an alderman', that is to say, to be a celebrity on the City Corporation. Clement stayed only a short time because he was offered the miserable wage of a guinea a week. He then went to Bramah's famous works and on the strength of his ability as a draughtsman quickly became chief draughtsman and superintendent of the Pimlico works at a wage of three guineas a week, increasing by four shillings a week each year for five years. Bramah said that if he had had his services five years earlier he could have been many thousands of pounds better off.

Before setting up his own business he made yet another move. This was to another famous firm, Maudslay and Field, where he was chief draughtsman and helped in the production of marine engines. Having saved enough money, Clement now started his own workshop in Newington Butts. He specialized in making small high-grade tools and machines required for a particular job.

He was often asked to make articles requiring special skill and which others had given up. This led him to invent many improvements. He continued and improved Maudslay's work in making screw-cutting more accurate. While he was manufacturing taps he invented the 'tap with a small square shank which would fall through the threaded hole instead of having to be screwed out'.

His chief invention was the metal-planing machine. This was not the first planing machine as several other engineers seemed to have invented it earlier, but it is the best known one. Clement finished it in 1825.

'The table of his planing machine ran on rollers, and the machine was bedded on a massive foundation of masonry. The machine was driven by hand and had two cutters, one for each direction of the bed. For ten years this machine was the only planer capable of taking large work – up to six feet square.

Clement charged 18s. a square foot. At this rate the machine could earn £20 a day, if fully employed, and it was his chief source of income.'

The kind of work he undertook when customers came to ask him to solve a difficulty can be shown by two very different examples. The Great Western Railway had recently opened. I. K. Brunel, the chief engineer, was unable to get locomotive whistles to make enough noise. Bramah agreed to make them and in accordance with his usual practice made a special tool to produce them. The whistles were so effective, and so carefully made, that the railway had to pay six times the old price.

Another example of his work was Charles Babbage's Calculating or Difference Engine. This engine invented by Babbage was the first attempt at making a computer. Babbage was a mathematician who undertook to design for the Government a machine for calculating mathematical and astronomical tables. He turned to Clement, and Clement made innumerable devices and special tools. It was a calculating machine using a series of revolving number-wheels. The job was highly complicated and costly and went on for ten years. Eventually the Government would pay no more and the Calculating Engine was never finished. Part of it may still be seen in the Science Museum.

Clement was notable for the high engineering quality of everything made in his workshop. Joseph Whitworth the famous engineer of the next generation, worked there and learnt from him.

At the same time as the new tools and machines were invented cast iron became available in large quantities because of the discoveries of Darby and Cort. The cast iron was cheap and so the machines were made of iron instead of wood.

With these new skills new trades began to appear. Instead of there being only millwrights, blacksmiths and carpenters, soon every workshop had turners, planers, vice men, and filers (the old name for fitters). Joshua Field, Maudslay's partner said:

'The rapid introduction of cast iron together with the invention of new machines and new processes called for more workmen than the millwright class could supply . . . a new class of workmen was found and manufacturing establishments arose to which were attached iron and brass foundries with tools and machines for constructing machinery of every description.'

As well as the changes in skills there was a change in the law affecting apprenticeship. Up to that time an old law of the time of Elizabeth I, the Statute of Artificers, had made it compulsory for those entering a skilled trade to serve an indentured apprenticeship. This law was repealed in the year that Bramah died. Now men could enter any trade without serving an apprenticeship.

The changes in the skills was seen very differently by the employers and by the workmen. The millwrights' monopoly of skilled work had gone. The employers hoped that the millwrights' power to enforce rates of wages had gone too and that the new men required would not have to be paid so much. One well-known employer, Alexander Galloway, whom Clement had described as 'a mouthing common-council man', remarked that 'engineers have become millwrights and we make our machines so much better and cheaper, that the trade that used to scoff and spurn at the name of an engineer are obliged to take up the name and conduct their business by the engineers' economy'. The engineer was replacing the millwright and his wages were only 18s. a week compared with the millwright's two guineas.

Another employer, a machine maker, said,

'Most of the tools or machines used in machine making are self-acting and go on without the aid of man; the man who works the planning machine is a labouring man earning twelve to fourteen shillings a week.'

Another employer, James Nasmyth, inventor of the steam hammer, pointed out the advantages, from his point of view, of machine tools over the old skilled workman.

'Shortly after the opening of the Liverpool and Manchester Railway there was a largely increased demand for machine-making tools. There was a great demand for skilled and even for unskilled labour. The demand was greater than the supply. Employers were subjected to exorbitant demands for increased rates of wages. The workmen struck and their wages were raised. The results were not always satisfactory. The workmen attended less regularly; and sometimes, when they ought to have been at work on Monday mornings, they did not appear until Wednesday. Their higher wages had been of no use to them. Their time had been spent for the most part in two days' extra drinking.

'The irregularity and carelessness of the workmen naturally proved very annoying to the employers. But it gave an increased stimulus to the demand for self-acting machine tools, by which the untrustworthy efforts of hand labour might be avoided. The machines never got drunk; their hands never shook from excess; they were never absent from work; they did not strike for wages.'

However, the engineering workers made progress, and for two reasons. It was true that less skilled men on the planer or 'go-cart' were needed for work which had been done by the skilled craftsmen with the chisel and file or hand lathe. On the other hand the new machines needed new skills of accuracy and speed to get the most work from them. Moreover much of the work – pattern making, fitting and erecting – still had to be done with hand tools.

Whereas in the old days the millwright had gone round with his tools from job to job, now hundreds of engineers were gathered together under a factory roof. This made it easy for them to combine into trade unions.

Thus in the 1820's the 'new class of workmen' referred to by Joshua Field formed many societies and unions. Among them were the Mechanics Friendly Union Institution in Bradford, the Steam Engine Makers' Society in Liverpool, and the Friendly Union of Mechanics in Manchester. The repeal of the Combination Acts in 1825 helped them and more societies were formed in the 1830's.

The new skills were shown in the names of these societies: the London Friendly Society of Engineers and Machinists, the Society of Friendly Boilermakers, the Amalgamated Society

87

of Metal Planers. The object of these societies was to look after their members in distress or unemployed, and to make fair contracts with employers.

The strongest of all these societies was the Journeymen Steam Engine and Machine Makers Friendly Society, known as the 'Old Mechanics'. It soon had 3,000 members. The man who founded the 'Old Mechanics' was John White of the Manchester 1st Branch. 'He campaigned enthusiastically in

[From *One hundred and fifty years progress, 1811–1961*, Amalgamated Engineering Union

Taking the oath

Manchester for the new Society, and on Saturday nights travelled to Stockport, Oldham and Bolton to advocate trade unionism, walking home on Sunday, but his task was far from easy. According to his son, he had to change his lodgings every three or four weeks 'to stop constables from tracing his movements', and even when the Society was well established, White, as treasurer, had to hide as much as £6,000 up the chimney and in the cellars of his house in China Lane, Piccadilly,

Manchester, as the trade unions had no legal security for their funds in the banks.'

Branches all over the country met in the local public house where the landlord held the box containing the funds based on the contributions of 6d. per week. The rule said 'The box shall contain three different locks and keys outside also three different locks and keys for the cash drawer which shall be kept by the president and the two acting stewards.'

When the new member received the password he had to swear secrecy with his hand on the Bible and a pistol pointing at him.

These articles can be seen written in the cash book of the Huddersfield Branch. Curtains to keep out prying eyes are also entered there.

The Society gradually developed its policy of keeping down the supply of skilled labour in relation to the demand for it, and thus maintaining wages. The aim was to ban systematic overtime, reduce hours, and limit the number of apprentices to one to every four men.

In London there was a strike in 1836. Maudslay's was one of the shops where work stopped. The men demanded a ten-hour day and special overtime rates after that. They had worked a regular ten and a half hour shift, often working longer at the ordinary rate. The strike went on for eight months and then the men won their demands.

The new combination of the 'new class of workmen' was as strong as the old combination of the millwrights against which the employers had petitioned Parliament forty years before; the Old Mechanics wanted to unite the new and the old class of workmen. It allowed machine joiners to become members; it also added the word Millwrights to the name of the society, thus bringing the old class into their ranks. In the earlier days the millwrights 'would not work with an engineer, they thought it rather a disgrace'.

The next step forward was towards amalgamation of the numerous societies in the engineering industry. The Old Mechanics took the lead. After many meetings and long arguments among the societies the new 'Amalgamated Society of Engineers, Machinists, Smiths, Millwrights and Pattern-makers' was established in 1851. (The title embraced the new and the old.) By the end of that year there were 10,841 members. It had a new trade protection fund to provide strike pay and not everyone would agree to this at first. The contribution was 1s. per week, much higher than usual at that time. The benefits covered unemployment, sickness, pension, accident, and funeral. This new amalgamated society became the Amalgamated Engineering Union eighty years later, in 1920.

Additional Reading

S. Smiles, *Lives of the Engineers: Toolmakers*, Murray 1904.
J. B. Jefferys, *The Story of the Engineers*, Lawrence & Wishart 1945.

CHAPTER FIVE

The Early Days
of Trade Unions
1825-1850

WE have seen how after the inventions were used in production the workers, often with new skills, were gathered together in large groups, in factories or on sites. They then formed societies and unions to protect their standards of living.

So far we have read about the iron workers, the millwrights, the spinners and weavers, the stonemasons, and the engineers. But there were many other groups of men and women – agricultural labourers, tailors, miners, potters, builders, cabinet makers, gas stokers, printers. All these people formed trade unions and so did many others.

The great effort of many of them in the 1830's was to combine many different trades in one big national union. This was to be a general union for all rather than a society of a particular trade; a trades union rather than a trade union. Some trades also tried to form national unions of their own.

There were repeated attempts to form a general trades union. An organization called the 'Philanthropic Hercules' was started by men from different trades in Manchester and spread to the Potteries and London. There it was led by the shipwright John Gast.

Next the cotton spinners centred in Manchester tried to form a national union. In 1829 they did form a 'Grand General Union of the United Kingdom'. Its aim was to get Parliament to reduce the hours of work. John Doherty, the Irish cotton spinner, was secretary and the union caused such alarm that the Boroughreeve and Constable of Manchester wrote to the Home Secretary, Sir Robert Peel, who had just started the Metropolitan Police:

'The combination of workmen, long acknowledged a great

evil and one most difficult to counteract, has recently assumed so formidable and systematic a shape in this district that we feel it our duty to lay before you some of its most alarming features . . . A weekly levy or rent of one penny per head on each operative is cheerfully paid. This produces a large sum . . . principally to support those who have turned out against their employers, agreeable to the orders of the committee, at the rate of ten shillings per week for each person.'

No more was heard of the Grand General Union but a bigger organization took its place. This was the National Association for the Protection of Labour. Doherty was again secretary. Its object was to resist reductions in wages. It grew rapidly and soon had enrolled about 150 small unions in Lancashire and the Midlands, with anything from 10,000 to 20,000 members. At first they were mostly textile workers of different kinds but there were also mechanics, moulders and blacksmiths. Later miners, woollen workers and potters came in. The Association had its own weekly paper, price 7d., which had a circulation of 30,000. This was very large for those days. It also worked to get Parliament to reduce hours, but like its predecessors it lasted only a short time because of lack of money.

While the National Association was growing the building workers established their own Builders' Union or General Trades Union. Its annual conference in 1833 was attended by 270 delegates representing 30,000 operatives. It was full of optimism. It started to build its own guild hall. Its own paper, the *Pioneer*, said

'A union founded on just and right principles is all that is now required to put poverty and the fear of it for ever out of society.'

But the employers replied with 'the document', which required all men employed to state they would not join a trade union. Strikes failed and the union faded out.

Other trades were stirring. The Northumberland and Durham miners had a strong union for two years. Their disputes caused marines to be sent from Portsmouth and squadrons of cavalry to be chasing over the two counties. The Potters Union had 8,000 members by 1833, coming from places all the way from Newcastle upon Tyne to Bristol.

All these attempts to form general trades unions or national trade unions led up to the biggest scheme of all. This was the 'Grand National Consolidated Trades Union'. It was the biggest attempt to establish a trades union combining all men and women workers of whatever occupation, as distinct from a trade union catering for one occupation or skill.

Immediately a great number of local unions joined the Grand National, and many previously unorganized trades and districts joined. Never before or since had men and women in so many different occupations come together. There were shop assistants, chimney sweepers, cabinet makers, ploughmen, shearmen, tailors (male and female), bonnet makers, hosiery workers, farm labourers, shoemakers, builders, and many others. Within a few weeks the membership rose to no less than half a million.

From the start the Grand National had ambitious aims. Led by Robert Owen, it aimed at nothing less than organizing industry in co-operatives which would take the place of the competitive capitalist system. It had much faith in its ideals. One of its rules read as follows:

'Although the design of the Union, is in the first instance, to raise the wages of the workmen, or prevent any further reduction therein, and to diminish the hours of labour, the great and ultimate object of it must be to establish the paramount rights of Industry and Humanity, by instituting such measures as shall effectually prevent the ignorant, idle, useless part of Society from having that undue control over the fruits of our toil, which, through the agency of a vicious money system, they at present possess; and that, consequently, the unionists should lose no opportunity of mutually encouraging and assisting each other in bringing about a *different order of things*, in which the really useful and intelligent part of society only shall have the direction of its affairs, and in which well directed industry and virtue shall meet their just distinction and reward, and vicious idleness its merited contempt and destitution.'

The Grand National was soon faced with disputes all over the country which were too much for it. It did not have the

93

money to support its members. Employers dismissed men unless they would sign the 'document'. This was the case of the Leicester hosiers, 1,300 of whom had to be supported. At Derby, 1,500 men, women and children were locked out by the employers for refusing to leave the Union. They were supported for four months by contributors from all over the country but then the money dried up and the employers won.

Then occurred the famous trial of the Dorchester labourers or 'Tolpuddle Martyrs'. In the village of Tolpuddle the farmers and the labourers had agreed that the wages paid should be the same as those in other districts, i.e. 10s. per week. The farmers then went back on their promise and reduced wages until they were down to 7s. per week. Two of the men, the brothers George and James Loveless, enquired about the trades union and two delegates from the Grand National visited them.

They formed a local branch with all the usual ritual and elaborate swearing of oaths of secrecy. The farmers were alarmed and the magistrates threatened to punish any members of the union. The men would not give way and six of them were arrested, tried and sentenced to transportation for seven years. Within nine months they had been put in a ship sailing for Botany Bay.

This is part of the evidence given at the Dorchester Assizes. The courtroom can still be seen today at Dorchester, just as it was then.

'John Lock. – I live at Half Puddle. I went to Toll Puddle a fortnight before Christmas. I know the prisoner James Brine. I saw him about a fortnight afterwards in a barn. James Hammet was then with him. Edward Legg, Richard Peary, Henry Courtney, and Elias Riggs were with us. They joined us as we were going along. One of them asked if there would not be something to pay, and one said there would be 1s. to pay on entering, and 1d. a week after. We all went into Thomas Stanfield's house into a room upstairs. I saw James Loveless and George Loveless go along the passage. One of the men asked if we were ready. We said, yes. One of them said, "Then bind your eyes," and we took out handkerchiefs and bound over our eyes. They then led us into another room on the same floor. Someone then read a paper, but I don't know what the meaning of it was. After that we were asked to kneel down, which we did. Then there was some more reading; I don't know what it was about. It seemed to be out of some part of the Bible. Then we got up and took off the bandages from our eyes. Some one read again, but I don't know what it was, and then we were told to kiss the book, when our eyes were unblinded, and I saw the book, which looked like a little Bible. I then saw all the prisoners there. James Loveless had on a white dress, it was not a smock-frock. They told us the rules, that we should have to pay 1s. then, and a 1d. a week afterwards, to support the men when they were standing out from their work. They said we were as brothers; that when we were to stop for wages we should not tell our masters ourselves, but that the masters would have a note or a letter sent to them.'

There was no law against trade unions but there was an old law forbidding the swearing of unlawful oaths and it was used against the labourers. The Government was alarmed by the growth of the Grand National and seized on this opportunity to check it. The Grand National fought back by organizing petitions and demonstrations to demand the return of the labourers from Botany Bay. In April 1834, 30,000 formed a great procession in London. After four years' work the Loveless brothers and their comrades were brought back free.

The Grand National then got into more difficulties. The unions belonging to it were in a militant mood but neither they nor it had the strength to succeed in their demands. The London tailors demanded shorter hours and 20,000 of them struck in April 1834. The Grand National made a levy of 1s. 6d. per member to support them but they could not keep it up and the tailors were defeated. A strike by Oldham spinners for shorter hours fizzled out. In London the workers employed by Cubitt the builder refused to drink the beer supplied because the brewers would not employ trade unionists. Cubitt locked them out and all the master builders insisted on 'the document' being signed. The struggle lasted for four months when the workers accepted partial defeat. Even when the Grand National refused to agree to a demand being made, as in the case of the London shoemakers, the shoemakers merely left the Grand National and went on with their dispute.

The Grand National had failed and it was disbanded in 1834. No such grand general union of all trades could have succeeded at that time. There was no other attempt to get unity of all unions until the appearance of the Trades Union Congress nearly forty years later.

Although the Grand National collapsed many quite strong trade unions remained. We have seen that the 'Old Mechanics' grew stronger. They had kept away from the Grand National. Among others who kept their organization going were the stonemasons, carpenters, cotton operatives, boilermakers, and potters. The miners formed a national body – the Miners Association of Great Britain a few years later.

These unions took hardly any part in the great political movement of working men from 1836 to 1848 known as Chartism. They had enough to do to build up their organization and strengthen their bargaining power, as the Old Mechanics did.

Additional Reading

G. D. H. Cole, *Short History of the British Working Class Movement*, Allen & Unwin 1937.
S. and B. Webb, *History of Trade Unionism*, Longmans 1920.

Plate 3

Above: Maudslay's original screw-cutting lathe, *c.*1800
Below: Brunel's mortising-machine, built by Maudslay in 1803, for cutting the slots in pulley blocks

Plate 4

Great Western Railway: 'Making a Cutting'. Watercolour by George Childs, 1841

(*Crown copyright*, *Science Museum, London*)

P.S. *Great Western*, 1837 (lithograph)

(*Photo, Science Museum, London*)

CHAPTER SIX

The
Railway
Engineers

GEORGE STEPHENSON (1781–1848)

GEORGE STEPHENSON, the 'father of the railways', made himself into an engineer, and became the first president of the Institution of Mechanical Engineers, without any education or training at school. This was possible because the locomotive and the railway were then in their infancy, and at their very simplest.

Stephenson's father was fireman of the pumping engine in Wylam Colliery, eight miles west of Newcastle upon Tyne. His wage for a 12-hour day was 12s. a week. All he could afford was one room in a stone cottage and in this room Stephenson was born and in it lived the whole family of eight.

There was no school for Stephenson. In any case his father was too poor to send him. Just in front of the house ran the colliery railway and he spent many hours watching the horses slowly drawing the wagons along the wooden rails from the pit down to the river Tyne. When the wagons arrived at the staithes on the river the coal was tipped into barges which went down the river to Newcastle.

At the age of eight he earned 2d. a day watching the cows. His hobby was modelling pumping engines out of clay. His wages rose to 4d. a day, for hoeing turnips. The Wylam pit became worked out and the family moved to another village. At the colliery Stephenson became a 'picker' at 6d. a day, picking stones and dirt out of the coal. From there he went to another pit where there was no steam winding engine and took charge of the horse gin.

When he was fourteen he took the first step towards being

an engineer. He became assistant fireman to his father, at a wage of 7s. a week. Two years later he was fireman at another pit at a man's wage of 12s., the same as his father's. This was a responsible job for a lad of sixteen, for the safety of the pit depended on maintaining steam pressure in the engine boiler.

Unlike many firemen he made a special point of studying the engine, stripping, cleaning and assembling it in his spare time. Thus in the following year he became engineman. He was now over his father who was fireman at the same colliery.

Stephenson then began to feel the handicap of never having gone to school. He could not read or write like some of his mates who could read in the newspapers about the conquest of Europe by Napoleon and the danger to England, and he had no hope of getting further as an engineer unless he could read the technical books he had seen. He went to night school three times a week, paying 4d. a week, and could soon read, write and do arithmetic.

Presently he got the more responsible job of brakesman, controlling the winding up and down in the pit shaft. Then, at the age of twenty-one, he married Fanny Henderson, a servant at a neighbouring farm, and they had a son, the famous Robert Stephenson. He supplemented his wages, which were now 17s. to 20s. a week, by repairing clocks and mending shoes.

Stephenson now became a brakesman at Killingworth, the place where he was to make his name. But he was not to settle down to happy family life. His wife died and the infant Robert was looked after by neighbours. His father was blinded in an accident and he had to support him. Then he was called up for the army. Characteristically, he had saved enough to pay a substitute to serve for him, as was then possible. Unfortunately for him, but fortunately for England this took all his savings. He had planned to emigrate to America, but now he could not pay the fare.

He had not yet achieved his ambition of working as a real engineer and the chances did not seem bright. He had not served any kind of apprenticeship. His opportunity did not come until he was over thirty. The colliery opened a new pit at Killingworth and installed a Newcomen atmospheric pumping engine constructed by Smeaton, the great engineer. Despite all the efforts of the engineers the engine would not work. At length Stephenson offered to put it in order, and after making changes to the injecting cock and the steam pressure he succeeded. When the engine-wright was killed in an accident Stephenson was appointed to the job. This was in 1812.

This was his first job with real engineering responsibility. For a salary of £100 a year he was expected to maintain the underground galleries, 160 miles of them, as well as the machinery for haulage and pumping. Now he had scope to develop his great abilities, and his attention was naturally drawn to the possibility of improving the haulage on the Killingworth wagon ways, which was the bottle neck in getting the coal away. He had read and heard about attempts to make a travelling steam engine and now he began to think about making one himself.

Stephenson was not the inventor of the locomotive. He improved on the earlier efforts of other men. It was Richard Trevithick who made the first railway locomotive in 1804. Before that he built at least two steam road carriages which ran successfully. Stephenson really went on where Trevithick left off, but he took a decisive step forward.

Trevithick, the Cornishman (1771–1833), had taken the necessary preliminary step when he introduced the use of high pressure steam. James Watt before him was unwilling to use any pressure more than a few pounds greater than atmospheric pressure, because he was afraid of explosions of the boiler, but without high-pressure steam there could have been no locomotive.

After constructing stationary high-pressure engines, Trevithick went on to locomotive ones. His stationary engines developed pressures up to 145 lb. per square inch. He made 50 or more of them: they were used for pumping and winding in mines, driving sugar mills, corn-grinding and rolling iron. These stationary engines were his main work but his locomotives were even more important.

The best known of Trevithick's locomotives was the one he made to carry iron ore along the cast iron tramway from the Pendarren ironworks to the Glamorgan canal. It was, as he said, 'the first and only self-moving machine that ever was made to travel on a road with 25 tons at 4 m.p.h., and completely manageable by only one man'.

Trevithick's engine was very heavy and broke the line under it. Trevithick himself was not interested in improving it, but it was important for two particular reasons. Firstly, it proved that smooth wheels would drive on smooth rails. (Many people would not believe this and even afterwards insisted that cogs were necessary.) Secondly, in his engine the exhaust steam from the cylinder was used, for the first time, to increase the draught for the fire. This was done by passing the steam into the chimney, thus forcing the smoke from the fire up the chimney. This idea was copied by Stephenson.

[From *Richard Trevithick*, by H. W. Dickinson and A. Titley

Side view and section of Trevithick's high-pressure engine with horizontal cylinder and dome-topped boiler, 1803

There is little doubt that Stephenson saw a Trevithick locomotive working at a nearby colliery. He also saw other types which men had tried to make locally with varying degrees of success, such as John Blenkinsop's engine with a cogwheel engaging in the teeth of a rack rail; and William Hedley's eight-wheeled locomotive at Wylam Colliery.

Stephenson's first locomotive, the *Blucher*, built in 1814 with the limited tools available in a colliery workshop, and the 16 others of its type he built subsequently were very much like the earlier engines made by these other men. But there were certain important differences which were his main contribution to the locomotive. The *Blucher*, unlike previous engines, had flanged wheels. His engines had a simpler transmission system, coupling the connecting rods direct to crank pins on the wheels. Because the cast iron rails broke so easily under the weight of the locomotive, his engines had 'steam springs'. These were a vertical cylinder filled from the boiler, in which worked a piston attached to the axle.

Stephenson was by now a well-known man in the north of England. This was due to his safety lamp as well as his locomotives.

Stephenson invented his safety lamp in the same year as Sir Humphrey Davy invented his famous lamp and quite independently of him. The difference was that Davy based his lamp on scientific principles and safe laboratory experiments, whereas Stephenson developed his lamp by trial and error in the dangerous conditions of the pits where he risked his life many times.

An under-viewer at Killingworth Colliery described how Stephenson experimented underground:

'I, John Moody do hereby certify whom it may concern that on the 21st of October 1815 at 6 o'clock that evening I accompany'd Mr. Stephenson and Mr. Wood down A Pit at Killingworth Colliery in purpose to try Mr. Stephenson's first safety lamp at a Blower. But when we came near the Blower it was making so much more gas than usual that I told Mr. Stephenson and Mr. Wood if the lamp should deceive him we should be severely burnt, but Mr. Stephenson would insist upon the tryal which was very much against my desire. So Mr. Wood and I went out of the way at a distance and left Mr. Stephenson to himself, but we soon heard that the lamp has answered his expectation with safety. Since that time I have been many times with Mr. Stephenson and Mr. Wood trying his different lamps. I likewise recollect Mr. Stephenson trying many experiments at Blowers long before we had any lamp.'

A Blower was a point where gas escaped into the pit through an opening in the rock.

Stephenson described how the gas put out his lamp before he could reach the blower and how he went forward to it a second time:

'I got my lamp trimm'd again and desir'd my companions to

accompany me to the blower a second time, but they would not altho' they did not leave me so far as before. When I approached towards the blower the second time I carried my lamp very slow and steady to observe the alteration of the flame in the lamp. As I went along I observed the flame increasing in size and change its colour to a kind of blue. I went a little further; the flame then went out. I then told my companions the effect and in a short time my companions became more bold so that they went up with me and seed the gas burn with the lamp.'

Davy's lamp had wire gauze surrounding the flame whereas Stephenson's had a metal plate perforated with small holes. There was a great argument about which of the two was the first to invent the lamp. Davy tried to make his case, but Stephenson kept silent and was content to let his lamp speak for itself. There was no doubt it saved many lives.

It was the Stockton and Darlington Railway, the first public railway in Britain to use locomotives, which made George Stephenson famous. Stephenson, as a well-known man in the north, was asked by Edward Pease, the Quaker financier of the line, to make a survey. He agreed in the following letter:

Killingworth Colliery,
April 28th, 1821.

Edward Pease, Esq.,
Sir,

I have been favoured with your letter of the 20 inst. and am glad to learn that the Bill has passed for the Darlington Railway.

I am much obliged by the favourable sentiments you express towards me, and shall be happy if I can be of service in carrying into execution your Plans.

From the nature of my engagement here and in the neighbourhood I could not devote the whole of my time to your Railway, but I am willing to undertake to survey and mark out the best line of way within the limits prescribed by the Act of Parliament and also to assist the Committee with plans and estimates and in letting to the different contractors such work as they might judge it advisable to do by Contract, and also to superintend the execution of the work. And I am induced to recommend the whole being done by Contract under the Superintendence of competent persons appointed by the Committee.

Were I to contract for the whole line of road it would be necessary for me to do so at an advanced price upon the Sub-Contractors, and it would also be necessary for the Committee to have some person to superintend my undertaking. This would be attended with an extra expense and the Committee would derive no advantage to compensate for it.

If you wish it I will wait upon you at Darlington at an early opportunity when I can enter into more particulars as to remuneration, etc.

I remain,
Yours respectfully,
George Stephenson.

Some kind of transport to carry the coal from the Auckland coalfield to the navigable river Tees at Stockton had been needed for many years. Pease and his friends first planned a tramway for horse-drawn wagons. Stephenson, however, persuaded them to have a much stronger railway on which locomotives would run. It was thanks to Stephenson's vision and determination that the Stockton and Darlington was the first public railway to have locomotives.

Stephenson completed his survey of the new line in a fortnight, with the help of his son Robert, then eighteen years old; his estimate of the cost was £60,987 13s. 3d. He was appointed engineer at a salary of £600 a year on condition that he spent one week in each month on the works.

The choice of permanent way was a difficult one to make. Although he would have made a good deal of money if his own type of cast-iron rail had been used, he recommended the new wrought iron rails, as a method of rolling them had just been invented. They were sunk in stone or wooden blocks, without any cross-sleepers, because it was intended to use horses as well as locomotives. The first rail was laid in May 1822 and the whole line was ready for use in September 1825.

In order to make the locomotives the new works of Robert Stephenson and Company were established at Newcastle. Robert was in charge of the works, although he was only twenty years old. The locomotives were made according to his father's design and patents. When the first engine, the *Locomotion*, was ready George Stephenson wrote to Pease from Newcastle:

'I beg to inform you that the Improved Travelling Engine was tried here last night and fully answered my expectations. And if you will be kind enough to desire Pickersgill to send horses to take it away from here on Friday it shall be loaded on Thursday evening. I calculate the weight of the Engine between 5 and 6 tons.'

When the *Locomotion* arrived from Newcastle by road she was unloaded on to the rails. One of the old navvies vividly described how she was got going by the burning glass he used to light his pipe:

'Number 1 came to Heighton Lane by road. We had to get her on the way. When we got her on the way we pump water into her. We sent John Taylor for a lantern and candle to Acliffe. When we done that I thought I would have my pipe. It was a very warm day though it had been back end of the year. I took me pipe glass and let me pipe. I thought to myself I would try to put fire to Jimmy Ockam*. It blaze away well the fire going rapidly. Lantern and candle was to no use so Number 1 fire was put to her on line by the power of the sun.'

The opening of the line on 27th September 1825, was a great event. Thousands of people from miles around lined the track. Three hundred tickets had been distributed to shareholders but hundreds more simply boarded the wagons so as to get the first ride to Stockton. George Stephenson drove *Locomotion* at the head of some thirty wagons with a load of nearly 100 tons. A horseman carrying a flag led the way along the track. A crowd of about 40,000 awaited the train at Stockton as it steamed slowly and safely in. George Stephenson had given a lead to the whole country.

Even before the Stockton and Darlington was finished Stephenson was working on a second railway, one which made him a national figure. This was the Liverpool and Manchester

* A wad of oakum packing.

104

Railway, famous for the Rainhill locomotive trial at which the *Rocket* showed finally that the locomotive had come to stay.

The Liverpool and Manchester Railway was projected because the Liverpool merchants had to pay high charges to the Bridgewater Canal Company which had a monopoly of carriage of goods between the two towns. Stephenson was appointed engineer but he found the task a far more difficult one than the Stockton and Darlington. On surveying the ground he met intense opposition. He wrote:

'We have sad work with Lord Derby, Lord Sefton and Bradshaw the Great Canal Proprietor whose grounds we go through with the projected railway. Their ground is blockaded on every side to prevent us getting on with the survey. Bradshaw fires guns through his ground in the course of the night to prevent the surveyors coming on in the dark. We are to have a grand field day next week. The Liverpool Railway Company are determined to force a survey through if possible. Lord Sefton says he will have 100 men against us. The Company thinks those great men have no right to stop a survey. It is the farmers only who have a right to complain and by charging damages for trespass is all they can do.'

Several times he was turned off the ground and threatened with a ducking in the pond. When the work was finished the surveying carried out by Stephenson and his assistants was shown to be so inaccurate by the professional engineers employed by the opposition in Parliament that the Bill was rejected. Stephenson had very little education or engineering training, and so the railway company had to employ professionally trained engineers to re-make the survey.

Stephenson was still, however, in sole charge of the construction of the Liverpool and Manchester Railway. It involved engineering works on a scale he had never tackled before. There were four major works. At the Liverpool end the Edgehill tunnel down to Wapping Dock, a tunnel 2,250 yards long, 22 feet wide and 16 feet high; the big cutting through the rock at Olive Mount east of the tunnel; farther east the Sankey Viaduct over the old canal; and at the Manchester end the bog of Chat Moss to be crossed.

Stephenson had no training to deal with this kind of civil

engineering but in spite of mistakes he pushed the work on and got it finished. Chat Moss was the worst problem. The experts said a line could not be laid across the bottomless bog. The engineers and labourers sank in and strapped boards to their feet so as to get about. At last Stephenson conquered by first draining and then pushing across the Moss closely woven rafts of heather and brushwood. On these soil was tipped and the lines laid so that the track was really floating on the bog. In spite of all this the 30 miles of track was finished in under four years.

The vital question whether locomotives were to be used had still to be settled. The opponents of locomotives wanted to use stationary haulage engines. A series of these along the line would haul the trains by ropes from point to point. The railway company settled the question by offering a prize of £500 for the best locomotive, to be won at the famous Rainhill loco- motive trials in 1829.

When the prize was won by the *Rocket* it was a triumph for Robert Stephenson, the son, rather than for George Stephen- son. It was Robert, still only twenty-six years old, who made revolutionary changes in the locomotive at his Newcastle Works and who designed and made the *Rocket*. This belongs to the story of his achievements.

The great day of the opening of the Liverpool and Man- chester Railway on 15th December 1830, was however another triumph for George Stephenson. It was not a happy day. At the beginning of the proceedings William Huskisson, a Tory leader and M.P. for Liverpool, was run over and fatally injured. The Duke of Wellington, the unpopular Tory Prime Minister, was on the train. At the Manchester end a great crowd, demonstrating against Wellington and demanding reform of Parliament, threatened to turn the proceedings into a riot. But eventually the eight special trains each drawn by its own engine the *Northumbrian*, the *Phoenix*, the *North Star*, the *Rocket*, the *Dart*, the *Comet*, the *Arrow* and the *Meteor*, got through to Manchester and back to Liverpool. The railway age had begun.

George Stephenson was now, at the age of fifty, the most famous railway engineer in Britain. As more railways were built, following the success of the Liverpool and Manchester, so he was more and more sought after as engineer, as consultant or merely to give the support of his name to a project. He bought land in Leicestershire and developed a coal mine on it. He became wealthy and famous.

He became very busy, travelling thousands of miles by post chaise, surveying, inspecting and giving advice on new railways. These were nearly all in the North Midlands. Many projects he started were built and completed by his son Robert. An example of these was the Newcastle and Berwick line which he surveyed. The line was strongly opposed by Lord Howick, son of the powerful Liberal leader, Earl Grey. This is what Stephenson thought about it, in writing to a friend:

'I am rather astonished at Lord Howick's observations about the line passing Howick. It does not go through any of their pleasure grounds, it passes over one of the drives which run down a dingle to the coast ... My senses are puzzled in judging how these people can set about making such paltry objections! It is compensation they want, nothing else. The line cannot be moved to the place Lord Howick alludes to, west of the house; it would require a tunnel a mile long. It would do very well for Lord Howick as it would pass through their limestone quarries ... This species of objection is a genteel way of picking the subscribers' pockets; there cannot be a doubt that it is meant to do so.

'Is the great thoroughfare through England and Scotland to be turned aside injuriously for the frivolous remarks made by Lord Howick? No! the times are changed. The legislators must look to the comforts and conveniences of the Public. Are hundreds and thousands of people to be turned through a tunnel merely to please two or three individuals?'

When he was fifty-six George Stephenson began to think about retiring and he wrote to the same friend:

'I intend giving up business in the course of the next two or three years when I shall be able to devote more time to my friends. I have had a most delightful trip among the Cumberland Lakes; I should like to have remained a month to fish ... I want to take thirty or forty thousand acres of land on the West Coast of England. I think it will be a good scheme.'

He still had much to do but when eight years later he went

to Spain, to survey a route for a Royal North of Spain Railway, he became seriously ill. He had only three years of complete retirement before he died in 1848 at the age of sixty-six. He left £140,000.

ROBERT STEPHENSON (1803–1859)

Robert Stephenson, the only son of George Stephenson, became an orphan when he was a baby for his mother died before he was two years old. But he was well looked after. His father wanted to keep his baby son with him and so he got his unmarried sister to keep house for him and she cared for Robert like a mother.

George Stephenson wanted his son to have the education which he himself felt the lack of. He was ambitious for his son and hoped that he would join him as a partner and bring with him the knowledge of a professional engineer. He always kept Robert hard at work at his studies or helping at home.

Robert was sent to the village school as soon as he could walk the three miles there and back. When he was twelve his father sent him to a private school for middle-class children which was considered better than the grammar school. It was at Newcastle, ten miles away, so Robert had a donkey to take him there. At first he was laughed at because of his Northumbrian accent and his rough clothes, miner's jacket, corduroy trousers and heavy boots, but not for long. His father could now well afford to pay the fees. He stayed at this school until he was sixteen and then he was apprenticed for three years at Killingworth Colliery. During his apprenticeship Robert often worked alongside his father who was chief engine-wright. He helped him in installing a system of underground haulage and learnt a great deal about the stationary steam engines for rope haulage and the rails and tramways which were laid down.

But Robert was not a strong lad; the time spent underground affected his health and there was frequent danger from accidents. His father therefore withdrew him from the apprenticeship before it was finished and took him out to help him with surveying the route for the Stockton and Darlington Railway. He now started his career as a railway engineer. So quickly did he become skilled that at the age of twenty-one he made by himself a survey of a branch line of the Stockton and Darlington and went up to London to see that the Bill for it got through Parliament.

Before this, at the age of nineteen, Robert Stephenson was assistant surveyor when the first route for the Liverpool and Manchester Railway was planned. Then his father sent him to spend six months at Edinburgh University to finish his education.

When he was only twenty he was made managing partner, at a salary of £200 a year, of the new firm of Robert Stephenson and Company, manufacturers of locomotives, which his father and his Quaker partners set up.

Stephenson now seemed well started on a career in England but the next three years of his life were spent in South America, at the remote silver mines of Santa Anna in Colombia. He wanted to go as engineer-in-charge and he wrote to his father for permission:

'Let me beg of you not to say anything against my going out to America, for I have already ordered many instruments that it would make me look extremely foolish to call off. Even if I had not ordered any instruments, it seems as if we were all working one against another. You must recollect I will only be away for a time; and in the meantime you would manage with the assistance of Mr. Longridge who, together with John Nicholson, would take the whole of the business part off your hands. And only consider what an opening it is for me as an entry into business . . .'

It was agreed and Stephenson sailed for Colombia. The only approach to the mines was by mule path over the mountains. He met great difficulties in restarting the mines. It was impossible to use the engines sent out from England, and he had difficulty in controlling the wild Cornish miners, 160 of whom had been attracted to Colombia by the high wages offered. At first they would not accept Stephenson as boss and several times threatened him with violence. Stephenson wrote:

'They plainly tell me that I am obnoxious to them, because I was not born in Cornwall; and although they are perfectly aware that I have visited some of the principal mines in that county, and examined the various processes on the spot, yet they tell me that it is impossible for a north-countryman to know anything about mining.'

He got control of the situation but the mines were a failure. After three years of adventure, including shipwreck off New York, and valuable experience, Stephenson returned in 1827 to be met by his father at Liverpool. He was now twenty-four.

It was not too soon. His father was so busy with the Liverpool and Manchester Railway that he could not attend to another of the early railways, the Canterbury and Whitstable. Robert therefore took charge of the works at that time.

More important than this he started building locomotives at the Stephensons' Newcastle works which had not done well in his absence. He developed new designs and under his direction the modern form of the steam locomotive gradually emerged. The following letter in 1828 gives a good idea of the way in which he began to revolutionize design and take the first steps towards the more advanced locomotives of the nineteenth and twentieth centuries:

'Since I came down from London I have been talking a great deal to my father about endeavouring to reduce the size and ugliness of our travelling-engines, by applying the engine either on the side of the boiler or beneath it entirely, somewhat similarly to Gurney's steam-coach. He has agreed to an alteration which I think will considerably reduce the quantity of machinery as well as the liability to mismanagement. Mr. Jos. Pease writes my father that in their present complicated state they cannot be managed by "fools", therefore they must undergo some alterations or amendment. It is very true that the locomotive engine . . . may be shaken to pieces; but such accidents are in a great measure under the control of the enginemen, which are, by the by, not the most manageable of beings. They perhaps want improvement as much as the engines . . .'

When the Liverpool and Manchester Railway ordered a locomotive Robert Stephenson was able to put his new ideas into practice and the result was the *Lancashire Witch*. This was a great advance on previous engines with their overhead beam arrangement. Its outside cylinders, at an angle of 45° above the rear wheels, drove direct on to the front wheels. It was also a working success and Stephenson built others like it.

And so when the railway announced the Rainhill locomotive trials and the prize of £500 for the best locomotive, Robert Stephenson's famous *Rocket* was a step forward from the *Lancashire Witch*. There were two great improvements. It had big, single driving wheels 4 feet 8 inches in diameter driven direct from the inclined cylinders, but the really important change was the new type of boiler. This was the multiple fire-tube boiler which replaced the boilers with only one or two flues. This was the new idea which gave the *Rocket* far greater capacity for raising steam and greater power than its rivals. The 25 copper fire-tubes in the boiler gave a much greater heating surface than any engine before and were the model for all later locomotive boilers.

It was a very difficult and long job to make a completely new type of engine such as the *Rocket* with the simple equipment available, but at last Stephenson could write:

'I daresay you are getting anxious but I have delayed writing you until I have tried the Engine on Killingworth Railway . . . The fire burns admirably and an abundance of steam is raised when the fire is carefully attended to . . . We went three Miles on this Railway . . . on a level part laid with Malleable Iron Rail we attained a speed of 12 miles per hour and without thinking that I deceived myself (I tried to avoid this), I believe the steam did not sink on this part. On the whole the Engine is capable of doing as much if not more than set forth in the stipulations, (of the Rainhill Trial). After a great deal of trouble and anxiety we have got the tubes perfectly tight . . .'

When the great day of the Trial arrived on 6th October 1829, Stephenson faced with confidence the four other competitors and the 10,000 spectators who came to see the strange new machines. Each locomotive had to haul its train 20 times to and fro over the $1\frac{1}{2}$ mile course. Each had to take its load of approximately three times the weight of the engine at an average speed of not less than 10 m.p.h. The *Rocket* achieved an average speed of 14 m.p.h. over the 60 miles but all the

The *Rocket* prototype: Robert Stephenson's *Lancashire Witch* for the Bolton & Leigh Rly, 1828.

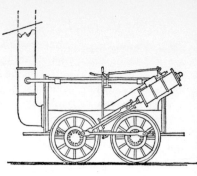

The Victor: Robert Stephenson's immortal *Rocket*, 1829

The *Rocket*'s two challengers at Rainhill: Messrs Braithwaite & Erickson's *Novelty* (above); Timothy Hackworth's *Sans Pareil* (left).

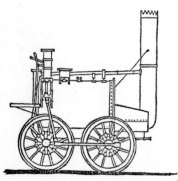

[From *George and Robert Stephenson*, by L. T. C. Rolt

The battle for the locomotive

other competitors either broke down or withdrew. It was a triumph for Robert Stephenson and his father.

For the next year or two Robert continued rapidly to improve the design of his locomotives. The *Northumbrian* of 1830 had a boiler with 132 tubes compared with the *Rocket*'s 25. In the *Planet* of the same year the basic form of the modern locomotive was reached. The cylinders were now underneath the smoke box instead of alongside it and they drove on to the rear wheels instead of the leading ones.

During these few years Robert had become the leading locomotive engineer in the country. However, he still found time to court the girl of his choice and marry her. Fanny Sanderson was the daughter of a city merchant. He had been anxious to be appointed engineer of the Canterbury and Whitstable Railway because this gave him opportunities to visit her home in the city. They were married in 1829. But although they were happy she died fourteen years later, having had no children, and he did not marry again.

He now turned to railway building. In 1830, when he was still only twenty-seven, he surveyed the whole route for the longest railway yet projected, the London and Birmingham Railway, 112 miles long. When this had been done successfully he became chief engineer for the construction at a salary of £1,500 a year. This was a great prize for a young man still under thirty.

The London and Birmingham railway was a tremendous task. It ran from Euston, through Camden Town, Watford, Tring, Wolverton, Blisworth, Kilsby and on through Rugby and Coventry. Work began in 1833 and the line was open in 1838. Throughout these five years Stephenson had to organize the whole work in districts and sections under his engineers. He let the work out to no less than 29 contractors. The total number of men at work varied at different times between 12,000 and 20,000. Enormous numbers of drawings and specifications were required.

When difficult pieces of work defeated the contractors Stephenson had to take them over. This happened with the Primrose Hill tunnel in London, the great cutting in the chalk at Tring, and the cutting through oolite rock and clay at Blisworth.

But the worst struggle of all was to make Kilsby tunnel, near Rugby, a struggle which lasted four years. It was 2,400 yards long. When the working shafts were sunk so much sand and water were met that work had to be abandoned. Stephenson took charge of the situation. He assembled 13 steam pumping-engines and by leaving them working for a year and a half the water was reduced so that work in the tunnel could go on. He had 1,250 navvies working round the clock and 200 horses on the site. At about this time he wrote to a friend:

'I sometimes feel very uneasy about my position. My courage at times almost fails me and I fear that some fine morning my reputation may break under me like an eggshell.'

Eventually the last brick was put in position in the tunnel and in June 1838 the first train ran through from Euston to Birmingham.

Because of all these difficulties the London and Birmingham railway cost far more than was expected. The cost was £5,500,000 or £50,000 per mile.

After this achievement Stephenson went north and built the Newcastle and Darlington Railway in 1844. This was a short line but it was important because now trains could run right through from London to Tyneside at Gateshead.

The next step in the rapid growth of the railway system was to extend north into Scotland and link up London and Edinburgh. Stephenson built the two big bridges needed. One was the high level bridge of cast iron, borne by piers of sandstone, over the Tyne to Newcastle. The other, built at the same time, was the Royal Border Bridge, the stone viaduct over the Tweed to Berwick.

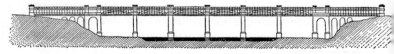

[From *A History of Technology*, Vol. IV

Robert Stephenson's high-level bridge, Newcastle upon Tyne, 1846–49

At a banquet at Newcastle to celebrate the new bridge Stephenson rose to speak. After comparing the engineers of his day with the early pioneers who had to do everything themselves he said:

'The principal engineer now has only to say "let this be done" and it is speedily accomplished, such is the immense capital, and such the resources of mind which are immediately brought into play. I have myself, within the last ten or twelve years, done little more than exercise a general superintendence and there are many other persons here to whom the works referred to by the chairman ought to be almost entirely attributed. I have had little or nothing to do with many of them beyond giving my name, and exercising a gentle control in some of the principal works . . . Beyond drawing the outline I have no right to claim any credit for the works above where we now sit.'

At the very same time as this work was going on Stephenson was building the two great bridges for which his name is famous. These were the two tubular bridges: the Conway bridge and the Britannia bridge at the Menai Straits. He was Engineer in Chief of the Chester and Holyhead Railway and the line had to cross the water at these two points, as Telford's Holyhead road had had to 20 years before.

Stephenson had to decide on the type of construction of these two bridges as well as the sites. He felt the responsibility very much, particularly because another bridge he had just built had collapsed while a train was going over it. This was the bridge of cast iron over the river Dee outside Chester. However, for the Conway and the Menai bridges he decided to use a completely new type of construction. This consisted of enormous rectangular tubes, made of wrought iron plates and angles, through which the trains would pass. They were extremely heavy and strong. Each of the main tubes of the Britannia bridge over the Menai Straits weighed about 1,500 tons, while even the smaller ones for the Conway bridge weighed about 1,000 tons. These tubes were constructed on the shores near the bridges, floated into position on pontoons and then raised to the top of the masonry piers. The central pier on the Britannia rock in the Menai Straits was over 200 feet tall. No such operation had been tried before.

No wonder that Stephenson wrote later on:

'It was a most anxious and harassing time with me. Often at night I would lie tossing about seeking sleep in vain. The tubes filled my head. I went to bed with them and got up with them. In the grey of the morning when I looked across the square it seemed an immense distance across to the houses on the opposite side. It was nearly the same length as the span of my bridge!'

After elaborate calculations and testing of models to destruction at the shipbuilding yard of William Fairbairn, Stephenson decided on the design of the tubes, the smallest of which was 230 feet long. The Conway bridge was a rehearsal for the bigger job of the Britannia. On a favourable tide in March 1848 the first tube was floated into position and raised on to the piers by hydraulic presses. Six weeks later the railway worked single line traffic over the bridge.

The Britannia bridge was a much more difficult operation because of the bigger and rougher stretch of water at the Menai Straits. Over this the four great tubes were floated on pontoons to the piers and then lifted by hydraulic rams 100 feet to the correct level. The first tube was floated out in June 1849. The carefully rehearsed operation was controlled by Stephenson. By his side, giving encouragement and advice, was his friend and rival the railway engineer, I. K. Brunel. The watching crowds saw the great tube on its pontoons swing out into the Straits. Then the capstan controlling it from the shore jammed its cable. The tube was drifting down out of control. The situation was only saved by the crowd on the shore laying hold of the cable and by sheer weight of numbers swinging the tube round into position. As the tide fell the tube landed on recesses in the masonry piers. It was then raised on to the piers by the hydraulic rams at the rate of 2 inches per minute. The second tube for the up railway line was in position six months later and the bridge was open in March 1850. The two tubes for the down line followed and by October of that year trains were steaming over the Britannia bridge on both lines. It was a great advance in the use of wrought iron for bridge building. As a result thousands of plate-girder bridges were built all over the world.

Stephenson was now forty-seven but he had only nine more

years to live. He had overworked so much that he was forced to slow down in the years left. He supervised the building of bridges abroad, in Canada, Egypt and Norway. At home he earned very high fees as a consultant and he became very wealthy. But he was a lonely man without wife or family.

He received many honours, including the Fellowship of the Royal Society. He was offered a knighthood but refused it. Even with all the tremendous amount of work he got through he found the time to be a member of Parliament for 12 years. He was a staunch and active Tory M.P. and as a Tory he opposed free trade and education for the people.

When he died on 12th October 1859, at the age of fifty-six, he was buried in Westminster Abbey beside Thomas Telford.

ISAMBARD KINGDOM BRUNEL (1806–1859)

Brunel knew well both George and Robert Stephenson. He was Robert Stephenson's great rival and yet his great friend throughout most of his life. Brunel is famous for his two 'greats' – the Great Western Railway and the Great Eastern Steamship.

His unusual name was partly French, partly English. He was named Isambard Brunel after his father Marc Isambard Brunel, a French refugee; Kingdom was his mother's surname.

The father, Marc Brunel, was a famous engineer who was knighted for the construction of the Rotherhithe tunnel under the Thames. He was able to give his more famous son a good start as an engineer. Marc Brunel's family had lived in Normandy for centuries. He was trained for the navy but as a young royalist officer he had to leave France in a hurry soon after the Revolution broke out. After several narrow escapes he reached New York where he made a name as an architect and engineer until he decided to go to England.

To England Marc Brunel took with him his designs for block-making machinery. An account of this complicated machinery has been given in Chapter four, with a description of the part Maudslay played. When the Government accepted the designs for Portsmouth Dockyard Marc Brunel married and started a family. He was able to give his son a very good education.

Young Isambard Kingdom Brunel showed his ability when very young. He was very good at drawing and learnt geometry very easily. He developed a habit of sketching and drawing buildings. First he was sent to a boarding school at Hove. When he was fourteen his father sent him to the College of Caen in Normandy. Later on he went to Paris and attended the famous Lycée Henri Quatre which was specially known for its teaching of mathematics. As well as this theoretical education he received a first class practical training under Louis Breguet, a famous maker of chronometers and watches. That was the end of his engineering training. He added to this, however, by spending much of his spare time with Maudslay's firm, Maudslay, Sons and Field, when he came back to England, and he began working in his father's office at the age of sixteen.

Brunel had been home only a year or two when he was fully involved in his father's last great project. This was the Thames Tunnel. A previous attempt, which Trevithick had been in charge of, to make a tunnel from Rotherhithe had failed. Marc Brunel invented and patented a tunnelling shield in 1818. This came to the notice of the financiers and they formed a Thames Tunnelling Company. Marc Brunel became Engineer at £1,000 a year and he received £5,000 for the use of his patent.

The tunnel was begun in March 1825, when Isambard Brunel was nearly nineteen: it was not finished until 18 years later. The difficulties and dangers were tremendous. There were frequent mishaps and many men died. Isambard Brunel nearly lost his life in the tunnel.

At the age of twenty he was for a time engineer in charge of the vast project at a time when his father was ill and the resident engineer had resigned. Brunel was involved in several accidents. In one of these when the water swept in from the river he saved the life of an old engineman. There was always a feeling of danger as the great tunnelling shield, consisting of twelve cast iron frames each 21 feet by 3 feet, pushed forward under the river. Sometimes the Irish labourers panicked on a false alarm. A miner told Brunel what happened on one of these occasions.

'I seed them there Hirishers a come a tumblin' through one o' them small harches like mad bulls, as if the devil picked 'un –

screach of Murther! Murther! Run for your lives! Out the lights! . . . My ears got a singing, Sir – all the world like when you and me were down in that 'ere diving-bell – till I thought as the water was close upon me. Run legs or perish body! says I, when I see Pascoe ahead o' them there miners coming along as if the devil was looking for him. Not the first, my lad, says I, and away with me – and never stopped until I got landed fair above ground.'

In January 1828 a real and serious mishap occurred which caused all work on the tunnel to be stopped for seven years. Brunel narrowly escaped drowning. The river bed was found to be unreliable; the clay had large patches of gravel and this had been dredged leaving large holes in the bed. Through one of these the river water poured into the tunnel. Brunel was in the shield. He was knocked over by the rush of water and his leg was caught under a beam. He managed to free himself and the water carried him up the shaft, but six others were drowned. Although in pain he refused to leave until he had found how much damage had been done. He was ill for some months, and he wrote down his impressions of those terrifying few minutes:

'When we were obliged to run, I felt nothing in particular; I was only thinking of the best way of getting us on and the probable state of the arches. When knocked down, I certainly gave myself up, but I took it very much as a matter of course, which I had expected the moment we quitted the frames, for I never expected we should get out. The instant I disengaged myself and got breath again – all dark – I bolted into the other arch . . . I stood still nearly a minute. I was anxious for poor Ball and Collins, who I felt sure had never risen from the fall we had all had and were, I thought, *crushed* under the great stage. I kept calling them by name, to encourage them and make them also (if still able) come through the opening. While standing there the effect was – *grand* – the roar of the rushing water in a confined passage, and by its velocity rushing past the opening was grand, *very grand*. I cannot compare it to anything, cannon can be nothing to it. At last it came bursting through the opening. I was then obliged to be off . . . Reaching the shaft I was much too bothered with my knee and some other things to remember much. If I had been kept under another minute when knocked down I should not have suffered more, and I trust I was tolerably fit to die.'

When he had recovered Brunel got several commissions, two for building docks, one for a conservatory, and one for drainage works on the Essex coast. But except for the last they came to nothing. He was an ambitious young man, in a hurry, determined to make a great career. He did not have long to wait for the first big opportunity. It came in 1829 when he was twenty-three.

The citizens of Bristol decided to build a bridge across the Avon Gorge, the Clifton Suspension Bridge. Brunel having spent his convalescence at Bristol, got to hear of the plan, and entered for the competition. He decided on a suspension bridge and submitted four designs for bridges at different points. Their spans were greater than any suspension bridge built so far, and ranged between 870 feet and 916 feet. He had some experience to go on for he had helped his father build suspension bridges in France. He had now the benefit of his father's advice and he studied closely a number of bridges of similar construction in England.

The designs were judged by Thomas Telford who was at the height of his fame but was also well over seventy. Telford rejected all the designs; Brunel's because he thought the spans were too long for safety. Telford then put in his own design which was also rejected, famous man though he was, and the competition was held again. Brunel revised his design, it won the competition and he was appointed engineer.

Work was delayed until more money could be raised. Then the Bristol Riots stopped work completely. These riots arose from the people's anger when the House of Lords rejected the Reform Bill. The prison was broken open and fired; the mansion house, bishop's palace and other buildings were burned. Brunel was sworn in as a special constable and helped the troops. However it was another five years before the foundation stone of the bridge abutment was laid with ceremony. Even after that there was not enough money and it was not until after Brunel's death that the bridge was at last finished and opened in 1864. During all that time alterations were made but today the Clifton suspension bridge is mainly as Brunel designed it when he was twenty-four years old.

Brunel was still without the big project he longed for and felt he was capable of carrying out. It was in Bristol, where he was already well known, that the really big project came his way. The merchants of that port had become alarmed at the way Liverpool had forged ahead of them. They had planned improvements to the docks and the new Clifton bridge but nothing had come of them. Most of the railways built so far had been in the north of England and the Midlands. Now it was time to plan a railway from Bristol to London, the longest of any so far built.

This railway was to be the Great Western Railway. At first it was called the Bristol Railway, when Brunel was appointed engineer in 1833, at the age of twenty-seven. He undertook to make a preliminary survey of the whole line for £500. For three months he toured over the whole country between London and Bristol, on horseback or in a coach by day, making estimates and calculations at night. He kept a diary:

'Saturday April 20th – Arrived at Reading late. Went to bed. After breakfast went in search of Hughes. After some trouble found him at "Black Boy", Shinfield, gave him maps. Went with him to Theale Road and into Pangbourne. Returned to Reading, went to Theale . . . Returned to Reading.

Sunday April 21st – Went to Church at the great Church – Dr. Millman. After Church lunched. Started on horseback for Wantage – baited at Blewbury and arrived late at Wantage.

Monday April 22nd – Started at 6.0 a.m. Examined the ground in the neighbourhood of Wantage – breakfasted at Streatley. Determined on the outer line winding round the undulating ground. Returned to Reading, dined, and went to Theale to meet Hughes . . .

Monday May 6th – Started by Emerald Coach to Newbury. Arrived there, mounted my horse and rode to Uffington, thence to Shrivenham. Slept there and in the morning proceeded to Swindon. . . . George came: our lines nearly met, but he has been winding round in a most curious manner. Directed him to point out his Bench Mark to Hughes at Wootton Bassett and then return over his ground to Chippenham following a line

I traced for him. Rode to Hungerford; thence to Newbury. Just as I got in sight of the Castle my horse came down – cut his knees and forehead dreadfully – just scratched my knee . . . Returned to town in Bristol Mail.'

The Great Western Railway Company was formed with twelve Bristol and twelve London directors. They now had to get a Bill through Parliament. Brunel now had to have his own office in London and he set himself up in style at 53 Parliament Street, near the Houses of Parliament, which he would have to attend frequently to give evidence for the railway. He had his own travelling carriage, a black one specially fitted out to take plans and instruments, which was nicknamed the 'Flying Hearse'. He had become a heavy smoker and the carriage had a cigar case holding fifty cigars.

The parliamentary Bill required a detailed survey and plans of the line and Brunel now carried this out, with assistants, covering the whole ground again as his diary shows. Some of the names are those of local landowners whose support had to be gained so that they would not oppose the Bill in Parliament.

'September 14 – Up at 5 a.m. Joined Place and Williams rowed on to the Island east of Caversham. Breakfasted and mounted. Called on Mr. Hawks, Surveyor; appointed to be with him at 8 p.m. Rode to meet Hughes; found him in barley stubble west of cottage. Directed him how to proceed and to meet me this evening at the Bear (Reading). Rode then to Purley Hall. Met Mr. Wilder just going in; spoke to him; found him very civil; gave him a prospectus. Rode in to Basildon Farm; left Mr. Hopkins' note and my card on Mr. Stone. Rode on to Streatley. Tried in every way to find a line round instead of crossing the river at Goring; found it impossible. On looking at the country from the high hill south of Streatley however, it was evident that much cutting might be saved by passing south-west of Streatley Farm and winding a little more east of Halfpenny Lane.'

The struggle to get the Great Western Railway Bill through Parliament was a keen one. It was rejected once and got through after a second attempt. It was opposed by landowners, coach proprietors, canal companies, rival railway companies.

The opposition tried to prove that the Box tunnel would be dangerous. Brunel himself, as the man who had made the plans, was cross-examined by counsel for 11 days. The cost to the company was more than £80,000 before a line of railway was built. While this was going on Brunel was already planning to extend the line in one direction to Exeter, Plymouth and beyond, and in another to Cheltenham and South Wales. Now he had the enormous task in front of him of carrying the line through from London to Bristol. This took five and a half years; it was the great work he had waited for.

He had been too busy to write in his diary but on 26th December 1835, he wrote:

'When last I wrote in this book I was just emerging from obscurity. I had been toiling most unprofitably at numerous things – unprofitably at least at the moment. The Railway certainly was brightening but still very uncertain – What a change. The *Railway* now is in progress. I am their Engineer to the finest work in England – a handsome salary – £2,000 a year – on excellent terms with my Directors and all going smoothly, but what a fight we have had – and how near defeat – and what a ruinous defeat it would have been . . .

I am just leaving 53 Parliament Street where I may say I have made my fortune or rather the foundation of it and have taken Lord Devon's house, No. 18 Duke Street – a fine house - I have a fine travelling carriage – I go sometimes with my four horses – I have a cab and horse, I have a secretary – in fact I am now somebody. Everything has prospered, everything at this moment is sunshine. I don't like it – it can't last – bad weather must surely come. Let me see the storm in time to gather in my sails.'

The question now to be settled was the gauge of the new railway. The Great Western Railway was chiefly famous for its 7-foot gauge. It was expected that the railway would use the 4-foot 8½-inch gauge of all those railways built so far. But Brunel thought otherwise. He was not the man to do anything merely because it had been done before. The 4-foot 8½-inch gauge had been used by George Stephenson simply because it was the gauge of the wagon ways of the collieries around

Newcastle upon Tyne. Other railways had copied it because of Stephenson's great reputation.

Brunel wanted for his Great Western Railway greater speed and smoothness than anywhere else and for this he wanted bigger and heavier locomotives and carriages. These could only be run on a broader gauge, and 7 feet it was. But there was a struggle to get it adopted even after the first section of line was opened. This event took place in May 1838 when the directors travelled from Paddington to Maidenhead, drawn by the *North Star* made by Robert Stephenson and Company, the first of the great broad gauge engines, with 7-foot single driving wheels. One of the directors described the event:

'A very pretty sight it was. At 11.30 we entered the carriages of the first train and, proceeding at a moderate pace, reached Maidenhead Station in 49 minutes, or at about 28 miles an hour. After visiting the works we returned to Salt Hill where a cold luncheon for about 300 was laid under a tent. After the usual complement of toasts we returned to the line and reached Paddington (19 miles) in 34 minutes, or $33\frac{1}{2}$ miles per hour.'

But even after this triumph the advantages of the broad gauge were not obtained until Brunel had made alterations to the engines and the permanent way. A party of shareholders tried to get another engineer appointed. Brunel was a very harassed man though he never showed it. He wrote a confession to his friend the railway secretary at the end of a long letter:

'I have spun this long yarn, partly as a recreation after working all the night, principally to have the pleasure of telling a real friend that I am sensible of his kindness, although he hardly allows me to see it, and partly because I wish you to know that if I appear to take things coldly it is because I am obliged to harden myself a little to be able to bear the thought of it . . .

If ever I go mad, I shall have the ghost of the opening of the railway walking before me, or rather standing in front of me, holding out its hand, and when it steps forward, a little swarm of devils in the shape of leaky pickle-tanks, uncut timber, half-finished station houses, sinking embankments, broken screws, unfinished drawings, and sketches, will, quietly and quite as a matter of course, and as if I ought to have expected it, lift up my ghost and put him a little further off than before.'

(The pickle-tanks were used for pickling or 'Kyanising' the timber for sleepers to preserve it.)

The Great Western Railway was pushed ahead from the London and Bristol ends at the same time. Going west from London, Brunel designed the Maidenhead bridge over the Thames and then came to the great cutting at Sonning east of Reading. (Plate IV.) This cutting through Sonning Hill was 60 feet deep and 2 miles long. Over 1,200 navvies and 200 horses had to be used to get through. In March 1840, more than four years after the railway was begun, the first train ran through to Reading. The permanent way had been improved. Brunel had decided to use a lighter rail, 62 lb. instead of 75 lb. On the return journey the *Firefly*, another of the engines with 7-foot single driving wheels, covered 31 miles at 50 m.p.h. This was what Brunel had aimed at and a speed which no other railway could maintain. The London division went as far as Shrivenham.

From the Bristol end there were some heavy works to be tackled. Between Bristol and Bath alone there were four bridges, seven tunnels and a viaduct to be made. Farther east there were numerous cuttings and embankments. Brunel was always up and down the line. From the temporary end of the line his travelling carriage rushed him to the sites. He writes to his wife from Wootton Bassett:

'My dearest Mary, I have become quite a walker. I have walked today from Bathford Bridge to here – all but about one mile, which makes eighteen miles walking along the line – and I really am not very tired. I am, however, going to sleep here – if I had been half-an-hour earlier, I think I could not have withstood the temptation of coming up by the six $\frac{1}{2}$ train and returning by the morning goods train, just to see you; however, I will write you a long letter instead . . .'

The last and most difficult stage of the London to Bristol line was the Box tunnel. The tunnel was nearly 2 miles long, far longer than any yet built, and it was on a gradient of 1 in

100. Much of the earth was soft but half a mile was through oolite rock. Over 100 tons of gunpowder were used in two and a half years to blast a way through. For the last six months Brunel employed 4,000 men and 300 horses on it, working round the clock. About 100 men died on the job, through accident or some other way. It was a tremendous task carried on in all weathers, with water sometimes rushing in from the overhead rock. At last, in June 1841, the first train steamed right through from Paddington to Bristol. The line had cost £6,500,000, more than double the original estimate. But such a line had never been built before.

The G.W.R. was immediately carried on to Exeter and to Cheltenham under Brunel's direction. The high speeds he hoped for from the broad gauge were obtained. The 194 miles from Paddington to Exeter were covered in four hours forty minutes, including stops for water.

Farther west Brunel was engineer to the South Devon, Cornwall and West Cornwall railway companies which continued the line to Penzance. There were some difficult engineering problems. The line had to cross many deep and narrow valleys which run down from the moors to the coast. Over these valleys Brunel built his famous timber viaducts. There were 50 or more of these viaducts. Some of them very high; near Liskeard there was one 153 feet high; on the Tavistock line there was a viaduct 132 feet high and 367 yards long. Their advantages were that they were much cheaper than stone or iron bridges, and they were very graceful structures. The timber was easy to get and it had a long life of up to 50 years. Great spars of yellow pine from the Baltic were used, but later on suitable timber for replacements could not be obtained. The last of them disappeared only about 30 years ago.

Brunel's last great railway work was the Royal Saltash Bridge over the river Tamar which barred the way of the line west of Plymouth. It was a difficult task because the river was over 1,000 feet wide and 70 feet deep at high tide, and the Admiralty required 100 feet headroom for ships. Brunel himself controlled the tricky operation in which the cast iron truss weighing 1,000 tons was floated down to the river to its position on the masonry piers. The bridge was triumphantly opened in 1859. By that time Brunel was a dying man.

To build the biggest railway in Britain was not enough for Brunel. He was also a designer of ships and he built the biggest ship of the time, the famous *Great Eastern*. But he wore himself out doing this. He designed and built his three great ships at the same time as the railway construction.

The idea of the first ship arose at a board meeting of the Great Western Railway when Brunel suggested that a steam boat should be built to go from Bristol to New York, to be called the *Great Western*. Brunel designed her to be very strong, built of oak strengthened throughout with iron and with the hull sheathed in copper, to face the Atlantic storms. Her length was 236 feet and her breadth over the hull 35 feet, over the paddleboxes 60 feet. The engines had to be nearly double the size of any marine engines made before. They were made by Maudslay, Sons and Field. Driven by her paddles the *Great Western*, the biggest steamship so far built made a record 15-day crossing on her maiden voyage in 1838. In the next eight years she made 67 crossings and she was the second ship to cross the ocean by steam power alone. (Plate IV facing p. 97.)

This was Brunel's first venture. But no sooner had the *Great Western* made her second voyage than he planned a larger and better ship. This was the *Great Britain*. Unlike the *Great Western* she was built of iron, and unlike almost every other sea-going vessel she was screw-propelled instead of paddle-propelled. She was greater than anything before in various aspects – her weight of 3,270 tons, her length of 322 feet, breadth of 51 feet, the tremendous strength of her hull with ten great girders running the length of her bottom, and her engines of 1,500 h.p. When she was launched in 1843 she got stuck in Bristol Dock. Brunel wrote:

'We have had an unexpected difficulty with the *Great Britain* this morning. She stuck in the lock; we did get her back. I have been hard at work all day altering the masonry of the lock. Tonight our last tide, we have succeeded in getting her through; but, being dark, we have been obliged to ground her outside, and I confess I cannot leave her until I see her afloat again, and all clear of her difficulties. I have, as you will admit, much at stake here, and I am too anxious about it to leave her.'

Three years later the *Great Britain* sailed for New York with

180 passengers when she struck rocks on the coast of Ireland. She lay there for a whole year, but she was so strong that there was no major damage. She was repaired and had another 40 years of active life. She sailed regularly to Australia, was used as a troopship, and only in 1886 did she end up as a store for wood and coal in the Falkland Islands. There she was sunk at last in 1937, nearly 100 years after her launching. She was the first iron ship and the first screw ship to cross an ocean.

The *Great Western* and the *Great Britain*, big as they were, only paved the way for Brunel's greatest ship of all, the *Great Eastern*. She was by far the biggest ship yet built. Her length, 692 feet, was more than double that of the *Great Britain*. When the contract for construction was signed it—

'Provided for construction, trial launch and delivery of an iron ship of the general dimensions of 680 feet between perpendiculars, 83 feet beam and 58 feet deep according to the drawings annexed, signed by the engineer, I. K. Brunel.

All vertical joints are to be butt joints and to be double riveted wherever required by the engineer. Bulkheads are to be at 60 feet intervals. No cast iron to be used anywhere except for slide valves and cocks without special permission of the engineer. The water tightness of every part to be tested up to the level of the lower deck.

The ship to be built in a dock . . .

The engineer to have entire control over the proceedings and the workmanship.'

Brunel decided that the *Great Eastern* should be propelled by both screws and paddles. He also decided that she should be launched sideways into the Thames from her berth at Napier's Yard, Millwall. Work on the hull began in July 1854 and the ship was ready to be launched three years later.

Everything in the *Great Eastern* was on a larger scale than anything before. The four screw engine cylinders, cast at Watt's Soho foundry, were 7 feet in diameter and 4 feet stroke. The four paddle engine cylinders, cast at the yard, were 6 feet 2 inches in diameter and 14 feet stroke. The crankshaft for the paddle engines required the largest forging ever yet seen, weighing 40 tons.

Brunel kept a close eye on the details, as shown by entries in his diary:

'March 3rd, 1854. Blake (an employee of James Watt & Co.) called with drawings of screw engines. Insufficiency of bearing surface. Crank pins 18″ × 18″ not enough: 24″ × 24″ barely sufficient. Problem: necessity of working crank between two piston rods limits dimensions.

March 7th, 1854. Have been thinking a great deal over Blake's arrangements and have come to conclusion that double piston rods carried through to the opposite engine *cannot* unless with a very low steam pressure, leave room for a properly proportioned crank. Wrote long letter to B. on necessity of resorting to two distinct connecting rods . . .

March 9th, 1854. Blake here again. Found, as I thought, a mistake of ten to one in his calculations of bearing surface.'

The launching of the great ship was the most difficult task of all. Never before had such a great mass been moved into the narrow and shallow waters of the Thames, or anywhere else. It was a complicated mechanical problem. The ship had to be eased gradually sideways down the launching ways, being checked under control the whole time. It was not possible to slide her off rapidly into the water.

The launching ways, on a foundation of two feet thick concrete, were constructed of timber baulks surmounted by iron rails. On these iron rails rested the iron bars of the two great cradles, each 120 feet wide, which supported the ship. The cradles were to be eased down the launching ways by gravity, by winches, and by hydraulic rams. Control was maintained by two huge checking drums, one at the head of each slipway.

The first attempt to launch the *Great Eastern* on 3rd November 1857 was a failure. Brunel had been compelled to make the attempt before he was ready. The operation was hampered by the big crowds which swarmed round the drums and the cradles. The public interest was so great that the company had sold three thousand tickets of entry into the yard. It was a bad day. One man was killed and four injured in moving the ship four feet. By 30th November the *Great Eastern* had been moved 33 feet down the slipway, and a week later another 44 feet.

More and more hydraulic presses were needed. Brunel sent an order to the newly established little firm of Tangye's. By January 1858 Brunel had eighteen presses in position. With their help the ship was got so far down the slipways that there was a danger of the high tide floating her off out of control. Water ballast was therefore pumped in. At last on 31st January everything was ready, the weather turned favourable, the *Great Eastern* was floated off safely and towed across the river to moor at Deptford.

The *Great Eastern* became famous as the layer of the first trans-Atlantic cable in 1866 and went on to lay cables all over the world. She was then fitted out for passenger services but she could not be made to pay. For a short time she was even a showboat anchored in the Mersey. At last, in 1888, 30 years after being launched, she was broken up and sold by auction.

Brunel lived only another year after the *Great Eastern* was launched. At the age of fifty-three he was worn out with the enormous work he had got through, with years of anxiety and exposure to weather in all conditions. Daniel Gooch, the locomotive designer and Brunel's best friend, wrote about him:

'By his death the greatest of England's engineers was lost, the man with the greatest originality of thought and power of execution, bold in his plans but right. The commercial world thought him extravagant; but although he was so, great things are not done by those who sit down and count the cost of every thought and act.'

NAVVIES AND RAILWAYMEN

These were the two classes of working men who came into existence as a result of the great engineering works of the Stephensons and Brunel.

Let us look at the navvies first, the men who built the railways. The railwaymen came after the railways had been built. The word 'navvy' was an abbreviation of navigator. This was the name of the skilled men who built the canals, but navvy came to be used of all the men, whether skilled or labourers, who worked in railway construction. There were about 150,000 of them working in Great Britain in 1848, the busiest year of construction (the population was then about ten million). The biggest contractors employed 10,000 men, most of whom would be digging and shovelling. In the north of England many of the navvies were Irishmen. In the south many were farm labourers whose wages were very low. They were a rough and tough lot, stout fighters and drinkers, and they led a hard life out on the wind-swept moors in the bitterest weather. One of them gave this account of himself to a journalist:

'The first work that I done was on the Manchester and Liverpool. I was a lad then. I used to grease the railway wagons, and got about 1s. 6d. a day . . . the next place I had after that was on the London and Brummagem. There I went as a horse-driver, and had 2s. 6d. a day. Things were dear then, and at the tommy shops they was much dearer; for there was tommy shops on every line then; and indeed every contractor and sub-contractor had his shop that he forced his men to deal at or else he wouldn't have them in his employ . . . Well, sir, I worked on that line through all the different contracts till it was finished; sometimes I was digging, sometimes shovelling. I was mostly at work on open cuttings. All this time I was getting from 2s. 6d. to 3s. and 3s. 6d. a day; that was the top price; if I'd had the ready money to lay out myself, I could have done pretty well, and maybe put a penny or two by against a rainy day; but the tommy shop and the lodging house took it all out of us. You see, the tommy shop found us in beer and they would let us drink away all our earnings there if we pleased, and when pay time came we should have nothing to take. If we didn't eat and drink at the tommy shop we should have no work. Of an evening we went to the tommy shop after the drink and they'd keep drawing beer for us there as long as we'd have anything coming to us next pay-day . . . and when we had drunk away all that would be coming to us, why they'd turn us out . . . Well, with such goings on, in course there wasn't no chance in the world for us to save a halfpenny . . . and now half of us walk about and starve, or beg, or go to the union.'

The tommy shop was a shop run by the contractor in out-of-the-way country where there were no other supplies.

The navvies were often exploited through high prices and inferior food. The above illustrates how the navvies saw them. In the following report to Robert Stephenson we see how the employer saw them:

'Ellison, one of the sub-contractors on No. 2 has a shop at his dwelling near Lee Hall which is kept by himself and supplies his men with shoes, bacon, bread and groceries. There is occasional grumbling amongst the men against the high prices they pay, but I cannot tell how far they are justified.'

A navvies' chaplain said 'they pay for the coarsest joint. what I pay for the best.' They often had to live in mere hovels. Some big contractors built stone cottages or wooden barracks but for many there were only mud and turf huts or a shared bed in an overcrowded village.

Some of the skilled men, such as tunnel miners, went abroad when the English contractors built railways in Europe. Four thousand of them worked on the Paris–Rouen line. There they astonished the French with their consumption of steak and whisky and their hard work.

The navvies never combined together in trade unions, although strikes did happen. But they did organize their own sick clubs and run them themselves.

'They support their sick extremely well,' said the chaplain, 'every man pays towards the sick . . . they make a little weekly payment.'

The railwaymen, unlike the navvies, were regular employees of the companies. They were in the railway service and they called themselves railway servants. It was a new kind of job in Britain, to go on the railway. Many village lads did this, so too did domestic servants and discharged soldiers, as the railways spread across Britain. By 1849 there were no less than 56,000 of them.

For most of them railway service was a good job. There was security of employment which was rare in those days, and wages which were regular and rather higher than the wages of farm labourers, a uniform and often a cottage. Railway jobs were much sought after. Here is a typical application for a job in 1842:

'The humble petition of William Bullock a resident inhabitant of the Parish of Steventon in the County of Berks. respectfully shewed that your petitioner is anxious to obtain employment as a Porter on your line of Railway. We the undersigned inhabitants of the said Parish recommend him as being a sober, honest, industrious person as a candidate for that office; he therefore solicits the kind approval of your honourable company hoping they will be pleased to grant him an early appointment and should he be the object of your choice will no doubt to the utmost of his abilities merit your confidence and approbation in discharging the duties committed to his care.'

But there were many drawbacks to the railwayman's life. Hours of work were very long; 12 to 14 hours a day was normal. Men felt the strain of the responsibility for the lives of passengers, particularly the signalmen and enginemen. Accidents were frequent and drunkenness was common. The railways had a strict system of discipline for its employees. Men were punished by dismissal or heavy fines for breaking the regulations; there were plenty of others ready to take their places. They had no unions to protect them when they asked for higher wages. Here is how the director of the Liverpool and Manchester Railway dealt with one incident as recorded in their minutes at the time:

8th February 1836
'The Treasurer reported that on Wednesday last there had been a turn out amongst the enginemen and firemen. On Monday several of the enginemen had given verbal notice that unless the firemen's wages were increased they would leave on Friday evening. On Wednesday morning the Treasurer asked one of the oldest enginemen whether he persisted in that notice and he answering that he did, the Treasurer discharged him instantly. Upon this the other enginemen refused to go with the trains. Other enginemen were however speedily engaged. Four of the enginemen who had entered into written agreements with the Company, viz. Charles Callan, Peter Callan, Henry Weatherbury and George Massey, had been apprehended and taken before the Justices of the Peace who investigated the circumstances of the turn out, and the breach of contract being

proved, committed the said offenders to Kirkdale Jail to be put to hard labour for one calendar month.'

15th February 1836

'Read a letter from Charles Callan, Peter Callan, Henry Weatherbury and George Massey, now confined in Kirkdale Prison expressing sorrow for their offence and begging to be let out. The Treasurer to reply that the Directors had no power to liberate them from their confinement.'

22nd February 1836

'Read a letter from the Chaplain to the Kirkdale Jail, communicating the petition of the two Callans, Henry Weatherbury and Massey to be relieved from the severe labour and fatigue of the treadmill, on which they were kept at work six hours a day. The directors were disposed to mitigate the severity of their labour for the remainder of their term of confinement and Mr. Currie (one of the directors) undertook as Chief Magistrate, to recommend to the Governor of the Jail that the Directors' clement disposition towards the prisoners might be attended to'.

There were very few strikes or disputes on the railways – the railwaymen were more satisfied than most workers. In the Chartist days they enrolled as special constables on the railways instead of joining the Chartists. They formed no trade unions in these early days, up to 1850. The enginemen, being the most independent and the best paid section, moved the farthest in that direction. They had their Locomotive Steam Enginemen and Firemen's Friendly Society with many branches and thousands of members. But the thousands of porters, platelayers, guards and signalmen were not able to form a union for twenty years.

Additional Reading

L. T. C. Rolt, *George and Robert Stephenson*, Longmans 1960.
L. T. C. Rolt, *I. K. Brunel*, Longmans 1957.

CHAPTER SEVEN

The
Machine-Tool
Makers

JAMES NASMYTH (1808–1890)

JAMES NASMYTH is famous as the inventor of the steam hammer. He also invented some important machine tools, a slot-drilling machine, a shaper, and a milling machine. He belonged to the school of Maudslay, having worked under him for several years.

Nasmyth was another of the Scots who made their name in engineering. Unlike many of them, his family were well off, with some influence, and this gave him a good start in life which many other inventors and engineers did not have. His father was a professional painter, with a big reputation in Scotland. He knew many of the famous men of the day. Of these James Watt and Sir Walter Scott made a great impression on young Nasmyth. He had a happy comfortable childhood, with his nine brothers and sisters. At the age of nine he was sent to Edinburgh High School but in the three years he was there he learnt a little Latin and not much else.

He did not attend any school after he was twelve, but was left free to follow his own interests. There were evening classes at the Edinburgh School of Arts, which was really like a technical college, and he went regularly to classes there in mechanics, mathematics and chemistry for five years, until he was eighteen. These were the subjects which interested him. He also learnt a great deal from his father who taught him drawing. He was free to use his father's workshop and he soon made himself into a good practical engineer at the bench and lathe. He made models of steam engines and at the age of fifteen he made his first working steam engine in the workshop. He made sectional models and sold them to technical schools for £10 each.

Nasmyth describes how he learnt to do this:

'I had the good luck to have for a school companion the son of an iron founder. Every spare hour that I could command was devoted to visits to his father's iron foundry, where I delighted to watch the various processes of moulding, iron-smelting, casting, forging, pattern-making, and other smith and metal work . . . I look back to the Saturday afternoons spent in the workshops of that small foundry as an important part of my education . . . By the time I was fifteen I could work and turn out really respectable jobs in wood, brass, iron and steel: indeed in the working of the latter inestimable material I had at a very early age (eleven or twelve) acquired considerable proficiency. As that was the pre-lucifer period, the possession of a steel and tinder box was quite a patent of nobility among boys. So I used to forge old files into steels in my father's little workshop, and harden them and produce such first-rate neat little articles in that line, that I became quite famous amongst my school companions . . .

'My first essay at making a steam engine was when I was fifteen. I then made a real working steam engine. $1\frac{3}{4}$-inch diameter cylinder, and 8-inch stroke, which not only could act, but really did some useful work; for I made it grind the oil colours which my father required for his painting.'

In this same foundry he learnt from the foreman in charge of the boring machines how to harden and temper steel. At the home of another school friend there was a laboratory where they could experiment in chemistry, making themselves the acids they used, instead of buying them.

Before he was twenty-one he made, with the help of a friend who ran a small works, working steam engines for the works and even a steam road carriage which ran successfully with eight passengers for short distances.

In Scotland the best engine makers had been trained at Maudslay's works in London. Nasmyth decided that if he were to be an outstanding engineer he must get a proper training there. In 1829, when he was twenty-one, he sailed from Leith to London. But before leaving, realizing it would be difficult to be accepted at Maudslay's works, he made a complete working model steam engine and prepared examples of his skill as a draughtsman in order to show Maudslay what he could do.

Maudslay refused to take pupils, or premium apprentices as they were called. Nasmyth's only chance to be taken on at the famous workshop was as an assistant to the great man himself. Fortunately his father had met Maudslay. This alone would not have been enough, but the work Nasmyth took with him so impressed the master that he was taken on as an assistant without serving an apprenticeship.

Maudslay's works were at that time famous for the accuracy of the tools made there, and Nasmyth had a wonderful training in helping Maudslay make many machine tools, such as the screw-cutting lathe and the collar-nut cutting machine. At first his wage was 10s. a week. When Nasmyth had been there two years Maudslay died and he then assisted the other partner in the firm, Joshua Field. Field was as kind to him as Maudslay had been. Nasmyth wrote about him later on:

'He gave me many most valuable hints as to the designing of machinery in general. In after years I had many opportunities of making good use of them. One point he often impressed upon me. It was, he said, most important to bear in mind the *get-at-ability* of parts – that is, when any part of a machine was out of repair, it was requisite to get at it easily without taking the machine to pieces. This may appear a very simple remark, but the neglect of such an arrangement occasions a vast amount of trouble, delay, and expense.'

When Nasmyth was twenty-three he decided to start his own business. He was allowed to take away with him castings of a Maudslay lathe and, having erected a temporary workshop at home, he soon completed it. With it he made a planing machine and after acquiring other machines he was ready to start. He decided to settle at Manchester where there was a great demand for machine tools, and rented one floor of a factory building. The floors were let separately and power was supplied to them all from a shaft connected with a near-by mill. The tenant of the floor below Nasmyth was a glass cutter.

Orders soon came in and the business flourished. Nasmyth described how this happened:

'I had plenty of orders, and did my best to execute them

satisfactorily. Shortly after the opening of the Liverpool and Manchester Railway there was a largely increased demand for machine-making tools... There was a great demand for skilled, and even for unskilled labour. The demand was greater than the supply. Employers were subjected to exorbitant demands for increased rates of wages ... The irregularity and careless-ness of the workmen naturally proved very annoying to the employers. But it gave an increased stimulus to the demand for self-acting machine tools, by which the untrustworthy efforts of hand labour might be avoided. The machines never got drunk; their hands never shook from excess; they were never absent from work; they did not strike for wages ...

'Most of my own machine tools were self-acting – planing machines, slide lathes, drilling, boring, slotting machines, and so on ... They were their own best advertisements. The consequence was that orders for similar machines poured in upon me, and the floor of my flat became completely loaded with the work in hand.'

One day the beam of a 20-h.p. steam engine crashed through the floor on to the glass cutter below. Nasmyth had to move. He was lucky in finding a six acre site at Patricroft in an ideal situation. It was bounded on three sides by the Bridgewater Canal, the railway, and a good road. Here he began to build his Bridgewater Foundry in 1836, at the age of twenty-eight, and before long it covered, with workmen's cottages, the whole six acres. At the foundry he invented his screw safety ladle. This removed a good deal of danger from the operation of pouring molten iron. It also saved labour.

As the Bridgewater Foundry became a large firm so Nasmyth employed many more men from different parts of Lancashire. His policy was to employ unskilled men on the machine tools, and to select from the labourers those men who were able to operate the planers, lathes and boring machines. This led him into conflict with the trade unions. This is his account of the strike.

'I had no difficulty in manning my machine tools by drawing my recruits from this zealous and energetic class of labourers. It is by this "selection of the fittest" that the true source of the prosperity of every large manufacturing establishment depends . . . But here I came into collision with another class of workmen – those who are of the opinion that employers should select for promotion, not those who are the fittest and most skilful, but those who have served a seven years' apprenticeship and are members of a Trades Union.

'The men who waited upon us were deputed by the Engineer Mechanics Trades' Union to inform us that there were men in our employment who were not, as they termed it, "legally entitled to the trade"; that is, they had never served a regular seven years' apprenticeship. "These men," said the delegates, "are filling up the places, and keeping out of work, the legal hands". We were accordingly requested to discharge the workmen whom we had promoted (to the machines) in order to make room for members of the Trades' Union.'

Nasmyth refused to agree and all the trade union members struck and picketed the works. He broke the strike by bringing 60 men down from Scotland. Nasmyth refused to employ apprentices. As he said he preferred to employ men who had learned the necessary skill in two years rather than those who were stupid enough to need seven years. He did, however, employ pupils who paid premiums.

In 1839, when he was thirty-one, Nasmyth made the in-invention for which he is famous, the steam hammer. The idea came to him in this way. One of I. K. Brunel's great ships, the *Great Britain*, was being built. It was to be driven by paddle wheel and a wrought iron paddle shaft was required far bigger than any before. It was so big that no forge hammer could forge it. This stirred him to design a hammer that could do the job. He describes what happened:

'How was it (he asked himself) that the existing hammers were incapable of forging a wrought iron shaft of thirty inches diameter? Simply because of their want of compass, of range and fall, as well as of their want of power of blow. A few moments' rapid thought satisfied me that it was by our rigidly adhering to the old traditional form of a smith's hand hammer – of which the forge and tilt hammer, although driven by water or steam power, were mere enlarged modifications – that the difficulty had arisen; as, whenever the largest forge hammer was tilted up to its full height, its range was so small that when a piece of work of considerable size was placed on the anvil, the hammer became "gagged"; so that, when the forging required the most powerful blow, it received next to no blow at all, as the clear space for the fall of the hammer was almost entirely occupied by the work on the anvil.

The obvious remedy was to contrive some method by which a ponderous block of iron should be lifted to a sufficient height above the object on which it was desired to strike a blow, and then to let the block full down upon the forging, guiding it in its descent by such simple means as should give the required precision in the percussive action of the falling mass. Following up this idea, I got out my "Scheme Book", on the pages of which I generally *thought out*, with the aid of pen and pencil, such mechanical adaptations as I had conceived in my mind. . . . I then rapidly sketched out my Steam Hammer, having it all clearly before me in my mind's eye. . . . The date of this first drawing was the 24th November, 1839.

My Steam Hammer, as thus first sketched, consisted of, first, a massive anvil on which to rest the work; second, a block of iron constituting the hammer or blow-giving portion; and, third, an inverted steam cylinder to whose piston-rod the hammer-block was attached. All that was then required to produce a most effective hammer was simply to admit steam of sufficient pressure into the cylinder, so as to act on the under-side of the piston, and thus to raise the hammer-block attached to the end of the piston-rod. By a very simple arrangement of a slide-valve, under the control of an attendant, the steam was allowed to escape, and thus permit the massive block of iron rapidly to descend by its own gravity upon the work then upon the anvil.'

Nasmyth took out a patent for the steam hammer. It so much increased the size of forging possible that all the iron works and foundries in Britain wanted it, and many were exported. Its great advantage was, as Nasmyth said, that 'the machine combined great power with gentleness. The hammer could be made to give so gentle a blow as to crack the end of an egg placed in a wine glass on the anvil; whilst the next blow would shake the parish . . .'

He soon developed from the steam hammer his second invention of the steam pile driver. This reduced the time

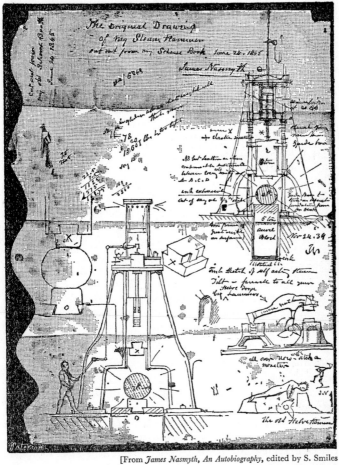

[From *James Nasmyth, An Autobiography*, edited by S. Smiles

Nasmyth's first drawing of steam hammer, 24th November 1839

required for driving in a pile to a small fraction of what was required before. It revolutionized the construction of bridges and docks.

Because of these two inventions Nasmyth became closely connected with the royal dockyards and workshops, where he was asked for his advice on modernizing them. He was amused by the strict observance of rank and status in dealing with people in the dockyards. He described what happened in church:

'The first Sunday that I spent at Devonport I went to the dockyard church – the church appointed for officials and men employed by the Government. The seats were appointed in the order of rank, employments, and rate of pay. The rows of seats were all marked with the class of employees that were expected to sit in them. Labourers were near the door. The others were in successive rows forward, until the pew of the "Admiral Superintendent", next the Altar rails, was reached. I took my seat among the "artificers", being of that order. On coming out of church the master-attendant, next in dignity to the admiral-superintendent, came up to me to say how distressed he was to see me "among the artificers", and begged me in future to use his seat. No doubt this was kindly intended, and I thanked him for his courtesy. Nevertheless I kept to my class of artificers . . . No doubt the love of distinction, within reasonable limits, is a great social prime mover, but at Devonport, with the splitting up into ranks and dignities even amongst the workmen, I found it simply amusing.'

As the Bridgewater Foundry grew and flourished Nasmyth became rich, but the years of continual strain and effort injured his health. In spite of great physical strength his nervous system was affected. He therefore decided to retire at the early age of forty-eight. He enjoyed his retirement for another 34 years, until his death at the age of eighty-two. Leaving Lancashire behind him he bought a large house in Kent and settled down to his many interests. His chief occupation was astronomy. His observations by means of a 20-inch diameter telescope that he erected in his garden contributed useful knowledge to the study of the surface of the moon and the sun.

SIR JOSEPH WHITWORTH (1803–1887)

The name of Whitworth is known today mainly because of the Whitworth scholarships and prizes awarded every year to the best students of engineering. Whitworth founded these scholarships in 1869 and they have been awarded every year since. Whitworth was himself a great mechanical engineer who became a Fellow of the Royal Society. As an engineer he became famous for the new standards of accuracy he initiated. The Whitworth thread – his standardization of a screw thread – is an example.

Whitworth started life with some advantages. His father kept a large private school in Stockport for the children of middle-class people. He later became a non-conformist minister but Whitworth had his first education in his father's school. When he was twelve years old he was sent as a boarder to another private school at Idle, near Leeds.

At the age of fourteen he was taken away from school and sent to live with an uncle who owned a cotton mill at Amber-gate in Derbyshire, to learn the business of cotton spinning. After four years he had learnt all he could, but cotton spinning did not satisfy him. It was too much of a routine business although there were prospects of becoming a partner. He decided to strike off on his own and begin his chosen career as an engineer.

He went to Manchester, where there was ample scope for an ambitious mechanic, and got himself a job at the bench with a firm of machinists. He stayed in Manchester another four years, working for several firms and getting varied experience. He saved enough to get married. Then, like many others, having heard much of the famous workshops of Maudslay and Clement in London he decided to go south and get the best training in mechanical engineering available at that time. And so in 1825, when he was twenty-two, and soon after getting married, he moved to London.

London was the centre of the best workshop practice and Whitworth soon made his way. He got a job at Maudslay's workshops in the Westminster Bridge Road, famous for the accuracy and quality of the tools made there. Maudslay had made the first screw-cutting lathe some years before. After several years with Maudslay, Whitworth worked for Joseph Clement, who had invented a planing machine and whose workshop was almost equally famous.

During his eight years in London Whitworth discovered the method of making true surface plates. Up to that time the most accurate plates had been obtained by first planing and then grinding. They were never true and Whitworth, realizing that true planes were the first thing needed to improve engineering, determined to produce them. He discussed it with his mate on the next bench, a Yorkshireman. 'If these planes were true,' he said, 'one of them ought to lift the other.' 'Tha knows nowt about it,' was the reply.

His first step was to use scraping instead of grinding. 'Taking two surfaces,' he said later on, 'as accurate as the planing tool could make them, I coated one of them with colouring matter and then rubbed the other over it. Had the two surfaces been true, the colouring matter would have spread itself uniformly over the upper one. It never did so, but appeared in spots and patches. These marked the high spots, which I removed with a scraping tool until the two surfaces gradually became more coincident.' He then realized that two surfaces might fit perfectly and lift each other and yet not be true planes. One might be convex and the other concave. The answer came to him – to make three surfaces and if each would lift either of the others they must be true planes. He made them, and said to his mate, 'John, come to my house; I've something to show you.' He showed John the three true planes. 'Ay! that's done it,' said John. It was a great moment for Whitworth, and also for the future of mechanical engineering.

When he was thirty Whitworth was ready to start his own business. He returned to Manchester, rented a room in Chorlton Street with power from a steam engine laid on, and put up a sign – 'Joseph Whitworth, Toolmaker from London.' From this small start his business grew quickly. There was a great demand for machine tools. Whitworth built them for sale to other manufacturers. By 1844, ten years after he started his business, he was employing nearly 200 men.

By 1851, the year of the Great Exhibition at the Crystal Palace in Hyde Park, he was easily the chief machine tool maker in Britain. At the exhibition Whitworth had twenty-three exhibits, many more than anyone else. They included lathes and machines for planing, shaping, slotting, drilling, punching and shearing. At the next great international exhibition, in 1862, Whitworth was still in the lead, although many more firms were now making machine tools. He employed 600–700 men.

Many of the machine tools Whitworth showed in the exhibition were based on his own inventions. His planing machine, a power-driven self-acting machine, was made under his patents; its new feature was that it cut both ways, by reversing the tool after each traverse of the bed.

He also introduced an important new feature into his lathes. This was the hollow-box design of lathe-bed. It was a big advance on the earlier triangular-bar type of construction, as it was more rigid and made accurate work more possible.

To illustrate the progress made in the workshop, Whitworth said in 1856:

'Thirty years ago the cost of labour for facing a surface of cast iron, by chipping and filing by hand, was twelve shillings per square foot; the same work is now done by the planing machine at a cost for labour of less than one penny per square foot, and this, as you know, is one of the most important operations in mechanics.'

Whitworth became famous as a great engineer for his basic discoveries in increasing accuracy and measurement to fine limits. The production of true planes was the first of these. The second step was to design machines which would measure accurately. Very soon after he set up as a toolmaker in Manchester he built a machine capable of measuring to one-ten-thousandth of an inch. Next he built a machine which could measure to one millionth of an inch. This machine was based on end measurement. He said:

'There is unsurmountable difficulty in converting line measure to end measure, and therefore it is most desirable for all standards of linear measure to be end measure. Line measure depends on sight aided by magnifying glasses, but the accuracy of end measure is due to the sense of touch, and the

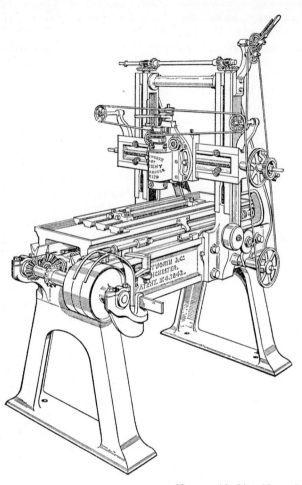

Whitworth's self-acting power-driven planing machine, 1842.
The tool is reversed after each traverse of the bed, so as to cut both
ways

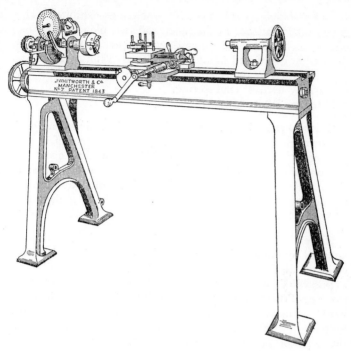

Whitworth's lathe, 1843. Note the hollow-box construction of the bed

delicacy of that sense is indicated by means of a mechanical multiplier.'

His millionth of an inch measuring machine was shown at the 1851 Great Exhibition. It worked by means of a steel bar as a feeling-piece held horizontally between two parallel surfaces. These surfaces could be moved a millionth of an inch by means of screws and wheels with marked divisions on their circumference. This movement was enough to make the feeling-piece stand or fall.

Whitworth next turned his attention to achieving accurate and standard gauges. There were many different standards of accuracy. Having worked on this problem he exhibited a ring gauge 0·5770 inches in diameter and two plug gauges, one 0·5769 inches and the other 0·5770 inches in diameter, to show what could and should be achieved. Whitworth gauges were accepted by the Board of Trade as standard and became universally used in engineering.

Later on Whitworth wrote:

'Prior to that time, every Engineer or Machinist had each his own peculiar screw thread, and when manufacturers obtained their Machinery from different makers, great loss was occasioned; the simple arrangement that every diameter of screw, bolt and nut should have a certain pitch and form of thread, has saved enormous sums of money to makers and users of Machinery.'

He realized the difficulty of getting standard screw threads adopted by industry in the existing chaos of screws. He there-collected all the screws he could find from as many workshops as possible throughout the country. He based his screws on an average of these, which could be adopted by most engineering works without too much difficulty. Then he laid down the number of threads to the inch for different sizes of screw, and the angle of 55° between the sides of the thread. Whitworth thread standards in engineering have remained in use to the present day; thus his general influence on engineering was enormous.

Whitworth also had a great influence in urging the benefits of standardization, dimensional tolerances, interchangeability of parts and what is now called simplification. The examples he used ranged from candlesticks to railway engines. Here he is writing about the first:

'Candles and candlesticks are in use in almost every house, and nothing could be more convenient than for the candle to fit accurately into the sockets of the candlesticks, which at present they seldom or never do. To this end I would propose the adoption for household purposes, of five sizes of Candles ranging, say, from 6/10ths of an inch to an inch in diameter, and each size varying from the next by precisely 1/10th of an inch. Whereas at present, in one large Candle Manufacturer, I find eleven sizes of Candles within the limit stated above, each of these sizes being of uncertain diameter, and none of them bearing any definite relation to the size of Candlesticks.'

Here he is speaking about locomotives:

'I think no estimate can be formed of our national loss from the over-multiplication of sizes. Take, for instance, the various sizes of steam engines – stationary, marine and locomotive . . . In the case of locomotives and carriages I would urge the subject on the attention of our members the engineers of the great lines of railway – the London and North Western, the Midland, the Great Northern, for instance. I hope they will permit me to suggest that they should consider and determine not only the fewest possible number of sizes of engines and carriages that will suffice, but also how every single piece may have strictly defined dimensions.'

Probably only since nationalization has this been carried out on the railway.

From about the time of the Crimean War, Whitworth became interested in rifles and artillery guns. Because of his reputation the Government asked him in 1854 to design and estimate for the machinery for the Enfield Royal Small Arms Factory. This led him to make his usual thorough examination of the basic requirements for an effective rifle, and from this he designed and produced the Whitworth rifle. It was superior to all others in existence but it was too novel for the War Office. Whitworth was not a diplomatic sort of man and he did not get on well with official committees. If he knew he was right he said so and stuck to it. However the Whitworth rifle was used in the big shooting competitions organized by the National Rifle Association of that day and was awarded as a prize to the best shots. It was adopted by the French government and Whitworth was made a member of the Legion of Honour. From then on Joseph Whitworth & Co. were closely connected with armament manufacture.

The growth of his firm had now made him a rich man but he was interested in social and economic questions outside his own profession and his own business. In his own business he tried to introduce co-partnership and profit sharing. At the same time he said, 'the artisan should be free to earn all he can without hindrance from his fellows'; in other words, trade unions should not control wages. He believed firmly that education, particularly technical education, could bring about progress.

Progress to him meant more and more people being relieved of the drudgery of labour by the use of more machines. Men who operated machines would receive higher wages than the labourer who used simple hand tools. He wrote:

'I believe that the science of mechanics, though a mere material power in itself, may, if rightly used, become a moral lever, by which, like Archimedes of old, we may seek to raise the world.'

It was natural, therefore, that Whitworth took the lead in expanding engineering training. He had ideas on liberal studies for engineering students. All engineers, he said, should study economics. They should understand tariff and customs barriers and the advantages of free trade. He offered to finance a number of scholarships and wrote to Disraeli, the Prime Minister, in 1868.

'Sir, – I desire to promote the engineering and mechanical industry of this country by founding thirty scholarships of the annual value of £100 each, to be applied for the further instruction of young men, natives of the United Kingdom, selected by open competition for their intelligence and proficiency in the theory and practice of mechanics and its cognate sciences . . .

'I venture to make this communication to you in the hope that means may be found for bringing science and industry into closer relation with each other than at present obtains in this country.'

The Government gratefully accepted the offer. This was the beginning of the Whitworth Scholarships and prizes which are still awarded.

On retiring Whitworth bought a large house and garden near Matlock, not many miles from Ambergate where he had had his first job. He married twice but had no children. He spent his leisure in landscape gardening and looking after his farm. He was a man of simple tastes. When he became old his doctor advised him to spend the winter on the Riviera; he died at Monte Carlo in 1887 at the age of eighty-three.

He left over a million pounds. His will provided that most of this should be used for education, colleges and schools, institutes and public parks. Whitworth's firm of Sir Joseph Whitworth & Co. was merged in 1897 with Sir W. G. Armstrong & Co. to become Armstrong–Whitworth. This in its turn was merged in 1928 with the Vickers Company to become Vickers–Armstrong. Whitworth's name survives in many places in Manchester, in the Whitworth Society, in the room named after him at the Institution of Mechanical Engineers and in his scholarships.

THE ENGINEERING WORKERS, 1850–1890

Whitworth, Nasmyth and many others introduced new types of machine tool and high standards of measurement and accuracy of working. These changes affected closely the work and lives of thousands of engineering workers.

The engineering industry grew tremendously in this Victorian age. If we look at the exports of machinery we find that, whereas in 1850 one million pounds' worth was exported, 40 years later the figure was fifteen million pounds. There were many more different kinds of product, at first mainly spinning and weaving machinery, steam engines and locomotives; later on machine tools, ship engines and hulls, and guns of all kinds. By the end of this period there was cycle manufacture and the beginning of electrical engineering.

If we look at the number of engineering workers we find that during the same 40 years it increased about five times, to about a quarter of a million.

The technical changes in one great city, Manchester, where Whitworth and many others had their businesses, are well illustrated by the following. It is part of an address by William Fairbairn, a noted engineer, in 1861.

'When I first entered this city (in 1814) the whole of the machinery was executed by hand. There was neither planing, slotting nor shaping machines; and with the exception of very imperfect lathes and a few drills, the preparatory operations of construction were affected entirely by the hands of the workmen. Now everything is done by the machine tools with a degree of accuracy which the unaided hand could never accomplish.'

These changes meant changes in the factories. There appeared separate shops for turning, for fitting and erecting, for patternmaking, etc. instead of the general shop. The work became more specialized. New skills were created. Where there were now five types of lathe instead of one, more specialized turning was required. The fitter, too, became more of a specialist. There were more different kinds of trade.

The employers wanted to take full advantage of the new machine tools. Some, like Nasmyth, wanted to employ on the machines labourers instead of men who had served an apprenticeship. Other employers wanted to introduce regular overtime or piece work.

As we have seen in Chapter four, the engineering workers' separate trade unions joined together into the Amalgamated Society of Engineers in 1851 (the same year as the Crystal Palace Exhibition where Whitworth and Nasmyth showed their inventions).

Straight away a head-on clash developed between the workers and the employers. The Amalgamated Society and its supporters requested abolition of regular overtime and piece-work and that labourers should not operate the machines. At first in Oldham a complete victory was won over the firm of Hibbert and Platt, the largest engineering firm in Britain, employing 1,500 men. Encouraged by this, the Society members in London and Lancashire, the two main centres of the industry, refused to work overtime. The employers closed their works, locked out the men and refused to take them back unless they signed 'the Document'. This was a promise not to belong to a trade union. The workers held out for six months but had to go back defeated. But in a few years the Society was stronger than ever.

During the next 40 years all these issues were settled in favour of the workers. Hours of work were reduced and overtime was paid for at a high rate. Piecework was not widespread, because there was never very much repetitive work. Apprenticeship was maintained because of the new skills and need for specialized craftsmen. An indenture in the 1870's said that the apprentice was to:

'Serve his Master faithfully, his secrets keep and lawful commands gladly obey and perform. He shall do no damage to his said Master nor see any done by others but to the utmost of his power shall prevent or forthwith give notice to his said Master of the same. The Goods of his Master he shall not waste nor lend them unlawfully to any. Hurt to his said Master he shall not do or cause or procure to be done. Taverns, Inns and Alehouses he shall not frequent. At cards, dice tables or any other unlawful games he shall not play.'

The Amalgamated Society improved its organization from year to year and increased its strength. It trained branch secretaries and built up its funds so that it was able to have full-time salaried officers at headquarters. Branch meetings were often held in public houses but the branch secretary could not keep a pub. The Society aimed at improving the behaviour of its members. Here is one resolution passed by the executive council:

'that the Executive Council does not approve of the language used by Francis Currie of the Greenock Branch for which he was fined, but as the expressions were used merely to illustrate the subject he was discussing, he be exempt from the fine. At the same time the Council trust that Francis Currie will never make use of such language again in our meeting rooms either in illustration or otherwise as it is bad taste to use such expressions.'

Branches were set up overseas by members who emigrated, in Australia, New Zealand and the U.S.A.

This was the age of the engineer. The engineering workers found it easier than most others to improve their wages and hours of work. They were very much in demand. The Amalgamated Society did not set out to use the strike as a means of improving conditions. They were able to get a good deal of what they wanted by negotiating with the employers and by using passive resistance in the works. By these means wage rates rose between 10 per cent and 15 per cent. At the same time hours of work fell from 58 to 60 hours per week to 54 hours.

A working week of 54 hours or the nine-hour day was not

won without a struggle. In fact, it took a strike in Newcastle and district lasting five months to achieve it. On the north-east coast hours were 60 a week. The building trade workers had demanded 54 hours and in some places got it, but in the engineering shops work was being speeded up all the time. At Sunderland the engineers struck on 1st April 1871, and the employers gave way very soon, but subsequently at Newcastle the request was refused by Sir William Armstrong of Elswick and other employers. The men formed a Nine-Hour League. They came out on strike on 2nd May, and at last on 9th October the employers agreed to introduce the nine-hour day from 1st January 1872.

During these five months of 1871 the employers tried to break the strike by importing foreign workers. It was no longer possible to bring in the Scots as Nasmyth had done many years before. The Scottish workers themselves were organized. Men were brought over from Germany and Belgium.

'The schools belonging to Sir William Armstrong were closed to the children and converted into barracks for the foreigner. Tenants living in Sir William's property received notice to quit if they did not return to work; the various foremen and clerks who would consent to the operation were sworn in as special constables, and preparations were made to guard the different factories much the same as if they were convict establishments.' (John Burnett, later General Secretary of the A.S.E.)

The Nine-Hour League and the Amalgamated Society countered this move by sending officials abroad to prevent recruitment there and by propaganda among the foreign workers at Newcastle. There was –

'a meeting of 120 of the Germans employed in Armstrong's factory. All the efforts of the heads of the firm were insufficient to quell the disturbances; they promised that the Germans should be allowed to smoke when they chose; in fact that they should have everything but the nine hours, which the Germans had by this time begun to shout for. The Nine-Hour League took advantage of this state of affairs and the next day shipped off nearly the whole of the 120 . . . amid such a scene of excitement as is seldom witnessed.' (John Burnett.)

The men won the strike because they were better organized than the employers were.

After this the nine-hour day was quickly and easily achieved throughout the whole country. In fact the Clyde, Dundee and other parts of Scotland achieved a 51-hour week.

Very soon, however, the nine-hour day had to be defended against employers who wanted to return to the longer working day. The workers formed Nine-Hour Maintenance Leagues and there were a number of strikes on this issue. The Amalgamated Society offered to accept reduced wages rather than lose the nine-hour day. 'We do sincerely wish to be allowed to leave work at 5 o'clock,' the members said. They realized that shorter hours were more important than money wages. Machine tools and mechanization had taught them that. By 1890 the 'twelve o'clock Saturday' had been won in some places and the eight-hour day was being discussed. By that time too, John Burns and Tom Mann had begun to lead the Amalgamated Society towards a socialist policy.

Additional Reading

S. Smiles (ed.), *James Nasmyth, an Autobiography*, Murray 1883.
J. B. Jefferys, *The Story of the Engineers*, Lawrence & Wishart 1945.

CHAPTER EIGHT

The Growth of Trade Unionism 1850-1890

As we have seen in Chapter five the trade unions in the eighteen thirties and forties had revolutionary aims. They tried to make industry co-operative instead of being under private enterprise. The workers set up grand general trade unions which were to do away with capitalist industry and put co-operatives in its place. But these grand general unions and their socialist ideas were before their time. When they were defeated the remnants reorganized into smaller, but stronger, unions.

From about 1850 onwards, however, the trade unions had quite different aims. Their aim was to improve the working conditions of their members and to do this gradually, without setting out to challenge the employers or change the whole basis of industry. They did not usually advocate striking; in fact they warned their members against it:

'Keep from it,' the Stonemasons' central committee warned, 'as you would from a ferocious animal that you know could destroy you . . . Remember what it was that made us insignificant in 1842 . . . We implore you, brethren, as you value your own existence, to avoid, in every way possible, these useless strikes. Let us have another year of earnest and attentive organization; and, if that does not perfect us, we must have another; for it is a knowledge of the disorganized state of working men generally that stimulates the tyrant and the task master to oppress them.'

Instead, the unions based their actions on the law of supply and demand. If they kept down the supply of their labour, then the price of it – the wages – would go up. And so as to keep the supply down they tried to limit the number of apprentices, to abolish overtime, and to help their members who wanted to emigrate.

For a long time the trade unions were only for skilled tradesmen, indeed right up to the end of this period. The weekly contributions were more than the unskilled men and labourers could afford. The unions had large funds; they gave regular friendly benefits to their members for sickness, unemployment and death. The unemployment benefits made the unions stronger when they negotiated with the employers for higher wages or shorter hours.

Foremost among these trade unions was the Amalgamated Society of Engineers. As we have seen in Chapter four, the engineering workers had formed their Amalgamated Society by joining together many small craft unions. As this society built up its organization so it became stronger year by year. It soon accumulated large funds; it could afford to pay salaried officials at headquarters and ample benefits to its members. It made a big impression when it paid £1,000 a week for three weeks to the building workers when they were on strike.

Thus so successful was the engineers' union that it became a model for other trades to copy. And they did take it as a model. The building industry was one of the biggest examples. The building workers were the first to campaign for a nine-hour day. Within that industry, the carpenters who were in innumerable tiny benefit clubs, took the engineers as their model and formed the Amalgamated Society of Carpenters. The tailors also formed an amalgamated society.

The other industries where trade unions were well organized were the cotton and the coal industries. The cotton operatives, spinners and weavers had always worked on piece rates. They were paid on the basis of very complicated lists of piecework rates. The unions had full-time officials who negotiated with the employers and who had to be very quick and clever at calculating the rates; the wages were looked after in that way. The main effort of the unions was to reduce hours and improve conditions through Parliament. They wanted to reduce the maximum working week from 60 to 54 hours. After a struggle they got the Factories Act of 1874 by which the 57-hour week became law.

The miners became more important as Britain used more and more coal for steam power and began to export it. Like their comrades in other industries they wanted to reduce hours of work. But the aim for which they had to fight 30 years was the right to have their own checkweighman. This was vital for their pay. The mineowners inspected the tubs of coal as they came to the surface and cut the pay if the tubs were not properly filled. Some mineowners made a practice of rejecting a percentage of the tubs so as to avoid paying wages for some of the coal hewn. It was vital to the miners that they should have their own checkweighman to inspect the tubs and see that the correct piecework wages were paid.

There were strikes about this in the 1850's, particularly in Yorkshire. Then, because of pressure from the miners' unions, the Mines Act of 1860 did give the miners at each pit the right to appoint their own checkweigher. But the mineowners obstructed the checkweighers and made it impossible for them to do their job. An example of this was John Normansell, a local trade union leader, whom the miners appointed checkweigher at Barnsley. He was sacked by the mineowner and not allowed to go near the pit. The employer was fined but he appealed against the fine. It took the union two years of costly struggle through the law courts to enforce the law on the mineowner. It was not until many years later that the Mines Act in 1887 made quite clear the miners' right to have a checkweigher at any pit, at the expense of the pit, to keep an accurate record of each man's work.

Apart from individual unions and industries, the trade union movement as a whole aimed at two important improvements. It was successful in getting both. Both were changes in the law and had to be made by Parliament, where the unions had several good friends such as Tom Hughes, the author of *Tom Brown's Schooldays*.

The first question was the legal position of the individual worker. The Law of Master and Servant was a survival from the Middle Ages. Under this law if a worker broke his contract of employment he could be, and often was, imprisoned for three months. The employer, however, could only be made to pay the wages due, or damages. In the worst cases workers could be immediately arrested. In a miners' dispute at a Durham colliery in 1863, 'In the middle of the night twelve of them were taken out of their beds by the police and lodged in Durham lock-up, on the charge of deserting their work without notice.'

The trade unions united on this issue. Great conferences were held. At one such conference all the following bodies came together:

The London Trades Council, Glasgow Trades Committee, Sheffield Association of Organized Trades, Liverpool United Trades Protection Society, Nottingham Association of Organized Trades, and the Northumberland and Durham United Trades and Labourers; the Amalgamated Societies of the Engineers and of the Carpenters, the National Societies of Bricklayers, Masons, Ironfounders, Miners, and Bookbinders, the London Society of Compositors, the Scottish Bakers, Sheffield Sawmakers, and others.

Eventually, in 1875 after continued pressure, an Employer and Workmen Act replaced the Master and Servant Law. This Act removed the unfair treatment of the workers by abolishing imprisonment for breach of contract. It gave employers and workmen the same legal rights.

The trade unions' second battle with the law was about their power to strike and their legal rights in conducting a strike. Their power to strike depended on the large funds they had accumulated with which they could give strike or unemployment pay. The unions had always thought that if an official stole any union money they could sue him for it. But now, in 1867, the judges laid it down in the case of Hornby vs. Close, that the unions could not do this and thus the unions' funds could not be protected. This was a severe blow to them. After much agitation, in 1871 a trade union Act reversed the judges' decision and gave the unions the security for their funds that they needed.

However, in the same year, Parliament passed another Act by which, when a strike had been called, picketing in a peaceful way by the strikers or persuasion of others to join the strike was illegal. This undermined the trade unions' power to organize a strike, as was shown by the frequent prosecutions under this law. The worst example was the case of six gas stokers employed by the Gas Light and Coke Company at Beckton Gasworks in London, who were sentenced to twelve months' imprisonment. From this crisis the trade unions again emerged victorious. After a long campaign Parliament, in 1875, passed another Act which made peaceful picketing legal and removed the unfair discrimination against unions and workers during disputes.

These achievements meant that the trade unions were now safe to continue their policy of gradual improvement in conditions of work and to grow stronger year by year.

The next big development in the trade unions was when the unskilled workers and labourers came into the movement. So far only skilled workers and tradesmen had been organized in unions. The turning point was the great dock strike of 1889. From then on the general labourers played an increasingly large part in the labour movement and the Trades Union Congress.

There were various reasons for the upsurge of the unskilled workers. From 1875 onward there were many years of trade depression and unemployment. A leader of the Lancashire cotton spinners described the conditions:

'Wages had fallen, and there was a great number of unemployed. Flax mills were being closed every day. All the building trades were in a bad position; iron foundries were in difficulties, and one third of the shipwrights were without work. With a few rare exceptions, the depression affecting the great leading trades was felt in a thousand and one occupations. Seeing that there was a much larger number of unemployed, the question naturally presented itself as to whether there was any chance of improvement. He considered there was no chance of improvement so long as the present state of society continued to exist . . .'

In the same year a leader of the United Society of Boiler-makers gave a similar picture:

'In every shipbuilding port there are to be seen thousands of idle men vainly searching for an honest day's work. The privation that has been endured by them, their wives and children, is terrible to contemplate. Sickness has been very prevalent, while the hundreds of pinched and hungry faces have told a tale of suffering and privation which no optimism could minimize or conceal. The workman may be ignorant of science and the arts . . . but he is not blind . . . he sees the lavish display of wealth in which he has no part. He sees a large and growing class enjoying inherited abundance. He sees miles of costly residences, each occupied by fewer people than are crowded into single rooms of the tenement in which he lives. He cannot fail to reason that there must be something wrong in a system which effects such unequal distribution of the wealth created by labour.'

The labourers suffered great hardships. They had no unions to rely on; they could only go to the workhouse. Charles Booth found that in London above one third of the people lived in abject poverty.

The amalgamated societies of the tradesmen did nothing much to help the labourers. In fact those societies could not do much to help themselves in the new conditions. They were criticized for their lack of action by their own most lively members. Such a one was Tom Mann:

'How long, how long, will you be content with the present half hearted policy of your unions? I readily grant that good work has been done in the past by the unions; but in Heaven's name, what good purpose are they serving now? All of them have large numbers out of employment even when their particular trade is busy. None of the important societies have any policy other than that of endeavouring to keep wages from falling. The true unionist policy of *aggression* seems to be entirely lost sight of: in fact, the average unionist to-day is a man with a fossilized intellect, either hopelessly apathetic, or supporting a policy that plays directly into the hands of the capitalist exploiter. . . . I take my share of the work of the Trade Union, to which I belong; but I candidly confess that unless it shows more vigour at the present time (June 1886) I shall be compelled to take the view – against my will – that to continue to spend time over the ordinary squabble-investigating, do-nothing policy will be an unjustifiable waste of one's energies. I am sure there are thousands of others in my state of mind.'

At the same time the ideas of socialism began to grow. Various socialist organizations, such as the Socialist League, appeared and increased their influence. Linked up with these were the unemployed demonstrations and marches in London. At one of these in Trafalgar Square on 'Bloody Sunday', 13th November 1887, held in defiance of the police ban, the cavalry and infantry were called out and many people were injured. At another a worker named Linnell was killed. The poet William Morris, himself a leader of the Socialist League, wrote the hymn for Linnell's funeral procession:

> 'Not one, not one, nor thousands must they slay,
> But one and all if they would dusk the day.'

These conditions encouraged men like Tom Mann and John Burns, both skilled mechanics, to organize the vast number of unskilled workers in London. Ben Tillett, a labourer in the tea warehouses, was trying to start a Tea-porters' and General Labourers' Union. The movement started with the strike of the match-girls in 1888. These girls made lucifer matches. They became diseased because of their working conditions and the phosphorus which was used. They struck against these conditions. They had no union, but although they were weak they won because public opinion and money supported them. Their example was followed by others.

The London gas workers formed the Gasworkers' and General Labourers Union. They demanded an 8-hour day instead of their 12-hour day and the gas companies gave way immediately.

Any morning in the early hours at London docks the casual dock workers could be seen fighting to get near the gates and obtain a job for the day. For some years socialist speakers had held dock gate meetings. On 12th August 1889, the dockers at West India Dock struck in order to get the proper bonus for a certain cargo over and above their 5d. per hour. Within a day or two 10,000 dockers came out in their support. Their demands were: 6d. an hour, extra pay for overtime, the minimum period for which they were taken on to be four hours, and abolition of sub-contracting and piecework. The struggle lasted for a month. Public opinion and the press were overwhelmingly behind the dockers. A public subscription for them raised nearly £50,000. With this money men could be given strike pay.

Finally the docks directors were compelled to agree to practically all the demands. The 'docker's tanner' was won.

After this victory it was easy to form more unions for unskilled workers and labourers and for the existing small ones to grow rapidly. Not only dockers, but labourers, agricultural workers, sailors and firemen came into new unions. These unions of the 1890's had quite different aims from those of the amalgamated societies of the fifties and sixties, just as the amalgamated societies had differed from the revolutionary general unions of the thirties. This was illustrated by the general secretary of the National Union of Gasworkers and General Labourers in 1889.

'We have at present one of the strongest labour unions in England. It is true that we have only one benefit attached, and that is strike pay. I do not believe in having sick pay, out-of-work pay, and a number of other pays . . . The whole aim and intention of this union is to reduce the hours of labour and reduce Sunday work.'

Within a year or so of the dockers' victory, trade union membership had grown by about 200,000, most of it in the new unions. Many of the leaders of these unions were socialists. They were bound to influence the policy of the whole labour movement. Its aims became more political. Hence the Independent Labour Party was formed in 1893. A few years later the Trades Union Congress agreed to organize the return of Labour Members to Parliament.

The employers did not form unions but associations to resist the unions' claims and to strengthen their own bargaining power. They did not have so much need to combine together as the workers had; in a strike the loss of profits was not so serious for the employers as the loss of livelihood was for the workers, and they had reserves on which to fall back. If there was a strike they could often hire unemployed men, blacklegs as the unions called them. Sometimes they brought these men from another part of the country, as James Nasmyth did. In Parliament there were many directors of companies but very few labour men. The employers' associations, therefore, became strong and permanent later than the trade unions.

There had been some earlier associations of employers. Before there were any trade unions a famous writer, Adam Smith, described the 'tacit, but constant and uniform, combination of masters not to raise the wages of labour'. Now numerous trade associations were formed.

An example was the Clyde Shipbuilders' and Engineers' Association in the 1860's, which said it was purely defensive and that it would stop if the trade unions did not exist. Another example was the Association of Midland Flint Glass Manufacturers which was formed to deal with a strike. The London master printers had an association to deal with the strong London Compositors' Society. The London master builders were another group. The General Builders' Association of 1865 was based on no less than eighty local associations of builders. These associations were rallying points for the employers when a dispute arose. They were not all of much practical use; in fact the tinplate manufacturers confessed that the wages they paid were not controlled by demand and supply but by a trade union.

A new way of settling disputes peacefully appeared in the sixties. Boards of arbitration and conciliation were set up jointly by some manufacturers and trade unionists. This started when, after years of bitter strikes, Mundella, a manufacturer in Nottingham, managed to set up a board of arbitration and conciliation for the hosiery and glove trade. The board was elected by both sides. It controlled the piece rates, and for twenty years it worked well.

Mundella's boards spread to other centres of the industry and then to other industries such as building. The Potteries, too, had such a board although it was nothing new there, as one employee said:

'Long before we had our board we settled our disputes on the same principle, by fixing on two workmen and two masters, and I never remember a single failure.'

It was in the iron industry that these boards of arbitration and conciliation became best known. Workers from Middlesbrough went to study the methods of the board at Nottingham.

Then the North of England Iron and Steel Board was set up. The industry was fairly young, without traditions, and unionism was not strong. The wages of the puddlers moved up and down a great deal in the next twenty years, but because of the board there were very few strikes. The big wage decisions went to outside arbitrators, usually men who were known to be sympathetic towards the workers; the smaller issues were dealt with by the board. There was also a conciliation board in Staffordshire.

In some parts of the coal industry also there were many joint committees of owners and miners which, for several years, dealt with hundreds of local claims about wages and conditions of work. They did not last long because they worked on the basis of a sliding scale on which wages changed according to the price of coal. This sliding scale made it impossible for the miner, who was working in a place where it was difficult to hew the coal to earn a decent wage. The unions therefore came out with a demand for a minimum living wage.

A hundred years ago, however, quite a number of men on both sides of industry thought out ways and means of reducing friction in industry and tried to put them into practice.

Additional Reading

G. D. H. Cole, *Short History of the British Working Class Movement*, Allen & Unwin 1937.
S. and B. Webb. *History of Trade Unionism*, Longmans 1920.

CHAPTER NINE

The
Steelmakers

SIR HENRY BESSEMER (1813–1898)

THREE men were the founders of the modern steel industry. They were Sir Henry Bessemer, Sir William Siemens, and Sidney Gilchrist Thomas. Bessemer invented the converter, Siemens invented the regenerative open-hearth process, and Gilchrist Thomas invented the basic process. These were the three great inventions which made it possible to make steel cheaply and in large quantities. Thus steel became the universal material of modern industry.

As we have seen in previous chapters, machinery, engineering and railways grew rapidly in the early part of the nineteenth century. This set up a big demand for iron and steel. The demand was met by wrought iron and cast iron. Little steel was made. About 100 years ago Britain, the biggest producer in the world, made about $2\frac{1}{2}$ million tons of iron but only about 60,000 tons of steel. The reason for this difference was that steel was very costly to make. Steel cost about £50 a ton while pig iron cost £3 to £4 a ton and wrought iron rails £8 to £9 a ton.

As steel was so expensive it could be used only for tools, weapons and instruments. Everything else, railway engines and rails, machinery, bridges, ships were of iron. The iron industry still depended on Henry Cort's puddling process and the puddler sweating at the furnace was still the key man. Steel was still made largely by the crucible method invented by Henry Huntsman, the instrument maker of Doncaster, 100 years earlier. This method was slow and expensive compared with the production of iron.

It is surprising that the big difference in the prices of two products, iron and steel, made of much the same material, did not tempt the iron makers to make an intense search for a new and cheaper method of making steel. But they were happy to go on as they were and so were the steel makers with a small but valuable product. The search and the discovery came from a man outside the industry, Henry Bessemer.

Bessemer's life was a good preparation for his invention of the converter when he was forty-two. His father was originally apprenticed to a mechanical engineer in Holland, and made several inventions. He was also a craftsman, and made gold chains. He was working in the Paris Mint when the French Revolution broke out and fled to England. Some years later he retired from business and settled down in the village of Charlton, near Hitchin in Hertfordshire. There Bessemer was born in 1813, and there he formed the interests which lasted the rest of his life. His father, using his experience at the Paris Mint, began cutting letters for the famous Caslon printing works and type foundry. Henry Caslon was actually Bessemer's godfather. After a time his father and the firm of Caslon set up a type foundry in the village. Against his parents' instructions Bessemer was often to be found in the foundry, watching the metal for the type being made in the furnace. He learnt the secret of the special alloy of the type: adding small amounts of tin and copper.

After leaving the village school he spent a year or two in the foundry, working at the bench and at a small, slide rest lathe which his father bought for him. He liked modelling all kinds of small objects and casting them from the foundry metal. He could often be found at the village mill, studying the simple but massive mechanism grinding the corn.

When he was seventeen his father decided to move up to London, the world of opportunity. Young Bessemer had already a good knowledge of type casting but he had no proper training for any trade or profession. He soon found a means of supporting himself. Developing his knowledge of casting, he went in for reproductions of works of art, casting them in a white metal alloy and coating them with a thin layer of copper. He became expert at using and improving metal alloys and gained a useful income from supplying dies to reproduce designs on books and cards. He began to make a good living from the die-making and stamping business he built up.

His business flourished, but for some years his inventive mind led him into various small projects without finding a really important one. He took up engine-turning, lead pencil making, medallion stamping, as well as developing improved alloys for type casting. As he said:

'I was always wanting and looking forward to the establishment of the one large and steady branch of business which I hoped would one day allow me to drop the many schemes which my versatile mind so easily created, seized upon and engrafted on the business I was carrying on; but this one great branch of trade, so earnestly desired, had not yet manifested itself.'

He went on searching in various directions for a really valuable discovery. In the meantime he got married and settled down. Then when he was thirty the opportunity came and 'the one great branch of trade' did 'manifest itself'. He had an idea which brought him a small fortune. Powder for making gold paint had been made for centuries out of leaf brass by a laborious hand process. It was imported from Germany and it was very expensive. Bessemer decided that he would try to make it by machinery.

This simple idea changed his whole life. It brought him the money with which he was able to experiment with iron and steel. It came about as follows. His sister was fond of painting flowers and she had a folder of paintings on which she asked her brother to put some ornamental lettering. He went out to buy some gold powder, as he described in his autobiography:

'How distinctly I remember going to the shop of a Mr. Clark, a colourman in St. John Street, Clerkenwell, to purchase this "gold powder". He showed me samples of two colours, which I approved. The material was not called "gold", but "bronze powder", and I ordered an ounce of each shade of colour, for which I was to call on the following day. I did so, and was greatly astonished to find that I had to pay seven shillings per ounce for it.

'On my way home, I could not help asking myself, over and over again, "How can this simple metallic powder cost so much money?" for there cannot be gold enough in it, even at this price, to give it this beautiful rich colour. It is probably only a better sort of brass; and for brass in almost any conceivable form, seven shillings per ounce is a marvellous price.

'I hurried home and submitted a portion of both samples to the action of dilute sulphuric acid, and satisfied myself that no gold was present. I still remember with what impatience I watched the solution of the powder, and how forcibly I was struck with the immense advantage it offered as a manufacture, if skilled labour could be superseded by steam power. Here was powdered brass selling retail at £5 12s. per pound, while the raw material from which it was made cost probably no more than sixpence. "It must, surely," I thought, "be made slowly and laboriously, by some old-fashioned hand process; and if so, it offers a splendid opportunity for any mechanic who can devise a machine capable of producing it simply by power.

'I adopted this view of the case with that eagerness for novel inventions which my surroundings had so strongly favoured, and I plunged headlong into this new and deeply interesting subject.'

He found out that the powder was made by a secret process in Nuremburg and he discovered the principles in old books which he hunted up in the British Museum. The problem was to reduce a piece of hard tough brass to thousands of minute brilliant particles as a powder. He produced a test sample which satisfied the dealers and decided to set up a plant. The important thing was to keep what he was doing absolutely secret. He felt there was no one on whom he could rely for secrecy except his three brothers-in-law.

'I proposed to do the work of seventy or eighty men, and I wanted this carried out by my three relatives without much labour or trouble to any of them. It simply meant this: I must design each class of machine to be what is called "a self acting machine"; that is, a machine that could take care of itself: and when a certain quantity of raw material has been put in place it must deal with it without a skilled attendant, do its appointed work with unerring certainty, and throw itself out of gear when its task was accomplished, to prevent injury to itself.'

So Bessemer designed an almost automatic plant. To

preserve secrecy he had the parts of each machine made by separate firms so that no one firm made any complete machine. The machinery he put in a small factory near St. Pancras. This building was deliberately made without any windows, the light coming only from skylights.

The plant was a complete success and the bronze powder undercut all competitors. The secret of the process was kept for forty years. Bessemer now had a good income; he bought a horse and carriage and a big house at Highgate. He described how this successful venture affected his future:

'Before long my bronze powder was fully recognized in the trade, and found its way into every State in Europe and America; it had, in fact, become the one staple manufacture I had so long and so earnestly sought for, and which I hoped would some day replace and render unnecessary the constantly recurring small additions to the business I had so laboriously built up. The large profits derived from it not only furnished me with the means of obtaining all reasonable pleasures and social enjoyments, but, what was even a greater boon in my particular case, they provided the funds demanded by the ceaseless activities of my inventive faculties, without my ever having to call in the assistance of the capitalist to help me through the heavy costs of patenting and experimenting on my too numerous inventions.'

In other words, he financed his own research and experiments in other fields, and particularly in steel.

Before, however, Bessemer invented the steel converter he was busy with two other and quite different projects. One of these qualified him well for the steel work for which he is famous. The first project was in sugar manufacture, an industry which was completely new to him. The West Indies sugar planters were very wealthy and influential but they were much concerned about the inefficient methods of extracting the sugar juice from the cane. Prince Albert, the Consort of Queen Victoria, offered a gold medal to whoever could invent an improved method. Bessemer knew a Jamaica sugar planter and so he decided to try his hand. Whereas only a low percentage of the sugar had been extracted from the cane by heavy roller mills, the machine Bessemer invented was a light press worked by steam which extracted much more sugar. It won the gold medal. He explained his success:

'In this particular competition, as in many other previous cases, I had an immense advantage over many others dealing with the problem under consideration, in as much as I had no fixed idea derived from long established practice to control and bias my mind, and did not suffer from the too general belief that whatever is, is right. Hence I could, without check or restraint, look the question steadily in the face, weigh without prejudice, or preconceived notions, all the pros and cons, and strike out fearlessly in an absolutely new direction if thought desirable.'

At the same time, about 1850, Bessemer became interested in glass manufacture. He had wanted to obtain powerful lenses to be used for burning small quantities of material in crucibles, and he tried to make more powerful lenses himself. This led him to think about the processes used for making ordinary commercial glass.

Again as an outsider he soon found he could improve on existing processes. The practice had been to mix together the materials, sand, lime and soda, shovel them into large glass pots which were heated in a furnace, and wait for the materials to fuse into glass. This took a long time. He found that by grinding the materials together very thoroughly he could make much more glass on the open hearth in a furnace, and much more quickly.

Then he took a further important step. This was a method of continuous casting of glass sheet, which is the basis of modern processes. The molten glass escaped from the furnace to pass through a pair of cold iron rollers. When he had patented this invention, the head of Chance Brothers, the biggest manufacturers of glass, visited him. Bessemer described what happened at the demonstration.

'When I said we had better get to work, there were myself, Mr. W. D. Allen, my eldest son Harry, a carpenter and my engine driver present in the small room in which the furnace and machine had been erected. As soon as the bar retaining the charge had been removed, and the tenacious semi-fluid glass touched the lower roll, the thick round edge of the slowly moving mass became engaged in the narrow space, where the second roll took hold of it, and the bright continuous sheet descended the inclined surface, darkening as it cooled slightly. I had intentionally omitted the cutter in the roll so as to make a continuous sheet; this had to be pulled away, for my little room was not half long enough to accommodate it. The heat suddenly thrown off from so large a white hot surface threatened our garments if we stood too near, and unfortunately some oily cotton waste took fire, causing a momentary panic. Mr. Chance called out, "Cease the operation, cease the operation!" We were all in a perspiration, and the long adhesive sheet of glass, 70 ft. long by $2\frac{1}{2}$ ft. wide, was gathered up before the door. The heat was very great, and throwing the rolls out of gear, we beat a hasty retreat. Notwithstanding the mistake of not putting in the cutter and making the glass into small sheets, I had the satisfaction of knowing that I has just made a sheet of glass more than three times the length of the longest piece that had ever been produced, and that Mr. Chance had seen, for the first time in his life, a continuous sheet of glass flowing from a machine, wholly without any skilled manipulation.'

The same day Bessemer sold the invention to Chance Brothers for £6,000.

When Britain entered the Crimean War in 1854 there was much concern about her weapons and armaments. These had hardly changed at all since the battle of Waterloo in 1815. The Duke of Wellington, the victor of Waterloo, had been Commander in Chief until 1852. The army leadership was incompetent and the War Office was buried in red tape.

Bessemer began to think how he could help to improve the cannon; the guns were all made of iron and they were smooth bore. Since it was not possible to make rifled gun barrels Bessemer designed and made a kind of shot which would have a rotary motion through the air It was an elongated round shot with channels on the side through which the gas in the barrel would escape and give it rotary motion.

The idea was rejected by the War Office but it was welcomed by Louis Napoleon, Emperor of France. Satisfactory tests with 24 lb. and 30 lb. shot were made at Vincennes. But the French said the existing guns were not strong enough for the shot to be used safely. They asked – could any guns be made to stand such heavy projectiles? This question started Bessemer on the train of thought which led to his converter. He wrote:

'This simple observation was the spark which kindled one of the greatest industrial revolutions that the present century has to record, for it instantly forced on my attention the real difficulty of the situation, how were we to make a gun that would be strong enough to throw with safety these heavy elongated projectiles? I well remember how, on my lonely journey back to Paris that cold December night, I inwardly resolved, if possible, to complete the work so satisfactorily begun, by producing a superior kind of cast iron. At that moment I had no idea whatever in which way I would attack this new and important problem, but the mere fact that there was something to discover, something of great importance to achieve, was sufficient to spur me on. It was a clear run that I had before me – a fortune and a name to win – and only so much time and labour lost if I failed in the attempt.'

Bessemer started immediately on his task. Eighteen months later he had found the process by which he could produce 'a superior kind of cast iron', and also, more important, cast steel. When he started he had very little knowledge of metallurgy.

All iron objects were made of one or other of two kinds of iron. Cast iron contained many impurities such as carbon and silicon and so it was brittle. Malleable or wrought iron, from which the impurities were removed, was made by the laborious puddling process from the pig iron which was smelted from the ore. The object Bessemer set himself was to produce a metal with the characteristics of wrought iron or steel, which could at the same time be run into a mould or ingot in a fluid state. In other words 'a superior kind of cast iron', since the malleable iron could not be cast.

The basic problem was to remove the carbon from the pig iron – all of it if he wanted malleable iron, all but a small amount if he wanted steel – and to have the result as a fluid. A greater amount of heat than before was required.

During his experiments an incident occurred which gave him

173

the clue. Two pieces of pig iron in the furnace had been subjected to gusts of cold air. He found these were completely decarbonized. The carbon in the hot pig iron had combined with the oxygen in the air and in intense heat was converted into a gas. He was now convinced that air brought into contact with molten pig iron would convert it into malleable iron and the high temperature resulting would keep it fluid.

Having achieved this result accidentally he set out to do the same thing deliberately by blowing air through little chimneys

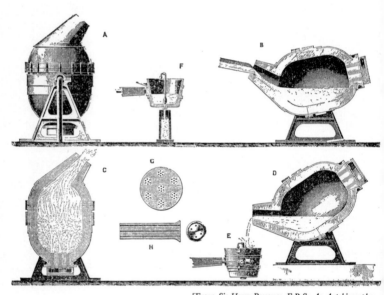

[From *Sir Henry Bessemer, F.R.S., An Autobiography*

The first form of Bessemer moveable converter and ladle

A: the converter before being charged.
B: the converter has been tilted and the molten iron is being poured in.
C: the converter is turned up and the blast of air is forced up through the tuyeres in the base and the molten metal.
D: the converter is turned down and the steel is poured into a ladle (E and F).
G, H: the bottom of the converter and the tuyeres.

or tuyeres in the bottom of the converter which contained molten pig iron. He tested that this was satisfactory and achieved the same result of producing malleable iron in a fluid state from pig iron in a short time. The next step was to find the best form of converter. He first used a fixed upright cylinder but it had disadvantages. He then designed the tilting converter, like a huge pear in appearance, known as the Bessemer converter. This converter is practically the same today.

Bessemer's discovery meant a revolution in every iron and steel works. He announced it to the world in a paper he read to a meeting of the mechanical section of the British Association in August 1856. He gave his paper the challenging title of 'The Manufacture of Iron without Fuel'. By fuel he meant the fuel which was required in the puddling process for making malleable iron or cast steel. His use of the air blast now made that process and the fuel unnecessary.

Bessemer told the following story about the morning when he was to read his paper:

'While finishing breakfast at the hotel, I was sitting next to Mr. Clay, the manager of the Mersey Forge at Liverpool, to whom I was well known, when a gentleman who turned out to be Mr. Budd, a well-known Welsh ironmaker, came up to the breakfast table and, seating himself opposite my friend, said to him, "Clay, I want you to come into one of the sections this morning for we shall have some good fun." The reply was: "I am sorry that I am specially engaged this morning." "Oh, you must come, Clay," said Mr. Budd. "Do you know there is actually a fellow come down from London to read a paper on the manufacture of malleable iron without fuel? Ha, ha, ha!" '

When Bessemer read his paper it made a tremendous impression and it was immediately accepted. The crucial part was where he explained how his invention applied to the making of steel as well as of iron, and the control over the blast could result in any quality of metal.

'At that stage of the process immediately following the boil, the whole of the crude iron has passed into the condition of cast steel of ordinary quality; by the continuation of the process the steel so produced gradually loses its small remaining portion of carbon, and passes successively from hard to soft steel, and from soft steel to steely iron, and eventually to very soft iron; hence, at a certain period of the process, any quality of metal may be obtained.'

Very soon the ironmasters flocked to Bessemer to buy rights to use his process. In one month after he announced it he gained £27,000 from the sale of licences to use the Bessemer process. He refused an offer of £50,000 to sell the patents outright. But then came failure.

When the various ironworks started to use his process it failed and it was impossible to make steel. Yet at his own works Bessemer made it work perfectly. This made a sensation and the Press was full of strong criticism of Bessemer. The explanation was simple. The pig iron which Bessemer had used had very little phosphorus in it and so steel could be made from it. But the pig iron used by the iron makers and most of the ores in Britain were heavily phosphoric. The old slow puddling process did remove the phosphorus but Bessemer's process did not.

Bessemer imported some pure pig iron from Sweden and proved that this explanation was true but the ironmasters dropped his invention as quickly as they had run after it. The steelmakers of Sheffield would have nothing to do with it and so Bessemer set up a works in Sheffield. He found out where phosphorus-free iron could be obtained, either in Cumberland or by importing from Spain and Sweden, and made better and cheaper steel than anyone. His works were very profitable for many years.

Much of the rest of Bessemer's business life was spent in overcoming the prejudice against his process and against the use of Bessemer steel. It was a long struggle, but Bessemer was a very determined and business-like man and the result was success. Twenty years after he announced his discovery nearly all the steel made in Britain was Bessemer steel. At the same time steel gradually replaced iron for many uses: for rails, ships and guns. If Bessemer had been a less determined man this changeover in industry from iron to steel would probably have been put off for years.

It took years for the endurance of the new material to be

thoroughly tested for railways, ships and construction. When Bessemer first proposed steel rails to the engineer of the London & North Western Railway he said, 'Mr. Bessemer, do you wish to see me tried for manslaughter?' The first Bessemer steel rail was laid at Camden Goods Station in 1862; in the following year the steel was first used in shipbuilding. Its use grew only slowly because of the great amount of capital locked up in the iron industry using the old puddling method, and the British iron industry was still dominant in the world markets.

Bessemer retired from business in 1873 when he was sixty, a very rich man. He had another 25 years of retirement. For such an energetic man it had to be an active retirement. He had a big house and grounds which he improved. When he had done what he could he filled his remaining years with four different hobbies. First there was the construction of an observatory and telescope which was never completed. Secondly there was his solar furnace with which he tried to use the heat from the sun to help in producing high temperatures. The next interest was his diamond polishing factory. He designed and established this in order to start his grandson in business and it was a great business success. His fourth interest in retirement was writing his autobiography, extracts from which are given in this chapter.

When an old man he wrote an account of his work in *Engineering*. This is from it:

'It is an interesting fact that at the international exhibition of 1862 I exhibited the first steel nails that were ever made.

'Those who have passed through Wolverhampton and the Black Country a dozen years ago must have seen the hundreds of young girls sacrificing all the feminine hopes and aspirations of their young lives, each one toiling from dewy morn to dusky eve, in smoky, grimy smithies, with a pair of iron tongs, holding the red hot nail in one hand, while with the other she showered upon it blows from the uplifted hammer in such rapid succession as to maintain the incandescence of the iron she was shaping, amid the ceaseless din of her fellow workers, who with grimy faces and horny hands, were reeking in the heat and foul air of the nailer's den.

'I have often felt that if in my whole life I have done no other useful thing than the introduction of unforged steel nails, this one invention would have been a legitimate source of self congratulation and thankfulness, in so far as it has successfully wiped out so much of this degrading species of slavery from the list of female employing industries.'

Because of Bessemer's converter the output of steel in Britain grew tremendously and steel replaced iron for many uses. In 1870 the total output was still only 250,000 tons; ten years later this amount had multiplied four times.

But Bessemer's victory was only a temporary one and the reign of the converter was short. It seemed an expensive and complicated machine to the conservative minded iron and steel makers. When a simpler method of making steel appeared, Siemens' open-hearth furnace, they welcomed it. The open hearth began to replace the converter during Bessemer's life-time. Whereas at the time he retired nearly all the steel made came from Bessemer converters, by the time of his death in 1898 only about a quarter of it was made in that way and the converter became less and less important.

SIR WILLIAM SIEMENS (1823–1883)

The second founder of the modern steel industry was William Siemens. Only eleven years after Bessemer announced success with his converter, the Siemens–Martin method of the regenerative open hearth came into operation. These two methods, the converter and the regenerative open hearth, were the basis of the modern steel industry. Steel took the place of iron as the basic material of industry.

The open hearth was quite different from the converter. The main difference was in the source of heat. In the open hearth the heat required for making the steel came from an outside supply of gas and air; for the converter the high temperature required for melting the charge came from the heat of the process in the converter.

The two inventors themselves were also quite different. Siemens was a German who became English. He was a trained engineer, unlike Bessemer who had little technical training. Unlike Bessemer he became well known for other things than

178

steel making. He was one of the founders of the great firm of Siemens Brothers, famous for development of the electric telegraph and electrical power industries.

One day in March 1843, a young man than known as Carl Wilhelm Siemens arrived in the Thames from Germany and lodged in a public house near the Minories in the east end of London. Siemens was twenty years old; he had come to sell an invention and to make his fortune. Let us see how he had reached this point.

Siemens was born near Hanover, where his father was a well-to-do farmer as his family had been for generations. There were 14 children of whom William was the seventh. Both parents died when Siemens was sixteen. The large family had to be split up among friends and relatives but the older brothers felt it their duty to support the younger children. Probably because of this there was always a very strong family feeling. The brothers were a team of energetic minds in all their industrial and scientific work.

The Siemens brothers were, in many ways, typical of the Germany of that time. Germany was then a collection of thirty separate states. Prussia, the largest, was leading them towards unity in a German empire under Bismarck. There was already a German Customs Union of the states, a sort of common market, which was helping towards unity. At the same time as this political movement there was a growing interest in science and technology in which Germany was to be so strong later. But Britain was still a long way ahead in manufacture, and so many young Germans came to Britain, bringing their inventions and their ideas with them.

At first Siemens was taught by a private tutor at home, along with his brothers. Then he was sent to a commercial school in Lübeck before going into a bank. But at this stage his elder brother took a hand in his education. This brother, Werner, had studied science and mathematics as a lieutenant in the Prussian artillery, and he decided that engineering was a much more promising career than commerce for his brother. Werner therefore arranged for his brother to go to a technical school at Magdeburg, where he stayed for three years. As well as science and mathematics he learnt English and French.

At the Magdeburg technical school he did not get on very

well at first, as the following letter from his father shows. By the time he left, however, he had done well.

'I have been sorry to see that you have been put into the third class. How long will it be before you get into the first, and how did it happen? Do your utmost to get out of it by Easter . . . Take care of your most valuable time; be frugal and economical, but without denying yourself anything absolutely necessary. If you find pleasure in follies, and in anything beside improving your mind, you will come to nothing . . . What sort of a fellow is Siemens' son? How is it that he, in his sixteenth year, is only in the third class? Is he wanting in brains?'

After his efforts in the technical school Siemens was able to go to the university at Göttingen for a year and successfully take a diploma in engineering. He was lucky enough to have a brother-in-law there as professor of chemistry, and he was financed by an uncle who was a banker. The next step was to get practical training as an engineer. Again through his brother he was taken for two years as a pupil or trainee at a factory making steam engines.

In the meantime and while he was still only nineteen he helped his brother Werner with his invention of a new process of electro-plating. This looked so promising, and money was needed so badly to bring up the younger brothers and sisters, that they decided to try to sell it. Siemens got leave from his factory and set off for England. On the way, at Hamburg, he obtained a contract with a manufacturer of metal window frames to gild two frames for him. From Hamburg he wrote to his brother:

'The life here is much more original than in Berlin . . . I am especially pleased with the free manner of thinking, and the independence of the Hamburg citizens. In all the beer-houses political matters are freely spoken of: the high and learned councillor is put down, if need be, by the plain citizen, even if ten of his fellow councillors are present. So it is also that in all public meetings and concerts where ladies go, the Hamburger keeps his hat on, while the unmarried ladies remove their head-covering.'

As we have seen Siemens arrived in London in March 1843.

He could not speak English well and he found his way around London with difficulty:

'I expected to find some office at which inventions were examined and rewarded if found meritorious, but no one could direct me to such a place. In walking along Finsbury Pavement I saw written up in large letters "So-and-So (I forget the name), Undertaker", and the thought struck me that this must be the place I was in quest of; at any rate I thought that a person advertising himself as an Undertaker would not refuse to look into my inventions with the view of obtaining for me the sought-for recognition or reward.'

He found his way to Birmingham and sold the brothers' invention to Elkingtons, the foremost electro-platers in the country, for £1,600. This was a great achievement for a young man of twenty; half of that sum would keep him for some years. Siemens returned to Germany to complete his training.

Because of this quick success Siemens and his brother felt sure that England was the country where they would make their fortune. They soon made two more inventions. The first was a new kind of governor to improve the pendulum governor invented by James Watt, called a chronometric governor. The second was a new copy-printing process. When Siemens had finished his training he left again for England with the intention of marketing these two inventions, and he meant to settle in England.

Siemens was not so lucky the second time. In fact he spent several troublesome and unsuccessful years trying to get these two inventions accepted. He could not sell them outright, as he wanted to, and he had to try to manufacture and operate them. He had to borrow money and he got into debt.

Writing home to Germany he expressed his disappointment:

'You took a part in these two inventions, which I wish, with all my heart, had never come to my knowledge. So long as my own property lasted I entertained no doubt that the patents would be sold for the price which they were worth at the time, before my means were exhausted. I was, however, disappointed ... I had to labour under the greatest disadvantages, and was constantly exposed to the meanest chicanery. When I came back from Germany I found the printing establishment much neglected, being left under the charge of a decayed school-master . . . In addition to all this which I had to encounter, I had sometimes not the means of living, my small paternal inheritance and all other property being entirely consumed. I have already been obliged to reject two offers which would have secured me a comfortable living . . . How I can, under these circumstances, prove my energy, I am at a loss to under-stand. I wish for work, and plenty of employment is the only thing that makes me happy.'

Siemens had several more years of frustration and unsuccess-ful attempts to get various inventions adopted. It was not until 1852 when he was thirty-one that he made his first invention to bring him an income. This was his water meter which was a commercial success and was widely used.

The water meter was immediately successful because it met a strong need. Twenty-one years before Siemens invented it there was an epidemic of cholera in London and only three years before his invention the dreaded cholera returned to London. Cholera was connected with drinking water contami-nated by sewerage. Many towns, therefore, had to start organizing water supply properly. Many attempts were made to make a machine which would register the quantity of water delivered. The first orders for the meter came from the Cor-poration of Manchester; many others followed. Over 100,000 were sold in due course. In the meter the flow of water turned a drum which by an arrangement of screws showed on an indicator the number of gallons consumed.

The water meter set Siemens on his feet and enabled him to continue his scientific experiments. He now had two main interests – heat and electricity. It was the second of these which helped to give him a steady income at this time.

His elder brother, Werner, had been developing the electric telegraph in Germany. Electric telegraphy was still in its infancy. The first small system had been installed by the Great Western Railway only ten years before. Werner Siemens invented several instruments and founded the famous firm of Siemens and Halske. The firm did so well that at the Crystal Palace Exhibition of 1851 it exhibited many instruments and 'gutta-percha coated electric line wire, first invented by Mr. Werner Siemens, and applied by him on a large scale'. The firm appointed Siemens as its English agent and very soon he became a partner in it. In this way Siemens now had a steady income to live on. Later on he made some important inventions in various fields of electrical current and power but now he began working on problems of heat.

The problem which interested Siemens was how to use the heat which was wasted in industrial processes. If he could prevent the wastage of heat there would be a big saving of fuel. His solution of this problem was vitally important to the whole steel industry, because at the same time a higher temperature was achieved than ever before, a temperature in which steel could be produced.

It was, of course, widely known that an enormous amount of heat was wasted in various machines and processes. The steam engine was an obvious example, and it was on the steam engine that Siemens first worked. The principle which he tried to apply was regeneration of heat. This meant that heat should not be allowed to escape from the process but should be used to help the process, for example by warming up incoming fuel and air in a furnace. In metal furnaces the hot gases, instead of escaping by the chimney could be used to heat bricks. Incoming fresh air and gas fuel could be passed over the hot bricks and thus be already warm before they were used in the furnace. In this way fuel could be saved.

When Siemens first tried to invent a steam engine using this principle of regeneration of heat he ran into many difficulties. He worked on it for more than ten years, but the engine could not be got to work satisfactorily. He and other members of his family lost a good deal of money.

Then in 1856, the same year in which Bessemer announced the success of his converter, another of Siemens's brothers, Frederick, took out a patent for a regenerative furnace. In the following year another inventor, Edward Cooper, with whom Siemens had worked, invented a regenerative hot-blast furnace. This was used for smelting iron and it resulted in a big increase in the output of pig iron.

For several years Siemens and his brother Frederick carried out experiments with their furnace based on the regeneration of heat, using the heat which had previously escaped up the chimney to pre-heat the air for the furnace. They soon realized that in doing this they could get higher temperatures in the furnace than ever before and this could be very important for steel making.

At first the Siemens brothers used solid fuel. Then they realized it would be a great improvement to convert the solid fuel into gas. This they did by means of a gas producer separate from the furnace. This had several advantages. Low grade coal could be used. Carbon and other impurities could be kept out of the furnace and away from the material being melted.

Siemens' famous patent of 1861 (he was now thirty-eight) was for the gas producer supplying gas to an open-hearth furnace. He described his invention at a meeting of the Institution of Mechanical Engineers:

'The fuel employed, which may be of a very inferior description, is separately converted into a crude gas, which being conveyed to the furnace has its naturally low heating power greatly increased by being heated to nearly the high temperature of the furnace itself, undergoing at the same time certain chemical changes whereby the heat developed in its subsequent combustion is increased. The heating effect is still further augmented by the air necessary for combustion being also heated separately to the same high temperature.'

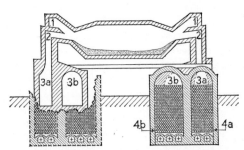

[From *Capital Development in Steel*, by P. W. S. Andrews and E. Brunner

Diagrammatic cross-section of open-hearth furnace

'Inside the furnace, air and gaseous fuel combine to form a flame which stretches about two-thirds of the length of the hearth and above the surface of its contents. The function of the ports (1 and 2) is to control the direction of the flame. The bath or hearth through which the flame passes is a shallow oblong box built of heat-resisting material. To prevent the waste gases from depositing all their solid content in the checkers, they are first passed through slag-pockets (3a and 3b) in which some of the solid material is deposited. On their way from the furnace to the chimney the waste gases give part of their heat to the incoming gaseous fuel and air as they pass through the checker-chambers (4a, gas; 4b, air). As a result, the temperature of the flame in the hearth is increased considerably, to about 1650° C. The flow of air and gas is reversed in direction at intervals.'

The first practical application of the furnace was at a glass works in Birmingham. It was so successful that it spread throughout the glass industry. The great Michael Faraday himself saw a furnace and was so impressed that he spent two days with Siemens to understand the process. The very high temperatures achieved were such a novelty that the manager of one glass works believed it was a fraud. He watched all through the night until he was convinced that the invention was genuine. Siemens said:

'The greatest heat that can be produced by direct combustion of coke and air is about 4,000° F. But with my regenerative furnace I should have no difficulty in going to 10,000°, in fact to any degree the material composing the furnace can be made to stand. The furnace melts the steel in pots (or crucibles) very well; the only difficulty experienced consists in occasionally melting the pots also!'

So great was the saving of fuel in quantity and quality that in a year or two over a hundred of Siemens' furnaces were in operation in other industries, such as iron, as well as glass. Siemens soon had a large income from his patent of this invention, which went on increasing over the years.

Then came the all-important use of the regenerative furnace in the steel industry. In the original patents Siemens always meant to apply the furnace to steel making but the problem was to find how it could be done. The main problem was to get a lining to the furnace which could stand up to the very high temperatures.

Siemens' furnace was first used in the steel industry, not to make steel, but to melt it in large quantities so as to produce cast steel. Up to this time this had been done in small quantities in pots or crucibles and it took a long time to deal with a large quantity; now it was possible to melt a large quantity in an open-hearth furnace. Various people tried to do this but it was two French iron and steel makers, Pierre and Emil Martin, who were successful first.

Pierre Martin was also the first to succeed in making steel, as well as melting it, with the Siemens furnace. Another Frenchman, Réaumur, had shown the way to make steel more than a hundred years before. The method was simply to fuse together wrought iron, with very little carbon in it, and cast iron with a lot of carbon in it. But it was not used on a big scale because suitable furnaces and temperatures could not be obtained. Then in 1856 Bessemer with his converter made possible steel making on a large scale and much cheaper. But the steelmakers were conservative and preferred to use the open-hearth furnace which they were used to, if a way could be found, rather than employ the new apparatus of the converter.

Pierre Martin succeeded in making steel in a Siemens furnace in 1864 by adding scrap iron to molten pig iron. Following this Siemens had experiments made in England but they were not successful because the furnaces gave way under the great heat. He therefore rented and altered a small furnace in Birmingham in order to show the steelmakers what could be done. It did not take long to get results. After a few months he wrote to a friend:

'The steel melting furnace which I erected at Birmingham has now been in full operation for some time, and is a most complete success. It has been working night and day for five weeks in melting extra soft steel for wire, and the furnace lining is still intact. The body of the furnace will last for several years, and the lining when it fails can be replaced in a day.

186

'The consumption of fuel does not exceed one-and-a-half tons of slack per ton of cast-steel of the softest kind produced . . . I can produce a ton of cast-steel for less money than Bessemer, and of superior quality.'

Siemens' own method of making steel in his furnace was different from Martin's. The basis was pig iron melted so as to form a bath in the furnace. The pig iron contained too much carbon and, in order to reduce the carbon to the small quantity required for steel, Siemens added iron ore to it. The oxide in the ore reacted with the carbon in the pig iron and reduced it to the required extent.

Martin's method of adding scrap metal to the pig iron, instead of iron ore, became more famous and more widely used. This was the famous Siemens–Martin process, conducted in open-hearth furnaces. The name Siemens stood for the regenerative gas furnace and Martin stood for the particular combination of materials.

This was the open-hearth process as compared with the Bessemer converter process. It soon spread throughout the steel industry. By 1900 it was more widely used than the Bessemer converter. There were several reasons for this. The open hearth had a great advantage because it could use scrap iron and cheap low-grade coal. Another important reason was that the steelmakers had a conservative outlook and they were used to the tradition of making iron in the open hearth. On the other hand Bessemer's process meant greater changes in the methods of production which the steelmakers were not so willing to accept.

At first Siemens did not want to enter the steel industry himself and compete with other makers. He wanted only to supply furnaces to steelmakers. But the success of his process tempted him to set up his own large steel works. This was at Landore, in South Wales, where production started in 1869. For some years the works flourished and it grew rapidly. It had a huge plant of 24 Siemens furnaces. It produced first-rate steel and it showed the industry what could be done with the open-hearth method. Then after 10 years there was a deep depression and falling prices, the Landore–Siemens Steel Company got into financial difficulties and after a few years went out of business. Siemens lost a great deal of money in this company.

Heat was one of Siemens' main interests. This had brought him fame and wealth. His other great interest was electricity. He made inventions in and developed electric telegraphy, electric light and power. These also made him famous.

The coming of the electric telegraph was a revolution in communication. It made many countries anxious to have international telegraph systems in order to increase their political power and their trade. Siemens and his brothers took full advantage of this situation. They built up their factories for the manufacture of telegraphic transmitters, cable and all kinds of apparatus. Siemens himself had a large part in organizing and managing this. The firm of Siemens Brothers were very busy for years laying submarine cables and international telegraph lines. Some of those it was concerned with were – between Malta and Alexandria, between Algeria and Spain, between Prussia and Persia which was part of a bigger telegraph system from England to India. Some idea of this last project can be seen from the following announcement in *The Times*:

'A prospectus has been issued of the Indo-European Telegraph Company, with a capital of £450,000, to carry out the projected lines, for which concessions have been granted to Messrs. Siemens by the Prussian, Russian, and Persian governments.

'The working is to be direct and under English management throughout, the concessions are to be made over to the company by Messrs. Siemens, in consideration of their receiving one-fifth of the surplus profits over twelve per cent; and the same firm have tendered to complete the whole undertaking during the year 1869 for £400,000, and to maintain it for a further sum of £34,000 per annum.

'The entire scheme appears to be honestly formed, and the board is composed of men of practical experience. In a commercial and political sense the importance of the work is unquestionable.'

As Siemens became more prosperous so he became more English. In fact he could use the English language better than most Englishmen. Until his early thirties he was struggling to make a living. He lived in lodgings until he was thirty-two when he was able to rent a house and share it with his brothers. His income from invention and trade began to grow. When he was thirty-seven he became a British subject and married a sister of the professor of engineering at Glasgow. As time went on he received many honours for his work in technology and science; he became an F.R.S. when he was thirty-nine, and he was knighted for services to science when he was sixty. He made and lost a great deal of money. It was said that he made three fortunes, of which he lost one, spent one, and kept one. The last of these was the £380,000 left in his will.

SIDNEY GILCHRIST THOMAS (1850–1885)

The last of the three inventions which revolutionized steel making was a way of getting rid of the phosphorous in iron ore. Until this was found, great quantities of phosphoric iron ores in Britain, Germany and U.S.A. could not be used for making steel. We have seen that the reason why Bessemer's converter was a failure at first was that phosphoric ores were used in it and produced very poor steel. An expert of the time said: 'The limit to the production of Bessemer pig is lack of ores free from phosphorus. What was wanted was a simple and inexpensive method of separating iron and phosphorus.'

The answer, the basic process, as it is called, did not come from the iron and steel industry at all. The inventor of the basic process was a junior clerk in an East End police court. Gilchrist Thomas was quite a different kind of man from Bessemer or Siemens. He was a part-time scientist. He combined his job as a police court clerk with research in metallurgy.

Gilchrist Thomas started life with certain advantages. His father was a Civil Servant; his mother was the daughter of a nonconformist minister and scholar. In their home there were often discussions on politics and literature. They were never very well off but they had enough money to send him to Dulwich College. He was a day boy at this public school while continuing to live at home in Camberwell with his two brothers and sister. His brothers became doctors and his sister eventually married a clergyman.

At school Thomas reached the sixth form when he was sixteen. He won the fifth form prize for Latin but his real interests were in a different direction. When he was about twelve he wanted to be a mechanical engineer, but later on at school he determined to become an analytical chemist. At school he was already interested in politics and he was always a strong radical. (He used to dream of doing something great in science and using the money he would make to bring about social reforms.) One of the burning issues in these years was the American Civil War; he argued for the North against the South.

When he was sixteen his father and the headmaster decided he should get a scholarship in science to Oxford or Cambridge. But Thomas thought otherwise; he said he would go to London University to study medicine.

These plans came to an end when Thomas's father died suddenly. He decided he must support himself by going into the Civil Service and, after a short spell as schoolmaster, at the age of eighteen he got a clerkship in the Metropolitan Police Courts.

It was while he was doing this job that he discovered the process of separating phosphorus from iron. As a junior clerk with a salary of £90 rising to £200 a year he was responsible for all the business side of the court; this included receiving money for fines etc., keeping records and examining witnesses to some extent. He was appointed to the Thames Police Court, Stepney, which was one of the busiest courts in London. He had to work hard during the official hours between ten and five, and often longer, in unhealthy conditions. The magistrates for whom he worked valued his work highly.

The misery and poverty of the East End impressed him deeply. He saw how useless was much of the work in the police court. Drink and drunkenness were then the great evils and Thomas decided he must be a teetotaller to help the temperance campaign. At the end of his life he left instructions in his will that his money was to be used to improve these conditions.

As soon as he started his job Thomas set up his own small chemistry laboratory in the basement at home and studied in his evenings. He attended evening classes at Birkbeck College. A lecturer there said: 'The man who eliminates phosphorus in the Bessemer converter would one day make his fortune.' This probably started Thomas on his life's work, not because he wanted the money for himself or his family but for the social reforms which his experiences in the East End convinced him were necessary.

It took him from 1871 to 1875 to work out the theoretical solution to the problem. Another three years for practical tests were necessary before he announced his discovery in 1878. He was then only twenty-eight.

In his spare time he took and passed several examinations in science. He did this so that the experts who had been baffled by the problem for years would be more ready to accept his research. They would not be likely to believe a mere police court clerk. When he was twenty-three he was offered a job as analytical chemist at a big brewery. He would not accept it because his police court experience had taught him the evil of drink.

As his work at home went on slowly but steadily he wrote to a friend:

'I am over ears in a technical experimental investigation on iron which is likely to last me considerably, and then perhaps to have no result; but, after all, life is very little else but the pursuit of crotchets, the pursuit being the best part of it. I recreated myself, after a long spell at references, at a rink yesterday.'*

As a result of intensive and lengthy reading he became very well informed about iron and its properties. He started writing articles for a periodical called *Iron* and continued this regularly for seven years. This helped to increase his income. From the beginning he realized he would need money for experiments. He therefore set himself to save all the money he possibly could, spending as little as possible on himself. During his ten years at the police court he saved £800 out of his salary, to be used for research.

Thomas also prepared himself by visiting mines and iron-works in England and on the Continent. Every year he spent

* Crotchet – the problem of separating the phosphorus.
  References – looking up previous research.

part of his holidays in this way. In August 1874 he went to Siemens' works, in 1875 to several ironworks in Wales. In the following year he made a tour in Germany, visiting many mines and works. On returning he wrote a series of articles about it called Technical Travel Talk. Here are two extracts:

'Some three or four miles from the town, (Blankenburg in the Harz mountains) among the hills, are great beds of iron-stone, in a situation almost inaccessible from the steepness of the roads leading to them. By means, however, of a tramway carried through the hills by an expensive tunnel, these have been reached, and two first-class blast furnaces erected on the edge of the plain to melt the ores raised from them . . . I could only get a general impression of the intended arrangement of the furnaces. The furnaces appeared to be designed as cupolas of good modern design, with four tuyeres, a slag-hearth at the back, a water balance hoist, a central gas-tube, and excellent blast-stoves . . .

'It was curious to find in the hills, not many miles away, another iron works, ancient, primitive, with no expensive plant or modern facilities for carriage, and yet busily occupied and flourishing exceedingly. The Rüheland Hütte in a beautiful situation in the valley of the Bode, almost confines itself to the manufacture of castings, for which it has a great reputation. The ore, partly haematite and partly iron ore, containing some thirty or forty per cent. of metal is brought in carts from workings in the vicinity, and smelted in low and old-fashioned blast furnaces, of which one is now worked with coke, the other with charcoal. The blast cylinder, a very ancient looking machine, is worked by a water wheel though this sometimes fails in dry summers and severe winters. The charcoal, of which large quantities are used, is made in iron retorts, the tar and other products of distillation being collected and sold . . . The manager, a Freiberg graduate, stated that it required something over twenty hundred weight of charcoal to produce a ton of pig-iron.'

By this time Thomas had solved the problem in his own mind. When the phosphorus in the iron was retained in the Bessemer converter during smelting the resulting steel was of no use. The question was why was the phosphorus retained in the converter. He saw that this happened because of the lining of the converter. This lining was acid in composition, e.g. silica bricks. But during the process the phosphorus in the iron became oxidized and formed phosphoric acid, and this phosphoric acid would not combine with the acid lining of the converter. Hence, it was necessary to have a non-acid lining, i.e. a *basic* lining which would combine with the phosphoric acid and make it harmless to the steel product. This is why the Thomas process was called the Basic process.

By experimenting at home he decided that the basic lining must be in some form of lime. He realized also that the phosphorus would be valuable. When the phosphorus combined with the basic material it would form a basic slag which would be valuable as a fertilizer.

This was Thomas's theory but he could not test it in practical conditions. He had a cousin, Percy Gilchrist, who was chemist to an ironworks at Blaenavon and he asked him to make experiments there. He wrote from the Thames Police Court:

'My impression is, a biggish wrought-iron crucible would be as good for an experimental converter as anything, and would be easy to try various linings in. The tuyeres (small air-holes), subject to your emendations, might be pieces of wrought-iron gas-pipe covered with fire-clay and with fire-clay stopper perforated thus – or laterally. I have not time enough to *do*. I only go home to eat and sleep. Most unsatisfactory.'

Percy Gilchrist carried on experiments with great enthusiasm. This went on for a year or two. He had to work in secrecy and at night. Thomas was in touch with him continuously. Often he would dash down to Wales for the week-end. Day by day, in his lunch hour, he wrote to his cousin with instructions and suggestions:

'Could it not be possible to try at what temperatures SiO_2 tends to displace P_2O_5 from phosphate of Fe? My theory of course is that at low temperatures (as in puddling) it does not, and that at very high temperatures (as in converter) it does displace P_2O_5; but I can find no records of experiments on this point, nor any statement or suggestion that it is so. Yet I firmly believe that it will be found to be so.' and again:

'I have nothing but translations and revisions, which don't take long, to divert me (from the research). Unfortunately "Thames" (the police court) is progressing fast in severity of work. We get now a thousand convictions a month, besides a multitude of cases, which though investigated at length, result in acquittal or dismissal. If additional coin will hurry up construction of blast engine do not scruple to use it. You must have worked tremendously to get such a magnificent crop of results. Take care of yourself. Have had two and a half hours interview with Patent Agents.'

The experiments proved that Thomas's theory was correct. He wrote to Gilchrist:

'You indeed have not been idle but worked to good purpose. The thing seems now to be as much settled as it can be, with present appliances. The only thing to be done is to find what lime mixtures and proportions, etc., for a durable lining is the sole hope we have of making coin (money) over the business. I will try some humble experiments in the same direction with small lined crucibles and such a furnace as I can extemporize.'

As one of the above letters shows, Thomas was already finding out how to take out a patent for his discovery. Unlike most inventors he made himself into an expert on patent law. His legal training in the courts helped here. He had to examine 600 patents in steel making taken out during the previous 20 years, in order to make sure that his patent would be accepted. He took out the first patent in November 1877. By now the cousins had proved their method to be successful on a minute scale, using a converter which held only eight pounds, instead of tons.

The work was now in danger for want of money; much of his savings had been spent. Fortunately the manager of Blaenavon works offered to help. Thomas and Gilchrist told him their secret and he helped them to carry out further experiments on a large scale at Blaenavon and Dowlais. Soon it was clear that the results proved the success of the basic method.

The time had come to announce the discovery publicly. In March 1878 the Iron and Steel Institute held a meeting at which Lothian Bell, a famous expert, read a paper on the separation of phosphorus from pig iron. At the end of the discussion Thomas got up and spoke. He was not yet twenty-eight years old.

'It may be of interest to members to know that I have been enabled, by the assistance of Mr. Martin at Blaenavon to remove phosphorus entirely in the Bessemer converter. Of course this statement will be met with a smile of incredulity, and gentlemen will scarcely believe it; but I have the results in my pocket of some hundred and odd analyses by Mr. Gilchrist, who has had almost the entire conduct of the experiments, varying from the very small quantity of 6 lb. up to 10 cwt., and the results all carry out the theory with which I originally started and show that in the worst cases 20 per cent of phosphorus was removed, and in the best I must say that 99·9 was removed; and we hope that we have overcome the practical difficulties that have hitherto stood in the way.'

Thomas thus announced the discovery which was to revolutionize the steel industry. The meeting did not believe him, and ignored what he said. He did not mind this because there was still much technical and legal work to be done.

All the time he was still working at the Thames Police Court. The following letter, a few days after his announcement, shows how the magistrates thought so highly of his work there that they tried to get him promoted to senior clerk out of his turn in seniority. It also shows his interest in the European situation at that time. There was a crisis in the Balkans and the government and the people were ready to declare war against Russia to prevent her setting up a satellite Bulgaria. The popular music hall song ran:

'We don't want to fight, but by jingo if we do,
We've got the ships, we've got the men,
     we've got the money too!'

Thomas wrote to a friend:

'My experiments are rather at a standstill. Some great works promised me a trial two months ago, but have not made the necessary preparations yet.

'However, nearly £300 has been spent in patents, in antici-
pation of things turning out well.

'I said a few words on the discussion on Bell's paper; but
we wish to keep quiet at present. I forget whether I told you
of the sudden death of my colleague as he was returning to the
office after a short holiday . . . His successor has only just come,
so I have been over full of work. The Magistrates went down
to the Home Office on their own account, to try and get the
rules of seniority set aside in my favour, which was rather
gratifying. Of course, they were unsuccessful . . .

'I utterly abjure all breath of war and slaughter, and am
utterly ashamed of the miserable position we have blundered
into. The Russian may be as black as he is painted, but neither
he nor we will be improved by slaughter.'

Meanwhile Thomas wrote a long account of his process in
detail, called 'The Elimination of Phosphorus in the Bessemer
Converter'. At the September meeting of the Iron and Steel
Institute it was not found interesting enough to be read. However Thomas met there the manager of Bolckow, Vaughan's
big works in the Cleveland iron field. The deposits of iron ore
there were very large but they contained a lot of phosphorus
and thus could not be used in the Bessemer converter. The
manager was so impressed by Thomas's discovery that he
arranged full scale tests at Middlesbrough. The main difficulty
was to get a basic lining for the converters, made of magnesian
limestone, which would stand up to the very high temperatures.
After this was overcome the tests were successful and the first
few tons of steel by the new process were made in April 1879.
Thomas wrote to a friend:

'Many thanks for your congratulations of tenth . . . Yes,
after some work, we have solved the greatest industrial problem
of England: so at least people say who have been themselves
trying the solution for twenty years say.

'We have certainly secured some reputation and may (or
may not) secure some money.

'This we shall know in two or three months, but not
before. Till this is ascertained I do not want to give up
"Thames", as I have to spend about £50 a month still
on one thing or another . . You may imagine I am pretty

busy; I spent three nights out of six on the rail last week.'

Immediately the continental and American steelmakers were after the process. Belgians, Germans and Americans came to see it in operation at Middlesbrough. In Germany and the United States there were very big deposits of phosphoric ores and the steelmakers there were naturally very anxious to use Thomas's process. After the Franco–Prussian war Germany had taken over the big Lorraine iron field. Thomas's process was protected by his patents. In some countries he sold his rights, as in America for 250,000 dollars. In other countries he gave licences and received the royalties.

Only after this was settled did Thomas resign from his job as clerk at the Thames Police Court, after twelve years of service. He would not give up the job until he was absolutely sure that he would have an income from his discovery. But the overwork during these years had affected his health. After a long and busy trip to Germany he had what seemed to be a heavy cold and troublesome cough. Before long, however, this was diagnosed as tuberculosis of the lung. At the height of his achievement he was stricken with a disease which, in those days, was often fatal. He was forced to take a rest.

The next year, in 1881, he went on a two months visit to the United States. This was partly for business, to arrange the terms on which the steelmakers would have the use of his process. The fame of his discovery preceded him and he was given a great welcome by the steelmakers, including Andrew Carnegie. He was news in the American newspapers. He wrote home:

'Dearest Mother, Have really had a good time for last three days following two days at Niagara ... Tuesday, 9 a.m. I, Carnegie and a Dr. Gilchrist started for a place near Tyrone on the Pennsylvanian Railroad. We arrived at 9 p.m. having picked up on our way a special car, with a railway man and two Pittsburgh partners of Andrew Carnegie. In this car we have slept for three nights, and fed gorgeously. Real fun. Gorgeous scenery, beautiful mines, grand furnaces, and lots of new people. Had several long drives and saw no end of the interior country. It has really done me good. I now go back again, three hundred miles or so, to Philadelphia, Washington, etc. The woods are delicious in their first greens, I am always longing for you two folk, which spoils my enjoyment and makes me look forward to 8th June.'

The trip was successful but tiring. On his return he was continually visiting works in Germany, Austria and France. But he had to slacken off. He was forced to spend the winter in Devonshire. In the meantime he wrote the following summary of phosphoric ores to show the vast use of his discovery.

'. . . the whole of the ores of Scotland, Yorkshire – including the vast deposits of Cleveland with its yearly output of 6,500,000 tons – North and South Wales, Shropshire and Staffordshire, and the great belts of country extending from Wiltshire across Oxfordshire and Northamptonshire to Lincolnshire, are phosphoric. In the continent also all the larger deposits, with the exception of those of Spain and Sweden, are phosphoric. The great phosphoric ironstone region shared between Luxembourg, the Meurthe-et-Moselle, Alsace-Lorraine, and Belgium, is alone more considerable than all the other deposits of Northern Europe together. In America . . . the great phosphoric ore tracts of Pennsylvania, Alabama, Tennessee and Virginia.'

His health did not improve but he was now kept very busy with correspondence all over the world. He also began to spend some of his royalties on schemes for social welfare as he had meant to. He wrote:

'You see, mother, I must, if I live show that I can work at other things besides dephosphorization. Because I must make more money still; I have really given so much away that we shall be hampered in our plans for colonization, workers dwellings, and what not, if I don't!'

Thomas was persuaded to go on a long cruise to improve his health. He went round the world, staying in South Africa, India, Australia and the United States on the way. In all those countries he took a hand in beginning or developing steel works. He was better when he returned home but the pressure of business soon made him worse and so he was driven abroad again. He spent the winter of 1883 and the following spring in Algiers.

The problem of the basic slag was his chief interest during the eight months in Algiers and until his death in 1885. The slag, or cinder, from steel making was regarded as rubbish which could only be dumped on waste ground or out at sea. However since the Thomas process had come into operation this slag was rich in phosphorus. It if could be made into a suitable form it would obviously be valuable as a fertilizer on the land.

Thomas had realized this right from the start of his research. The Germans now realized it and ground the slag to powder for use as a fertilizer. It was known as 'Thomas phosphate powder'. The British steelmakers were still getting rid of their slag as best they could, even selling it to Germany for whatever they could get. Thomas was convinced that the potential value of the slag as a fertilizer was just as important as the production of steel. While he was in Algiers he directed various experiments to find the best way of treating the slag. He wrote to his cousin:

'However laughable you may consider the notion I am convinced that eventually, *taking cost of production into consideration*, the steel will be the by-product, and phosphorus the main product.'

In Algiers he heard of a doctor in Paris who had a new treatment for lung diseases and decided to see him. From France one of his last letters in July 1884 said:

'We may stop only a week or two, or possibly two months, according as I think Dr. — has or has not anything useful, and as I can get over some business matters connected with France.

'I have been working a little at Algiers on an investigation which may, or may not, lead to a "discovery", but which has anyhow been very instructive (the main thing). It is a kind of offshoot of my old ideas, but in a different direction. I do not expect it will be finished for a year or two; anyhow it has served as an interest to keep me from stagnating, though it has absorbed a good deal of money.'

The new treatment for tuberculosis did not help him and he died in Paris in February 1885. He was thirty-four years old.

Thomas left all his considerable fortune to his sister so that she could use it for the social reforms which they both always meant to finance. This she did in many ways. The conditions of women workers in certain trades were very bad indeed. The worst of these were in the manufacture of phosphorus-tipped matches, fur-pulling, and china manufacture. These caused respectively diseases of the jaw, lung and stomach diseases, and lead poisoning among women workers. Investigations were organized and as a result conditions were improved. Enquiries were financed into the conditions in which shop assistants worked. Clubs were run for girls working in factories in the East End. Destitute families were helped to emigrate. Cottages for labourers were built, in the days before there was any council housing. Money was given to preserve open spaces; at Middlesbrough, where Thomas's discovery was first put into practice, there was a Sidney Gilchrist Thomas playground. At the police court where Thomas had worked his money was used to pay a police court missionary to help the general poverty and hardship. Thus, as he wished, the money made from his discovery of the separation of phosphorus from iron was used to improve some evil conditions and to give some people a better life.

Thomas's process could be used with the Siemens open-hearth furnace as well as with the Bessemer converter. It helped particularly the steel industry of Middlesbrough, of the Ruhr, and of the southern United States. The German steel industry grew rapidly, overtaking the British industry, and Germany expanded as a great power. This expansion was one of the causes of the 1914–18 War.

THE IRON AND STEEL WORKERS

The workers in the iron and steel works were closely affected by the inventions of Bessemer, Siemens and Gilchrist Thomas. The general effect of these inventions was to make it easier for the workers to form permanent trade unions. The inventions needed more capital to put them into operation, the works became bigger and hence employed more workers living and working together in one place. The works had been isolated in the country; now they were developed closer together and near the railway. All this made it easier for the early trade union organizers to get and keep together a stable membership.

As we have seen, steel began to replace iron in industry. In the same way steel workers began to outnumber the iron workers, who were mostly puddlers and their under-hands. The new steel workers either joined in the iron workers' trade unions or formed new unions of their own, such as the British Steel Smelters' Association.

Before Bessemer's time trade unions in the iron industry were rare. They were usually nothing more than small local friendly societies and they did not last long. There was an Associated Fraternity of Ironworkers in 1830. In 1842, John Kane, later a well-known leader, tried to form a union of iron workers but failed. The most important reason why this attempt failed, together with many others, was the way in which the puddlers were employed. It was a system of sub-contract. The puddlers were often under contract to the manufacturer to produce the pig iron, and they employed under-hands to work for them. They were small masters on their own and so were not likely to want a trade union. This system went on for some years after Bessemer's and Siemens' time.

The work of the puddler and of his under-hand, sweating at the furnace to make the malleable iron, was extremely heavy and laborious. The under-hands began to come together in trade unions from about 1860 onwards, a few years after Bessemer's invention of the converter. Disputes had been rare, though there was a bitter conflict at Dowlais in 1853.

Their first permanent trade union started at Darlington. At first it was called the Amalgamated Malleable Ironworkers Association. The fact that this union stayed in existence and grew was mainly because of the leadership of John Kane. An orphan when very young, he had a few years schooling, and then became a gardening apprentice. When he was sixteen he ran away to work in a Gateshead ironworks where he stayed for 25 years.

Kane led the ironworkers for twenty-four years. He was secretary of the union and he edited the paper, the *Ironworkers' Journal*. These were the men for whom he worked:

'With the exception of the collier, the ironworkers have been more handicapped than the members of any other trade; handicapped by and from long hours which have all but destroyed the desire for mutual improvement and gone far to brutalize and degrade the ironworkers; handicapped by low wages and excessive labour, resulting in premature old age when they ought to be in the prime of life.'

Kane wrote most of the *Ironworkers' Journal* himself. Through its pages he aimed to do two things: to draw his new union into the trade union movement as a whole and the broader question of politics in which it was involved; to lead his union away from strikes and towards arbitration and peaceful settlement of disputes.

One of the most important of these broader political questions was reform of Parliament. Working men were without the vote until the Reform Act of 1867 gave it to some of them. The older trade unions, such as the Amalgamated Society of Engineers, had played a big part in getting the Reform Bill through Parliament. Kane urged his members to take more interest in the vote. He told them about the new Parliament which was elected after the vote had been given to those working men who lived in the boroughs:

'In the present Parliament there are 110 men who are the sons of peers of the realm; there are brother cousins, sons-in-law and brothers-in-law of peers and there are 204 members who are directly related to peers, who chiefly represent the counties: in addition to 63 baronets and sons of baronets there are 50 professional men and 100 naval and military and, above all, 30 directly representing the iron and coal trades. All interests and all classes are represented except labour. There is not a single working man in Parliament, and yet the working men in the boroughs, if they had so willed it, could have sent 100 of their own representatives to the new Parliament.'

Kane always spoke of what he called the wasteful and cruel struggles of strikes and lockouts and he took the lead in asking for an arbitration board similar to the one set up successfully in the hosiery industry. After negotiation with the masters it was agreed in 1869 to set up a 'Board of Arbitration and Conciliation for the manufacturing iron trade of the North of England'. When the first wage claim was submitted to it the puddlers were awarded an advance of 6d. per ton and the millmen a 5 per cent advance.

Once arbitration was started it went on successfully to deal with disputes without their reaching the strike stage; as Kane said 'It is not likely to fail if men will be governed by reason. Reason and not force is the weapon men should use; if there is any sense in a man it will be brought out at the Arbitration Board.'

But there were difficulties on both sides in settling disputes peacefully. Kane had to explain continually the advantages. He was often hampered by the lack of discipline among the ironworkers. He wrote about:

'The old mischievous policy of throwing down the tools and suspending work if the slightest hitch should occur in the work, which still continues to the injury of the workmen and all connected with them. But for the first time in the history of the iron trade a basis has been laid down by which the wages shall rise and fall in accordance with the selling price (of iron) in the market, and it must not be forgotten that the men have got more frequent and better advances than they ever got at any former time by strikes.'

On the employers' side of the board there was a similar lack of discipline. A Darlington firm, the Albert Hill Company, had failed to pay an advance in wages awarded by the board. Kane fairly lashed the company when he wrote in the *Ironworkers' Journal*:

'We would like to know by what right this Albert Hill Company tramples on the rules of our board and the laws of our country, making reductions on whom they please and refusing the just advance to sections of the men. There are other cases to which we could refer of gross injustice which is a scandal to the firm and disgraceful to the manager, who is an actor once a week in the Primitive Methodist pulpit.'

When John Kane died in office his widow gave an account of the growth of the union under his leadership.

'The society was in a very low state when we took over the books in 1868; there were but twelve lodges which numbered not more than five or six hundred members and they were all in the North of England, excepting one in Sheffield. How we worked to raise the workmen once more and to give them an interest in themselves will be seen by the increased number of lodges and members we had in 1872. We had then above 200 branches with over 20,000 members not only in the North of England but in North and South Staffordshire, Wales and Scotland. He never tried to enrich himself . . . what he believed he practised . . . all the time you have suffered from depression of trade he charged me to take from his salary what would keep us and to let the rest go to the unemployed. He believed in the universal brotherhood of man, and tried to carry it out as fully as possible.'

The arbitration boards grew and were set up in various parts of the country where they went on doing useful work for many years.

As steel replaced iron and the industry grew rapidly the trade union decided to reorganize to bring in more workers. Its new name – The Associated Iron and Steel Workers of Great Britain – showed the greater importance of the steel workers. (Plate V, facing p. 224.)

Another sign of the growth of steel resulting from the inventions of Bessemer, Siemens and Thomas was the appearance of a new trade union of steel workers. This was the British Steel Smelters' Association. It started in Scotland, at Motherwell, in 1885. The firm of Colville demanded that the number of men on a furnace should be reduced from three to two and that wages should be cut by 20 per cent. The Motherwell men thereupon started a union. In the first year there were 300 members and John Hodge (later the Right Hon. John Hodge, P.C.) became secretary at £2 a week. From this small group of smelters the union grew so that 20 years later it covered all the steel districts and had 12,000 members. Two of its officials became Members of Parliament in the great Liberal victory election of 1906.

Additional Reading

Sir Henry Bessemer, F.R.S., *An Autobiography*, Engineering 1905.
W. Pole, *Life of Sir William Siemens*, Murray 1888.

L. G. Thompson, *Sidney Gilchrist Thomas*, Faber & Faber 1840.

J. D. Bernal, *Science and Industry in the Nineteenth Century*, Routledge & Kegan Paul 1953.

A. Pugh, *Men of Steel*, British Iron and Steel Trades Confederation 1951.

CHAPTER TEN

The
Trade Union
Movement
1890-1918

By this time the new trade unions of the general labourers and the older unions of the craftsmen, with their different aims and objects, had settled down together in the Trades Union Congress. The unions aimed at improving the conditions of work and of living in two different ways. The first was by putting the case for labour in Parliament and getting the legislation they wanted; the second was by claiming better conditions from the employers.

Many of the leaders of the new general trade unions were socialists. The economic depression of the 1870's and onward made more people think that socialism was necessary. A number of socialist leagues and societies came into being. The Independent Labour Party was started in 1893, led by Keir Hardie, known as 'the man in the cloth cap' because when he was elected to Parliament he insisted on still wearing his cap as he always had done. The Fabian Society had started earlier, led by Sidney and Beatrice Webb and Bernard Shaw. Both these bodies persuaded more and more trade unionists to be socialists. Socialism meant the public ownership and public control of the means of production, distribution and exchange.

Because of this the trade unions aimed at action in Parliament more than ever before. Whereas previously they had supported the Liberal Party, now they aimed at getting their own Members of Parliament elected. Accordingly in 1900 they set up a Labour Representation Committee to see that labour members were elected.

The attempt to have independent labour members of

Parliament got off to a slow start. Keir Hardie was the first to be elected, for West Ham in 1892. He wrote the following note about himself:

'Born August 15th, 1856, married August 3rd, 1879, began work as a message boy in Glasgow when 8 years and 9 months old, wrought for some time also in a printing office in Trongate, in the brass finishing shop of the Anchor Line Shipping Co., also as a rivet heater in Thompson's heat yard. Left Glasgow in the year 1866 and went into No. 18 pit of the Moss at Newarthill, from thence to Quarter Iron Works, and again to one or two other collieries in the neighbourhood of Hamilton. Was elected Secretary to the Miners' Association in 1878, and in the same position in Ayrshire in 1879; resigned April 1882, when got appointment unsolicited as correspondent to Cumnock News. Brought up an atheist, converted to Christianity in 1878.'

There were no more successes until the general election of 1900. This was called the Khaki election because it was during the South African War and the Conservatives took advantage of the war feeling to get back to power. The labour groups were opposed to the war and so the Labour Representation Committee was lucky to get two candidates elected out of a total of fifteen. These two were Hardie at Merthyr and the secretary of the railwaymen's union at Derby.

Then something happened which helped to change the whole course of events. In 1900 the railwaymen on the Taff Vale Railway in South Wales came out on strike. The railway companies did not recognize the trade unions and they insisted on a strict, military kind of discipline. After the strike had started the railwaymen's union, the Amalgamated Society of Railway Servants as it was then called, recognized the strike and tried to run it in an orderly way. There was, however, some violence. The Taff Vale Company then sued the union and was awarded damages of £23,000 by the court and, on appeal, this was upheld by the House of Lords.

This legal decision was a great surprise and shock to the trade unions because they had believed ever since the Trade Union Acts of 1871 and 1876 that they were not liable for damages arising from a strike. Now the trade unions' ability to carry on a strike was destroyed since they could not afford to pay heavy damages after each one. Their only solution to this problem was to get Parliament to pass a Bill to change the position. But the Conservative Government would not do this, and so all the unions made an issue of it at the next General Election at which they put up fifty candidates.

At this general election, the great Liberal victory of 1906, no less than 29 labour members were elected. The result was that the Trades Disputes Act of the same year removed altogether the liability of a trade union to be sued for damages. The labour members now formed themselves into the Labour Party.

The little Labour Party was not in a strong position and could not do much because the Liberals had an overwhelming majority in Parliament. However, as a completely new party it was regarded with alarm by both Liberals and Conservatives. The railway directors in Parliament found it a nuisance to have the railwaymen's secretary there. He had blocked one railway Bill of theirs because it was harmful to the railwaymen's interests.

The Labour Party, in the next few years rather disappointed the trade union members who supported it because it could not get much done in Parliament about wages and conditions of work. Then came another legal case which, although it had a bad effect on the Labour Party at first, drew the trade unions closer to it and strengthened it. This was the Osborne Judgement of 1909.

Again the railwaymen were involved. Osborne was the secretary of the Walthamstow Branch of the Amalgamated Society of Railway Servants. He objected to the union using part of its funds to finance any political movement, especially the Labour Party. He brought an action against the union to stop it doing this and the judges ruled that no union could use any of its funds in this way. This was now the law and it was a great blow to the Labour Party since it depended on the unions for its finance.

The effect was to swing over to the Labour Party the support of many active trade unionists who felt that the judgement was wrong, and the party grew rapidly in number. It took a campaign lasting four years before the Government passed a bill which changed the law. The Trade Union Act of 1913 allowed unions to pay money to a political party; but it also said that any member could stipulate that his own contribution was not to be used in this way by signing a form on which he contracted out. This remained the law until 1927. As a result of the general strike the year before, the law was changed, so that trade union members had to contract in instead of contracting out, i.e. if they agreed to payments to a political party they had to sign a form which said so. Then 20 years later the law was changed back again to what it had been in 1913, and so it remains today.

In the meantime the Labour Party in Parliament grew to 40 members by the eve of the First World War.

In industry the trade unions had a more stormy time. This was because of the economic situation. Before the period we are discussing prices and the cost of living had been falling or stationary, and the trade unions did well if they kept wages steady. Now, in most years, prices and the cost of living rose. Wages rose too (partly because of pressure by the trade unions), but not as much as prices. The result was that real wages were less and the standard of living fell. This set-back was only slight, but it was felt keenly because until then there had been a general improvement. The trade unions were now stronger than ever before; the employers and the government would not grant their demands without a struggle. The inevitable result was many serious strikes which were only halted by the war of 1914.

The conflict between the big trade unions and the employers did not come to a head until the last few years before the war. In the eighteen-nineties and the first few years of the twentieth century things were fairly quiet, but there were two big exceptions to this, in the mining and engineering industries.

The miners' wages had risen or fallen, on a sliding scale, according to the price of coal. Dissatisfaction with this arrangement led the miners to form the Miners' Federation of Great Britain. Then in a year of bad trade, 1893, they struck to resist a fall in wages. They lost the dispute but the owners accepted the principle that there must be a minimum wage below which the sliding scale would not fall.

With the engineering workers the problem was a different

one. As a result of the inventions in engineering more and more new and specialized machines were brought into the workshops. Capstans, turret lathes, millers and borers took the place of the planers and centre-lathes of the earlier years. The 'machine question' came to the fore again. Should the employers be allowed to put unskilled men on the new machines which were doing work formerly done by craftsmen? At one place, Earle's shipbuilding and marine engineering works at Hull, there was a strike which gained 'recognition of the principle that machines which supersede hand-skilled labour should be manipulated by skilled and full-paid men'.

When it came to a country-wide strike, however, the men were defeated after being out for seven months. They had to accept the employers' right to 'determine the conditions under which such machine tools shall be worked'. At the same time, however, the employers and the Amalgamated Society of Engineers agreed to negotiate in future so as to avoid disputes.

The big conflict in industry did not begin until three years before the First World War. Profits were bigger and wages still did not keep up with prices. First the sailors and firemen struck and won increases from the shipowners. Then the dockers in most parts came out. They were still on the basic dockers' tanner, the 6d. an hour which they had gained in the big dock strike of 1889. In London the dockers were followed by all the different waterside workers, stevedores, lightermen, coal porters, grain porters, tug-enginemen, and the whole of the port of London was at a standstill. The Port of London Authority refused to negotiate. The Home Secretary, Mr. Winston Churchill, had troops brought to London. Then the Government gave way and brought pressure to bear on the Port Authority. The dockers won the whole of their claim; they got 8d. an hour, and 1s. per hour for overtime. In the meantime the various waterside unions formed a federation of transport workers. In the next year, however, they failed in another strike to get the Port Authority to recognize it.

The second big section of labour to take part in this movement were the railwaymen. In the month after the dockers' strike 150,000 railwaymen stopped work. The railwaymen had always found it difficult to form trade unions. The companies insisted on a military kind of discipline and even at the time of this strike refused to recognize the railway unions. Four years earlier, Lloyd George, a member of the Government, had forced the companies to set up conciliation boards. These did not work well. Now the strike was called to make the companies meet the unions and discuss wages. Again the Government had to force the companies to give way and recognize the unions. Another result was that, as with the dockers, a new big union was formed by combining various small ones, the modern National Union of Railwaymen.

In the next year it was the turn of the miners. There were now large exports of coal, the production of coal increased rapidly and with it the number of miners. The miners' unions had become stronger and they had combined into the Miners' Federation of Great Britain. Their wages had been on a sliding scale according to the price of coal. There was much dissatisfaction with this because it was impossible for the miner working in a place where the coal was more difficult to hew than normal to get a proper wage. The miners' union therefore demanded a national minimum wage. The owners, through their Mining Association, refused to negotiate and more than a million miners struck for over a month. This was the biggest strike there had ever been in Britain. The Prime Minister, Asquith, himself intervened and as a result the Coal Mines Minimum Wage Act was passed. This said that a minimum wage must be settled on a local basis and if the owners and the miners could not agree the Government would decide.

These were the three chief outbreaks in the industrial strife of the pre-war years. There were many other smaller strikes, among the jute and flax workers of Dundee, the West London and the East London tailors, the London taxi-drivers, the Yorkshire dyers, the London printers, the Leeds municipal employees, and even, in Lancashire, the agricultural workers.

Because of the upheaval in industry during these years both the Government and the big trade unions tried to improve matters for the future, but in different ways. The Government set up an Industrial Council. This was composed of employers and Union leaders and its object was to settle disputes without strikes. It turned out to be of little use.

The three biggest unions, on the other hand, the transport workers, railwaymen and miners, made an agreement called the Triple Alliance. During the recent strikes, when one group went on strike many men in the other groups were thrown out of work. The object, therefore, was to arrange that their agreements with employers should be due to end at the same date. They could thus all strike at the same time, although each group would be striking for its own claim. The Alliance was not intended to organize a combined strike but men began to think more and more about a big sympathetic strike in which one group would be supported by the other two. Nothing came of this for 12 years, until the General Strike of 1926.

When the war began in 1914 the trade union movement put its whole strength behind the war effort. Trade unions encouraged their members to join the services until it became obvious that there was a danger of a shortage of labour. Then miners, railwaymen and engineers were refused as recruits and exempted from conscription, when it was introduced half-way through the war.

The Government made an agreement with the unions that their peacetime rules and practices should be suspended during the war. The unions agreed to suspend the rules about apprenticeship and about certain kinds of work being done by skilled men, not to object to overtime and even to relax some health regulations under the factory Acts. They also agreed to give up the right to strike and to accept compulsory arbitration by the Government. The Government, on its side, promised that all these rules and practices should be restored when the war was over.

At the same time the shop steward movement came to the fore. Although the trade unions co-operated with the government and there were very few important strikes, there were quite a number of unofficial strikes. Wages did not rise as much as the cost of living, and big profits were made. There had been shop stewards for a long time but they had been mainly collectors of dues. The shop stewards in the engineering and shipbuilding industries now formed their own movement and led the unofficial strikes. This happened at Coventry, Sheffield and at Glasgow where they set up the Clyde Workers' Committee. At the Parkhead Forge, Glasgow, there was a strike about the position of the chief shop steward; there were others at Barrow and on the Tyne. At the end of the war the engineering employers agreed to recognize the shop stewards and negotiate with them as part of the official trade union leadership.

The unions became much stronger because of the war. Their membership increased by about 60 per cent. But, more important, they took part in many government committees dealing with rationing, forces pensions and employment, and so became temporarily partners with the Government. Thus their status in the community rose, for the time being at least.

As the unions became stronger and amalgamated themselves into national bodies, so the associations of employers came more to the fore. Big firms such as Whitworth and Armstrong amalgamated and the fewer, but larger, employers found it easier to join together.

In engineering there had been local associations of employers for some years. As the machine question and the eight-hour day came to a head, the employers combined in 1896, to form the Employers' Federation of Engineering Associations; this included employers from the Clyde, the North East, Belfast and Barrow, Manchester and London. In the strike of 1897, mentioned earlier, the Federation persuaded firms which were not members to lock out their men. The stated object of the Federation was 'to resist the attempt made to deny to British Employers the same freedom in managing their works which is enjoyed by every manufacturer with whom they have to compete'. Another object, however, was told to the Press by one of the Siemens brothers – 'to get rid of trade unionism altogether'.

The Federation won the day. Part of the settlement was the machinery set up for avoiding disputes. If disputes could not be settled by local officials of both employers' associations and trade unions, then they were to go before a central meeting of the federation and the union.

In the coal mining industry the district associations of colliery owners founded the Mining Association. It was this body which refused to negotiate on a national basis with the miners about the minimum wage. In nearly all trades there was an association of some kind. Many of them had been set up to negotiate with organized workers. Others had been started in order to control the prices of their products. Many associations did both these things.

During the stormy years of 1910 to 1913 there were 3,686 disputes. Of these, 15 per cent were victories for the employers, 74 per cent were settled by negotiation between employers and unions, 8 per cent were settled by conciliation and 3 per cent by arbitration, these last two usually effected by the Board of Trade.

Conciliation by third parties in disputes took place more often than before. Parliament passed a new Conciliation Act which gave the Board of Trade more opportunity to intervene and effect conciliation. This was mostly in smaller disputes where there was room for give and take on both sides. In the big issues, like recognition of the union, a minimum wage, or the eight-hour day, it had to come to a struggle.

Additional Reading

G. H. D. Cole, *Short History of the British Working Class Movement,* Allen & Unwin 1937.
S. and B. Webb, *History of Trade Unionism,* Longmans 1920.
J. B. Jefferys, *Story of the Engineers,* Lawrence & Wishart 1945.

CHAPTER ELEVEN

Motive
Power
Inventors

NONE of the inventions or engineering achievements mentioned in this book would have been possible without the use of power. James Watt brought steam power into use. The work of the three men described in this chapter brought about great changes in the use of power in modern times. They are Sir Charles Parsons, F. W. Lanchester, and Sir Frank Whittle. Parsons invented the steam turbine; Lanchester, many of the basic parts of the internal combustion engine and the motor car; Whittle, the jet engine.

SIR CHARLES PARSONS (1854–1931)

Charles Algernon Parsons was born on 13th June 1854 in London. He grew up in the era of steam power, but by the time he was a young man engineers and scientists were beginning to wonder what the future of power would be. Britain had led the world in steam power ever since the days of James Watt. The reciprocating steam engine was in use everywhere and it had made possible Britain's manufactures and her exports to the world markets. Britain had become a wealthy country by means of 'the snorting steam and piston stroke'. Coal was cheap.

Everyone knew, however, how wasteful of power even the best steam engines were. New sources of power had been discovered and inventors had begun to show how they could be used. Lenoir had invented the gas engine in 1860. When this gave way to the Otto engine, it was soon widely used in factories, particularly in the light metal works of the Midlands. Electricity had already been used for lighting and electric power was on the way. The dynamo had been invented and experiments in transport had been made.

Leading engineers were prophesying the end of steam, but they thought that the internal combustion engine, i.e. the gas engine, would replace it before electricity. Britain had plenty of steam coal and gas coal but as other countries, with more water power, began to use electricity for power, Britain lagged behind.

Parsons' invention of the steam turbine came at the right time. It was a vital link between steam and electricity for it was invented to drive the dynamo.

Charles Parsons was the sixth son of the third Earl of Rosse. His family traced a long line of descent back to the sixteenth century. His father was not only an aristocrat but also a distinguished scientist and president of the Royal Society.

He had a happy carefree boyhood at the old family home at Parsonstown in Ireland. This was the moated Birr Castle which had stood for centuries and survived a siege by Cromwell's army. As his father did not like public school education, Parsons had a private tutor at home until he went to university. There was a workshop as well as a library at Birr Castle. When he was seventeen he went to the University of Dublin where he won a prize for mathematics. Two years later he went on to Cambridge University where he won distinction in mathematics.

Parsons might then have begun an academic career in mathematics or science but he preferred practical engineering and he went as a premium apprentice to the famous works of Sir W. G. Armstrong at Elswick. He described his education as follows:

'I was educated on what is called among engineers the "sandwich" system. My father had, rightly or wrongly, a rooted objection to public school education, and consequently with my brothers, I was taught by tutors at our home in Ireland. Concurrently I had the advantage of working in well-equipped workshops where my father had constructed his telescope, and from him I learnt the first principles of mechanical construction and engineering, for he was a skilled engineer as well as a scientist and an astronomer. After that were interposed five years of pure and applied mathematics including the Cambridge Tripos; and I recall that the strain was more severe than anything I have sustained in business life. Luckily for me, boat racing interfered with reading.

'I entered Elswick works as a premium apprentice, and served three years. During this time I learned from Sir William Armstrong and his staff . . . the methods of mechanical research and construction that have made the works famous throughout the world . . .'

He began to show his powers of invention while serving his apprenticeship. Various attempts were being made to design a high speed steam engine for driving the dynamo, of which the armatures rotated at high speed. Parsons made a model of an engine while he was at Cambridge and built it at Elswick. It was an 'epicyloidal' engine of 10 h.p., in which the four cylinders revolved at half the speed of the crankshaft. He used it to drive a Siemens dynamo. Later the firm of Kitson's took up the invention and made about 40 engines which were used for driving dynamos. Soon afterwards he turned away from this type of engine to work at the invention of the steam turbine.

When Parsons finished his apprenticeship at the age of twenty-seven he received the following letter:

Elswick Works,
Newcastle-upon-Tyne
June 3rd, 1881.

The Hon. C. A. Parsons,
Dear Sir,
In reply to your request for a recommendation from our firm to assist you in your search for a partnership in an engineering firm, pray make use of this letter in which we have the pleasure of bearing testimony to your high theoretical knowledge, your constructive abilities, and your promising business qualifications.

With this letter we hand you your indentures, which you will observe Sir William Armstrong has kindly certified.

We are, dear Sir
Yours faithfully,
W. G. Armstrong & Co.

217

Torpedoes had recently come into use by the Navy. At first Parsons was interested in rocket propulsion for torpedoes. He spent two years at Kitson's working on this problem but without success. In the meantime he got married and made his home at Elvaston Hall, Ryton-on-Tyne; there two children were born.

After leaving Kitson's he joined the firm of Clarke, Chapman & Co., of Gateshead, as a junior partner. This firm set up an electrical department and Parsons turned his energies to the problems of the generation of electricity. He soon realized that the electric lighting of ships had possibilities; here was scope for a steam turbine driving a dynamo. He was now thirty years old. He described what happened:

'About the year 1884, circumstance being favourable, I determined to attack the problem of the steam turbine and of a very high speed dynamo and alternator to be directly driven by it . . . the efficiency of this dynamo was about 80 per cent and the steam consumption of the plant about 150 lb. per kilowatt-hour. This little turbo worked satisfactorily from the start.'

In the very next year a Chilean battleship was the first warship to be fitted with a Parsons' turbine and dynamo set for electric lighting.

The turbine was a very old device, known to the ancient world. A certain Hero of Alexandria in 130 B.C. made a simple steam turbine engine.

'It consisted of a boiler from which rose a vertical tube bent at right angles at the upper end. The horizontal end was inserted, not too tightly, into a hollow sphere, which was supported by a pivot opposite the steam tube, so that the sphere was free to rotate on a horizontal axis. Two other short tubes were fitted radially to the sphere at opposite sides and at right angles so that the steam issued from them tangentially to the sphere. As, according to Newton's Third Law, action and reaction are equal and opposite, the force of the steam upon the atmosphere reacted upon the tubes and caused the sphere to spin round.'

In this simple engine the turbine was of the reaction type,

since the rotation was caused by the reaction, or back pressure, of the steam against the tubes. The Hero engine was not developed any further. Many inventions were made in the ancient world but slave labour was so plentiful that they were not used.

[From *A History of Technology*, Vol. IV

Branca's proposed stamp-mill, to be worked by steam

Much later, at the time when Francis Bacon was developing science in England, an Italian called Branca invented a steam turbine. This turbine was of the *impulse* type. Direct impact of steam on the vanes of a wheel gave it rotary motion. This was geared to a pair of drop stamps. It was too crude to be successful and nothing more was done until the nineteenth century.

Many men, including James Watt and Trevithick, tried to

invent a practical steam turbine but gave up the attempt. By the time Parsons turned his attention to the problem the difficulties were generally understood, but no one had been able to find a solution. The main difficulty was that the turbine turned too quickly and was extravagant in the use of steam. This was because of the very high speed at which steam, under only a moderate pressure, escapes from a nozzle. This speed was very much more than the velocity at which the turbine wheel was required to move. It was therefore a problem of absorbing the steam energy.

A Swedish inventor had solved the problem with the impulse turbine by means of special reduction gears. In his engine, expansion of the steam took place and the energy of the steam was expended on one wheel, in one operation. The drop in steam pressure took place in only one stage.

Parsons had the brilliant idea of dividing the drop in the steam pressure into stages; the energy of the steam was given up in stages instead of in one tremendous blast. The result was that the turbine rotated at a moderate speed instead of the very high speed which was obtained by allowing the whole drop of pressure to take place in one stage.

He achieved this effect in his first turbine, in 1884. In this engine the steam was supplied from the boiler continuously. Inside the turbine it passed alternately through a series of fixed blades which were attached to the shaft casing, and moving blades attached to the turbine shaft. This produced a reaction effect between the fixed and moving blades, which rotated the shaft (Plate VI, facing p. 225).

This small engine, only 5 feet 8 inches long, was the father of some of the most powerful engines in the world.

Parsons' next task was to design the right kind of dynamo to be driven by this turbine. The maximum speed of existing dynamos was not high enough and therefore he designed a new high speed dynamo. This was as revolutionary as the turbine. It ran at 18,000 r.p.m. Engineers at that time who read an account of Parsons' invention thought that an extra o had slipped in through a printer's error.

Once the first engine had been found to be sound and able to generate current, Parsons was able to make many improvements. Turbo-generators for lighting were installed in warships during the next year or two. At an exhibition at Newcastle ten of Parsons' turbo-generators supplied current for lighting, and his name became more widely known.

There now began to be enormous scope for the growth of electrical power and lighting. The problems of the incandescent lamp, and of power transmission had been solved by the inventions of Edison, Swan and others. Power began to be used in industry and for lighting in houses. This was a new and profitable industry.

Power stations began to appear. Only four years after the first engine was built Parsons installed a turbine-driven generating set in the Forth Banks Power Station of the Newcastle and District Electric Lighting Company. A year or two later a set was supplied to the Cambridge Supply Company. Then came others. Two 350 kilowatt sets were built for the Metropolitan Electric Supply Company's power station in London. By now the steam turbine was established as the best prime mover for electrical power stations.

The turbines for power stations became more and more powerful. The biggest unit at Newcastle in 1888 was 200 h.p. Sixteen years later at Wallsend the largest unit was 6,000 h.p.

In the meantime Parsons left Clarke, Chapman and Co. at Gateshead. He started his own works, C. A. Parsons & Co., at Heaton, near Newcastle, to make steam turbines and high speed electrical machinery. About fifty people were employed on a site of about two acres, with a fitting shop, pattern and blacksmith's shops, testing room and offices. Forty years later there were 2,000 people working on a site of 20 acres.

Along with all this tremendous effort and activity Parsons led a happy domestic life with his family. He constructed power-driven and mechanical toys for his two children. He even experimented with a power-driven model aeroplane. (Plate VII.) This was ten years before the famous first flight of the Wright brothers. He described this experiment:

'Steam was raised by placing the boiler on a spirit lamp, and when 50 lb. was registered on the gauge, and the engine started, it raised itself in the air vertically to a height of several yards – the revolutions of the engine were about 1,200 and the I.H.P. $\frac{1}{4}$ horse power. The same engine was then mounted on a framework of cane covered with silk forming two wings of 11 feet span and a tail, the total area being about 22 square feet. The total weight was now $3\frac{1}{2}$ lb. When launched gently from the hand in an inclined direction, it took a circular course, rising to a maximum height of about 20 feet. When the steam was exhausted, it came down, having traversed 80 yards.

'The difficulty in maintaining the steam by a lamp was not satisfactorily overcome, but very satisfactory results were obtained by using methylated spirit in the boiler instead of water, and burning the exhaust under the boiler. Great difficulty was experienced in maintaining the flame when the apparatus was flown, owing to the currents of air from the propeller.'

He ended:

'It seems to me that the problem of aerial flight can be attacked much more favourably by means of cigar-shaped balloons propelled by gas or oil engines.'

The steam turbine was now put to another use. Parsons turned to the marine turbine and was the first man to use the turbine to drive a ship. For Britain, a maritime and shipbuilding nation, this was tremendously important. The existing compound steam engine in ships had been made as efficient as was possible. The marine turbine was a completely new means of propulsion.

Parsons described how he started thinking about the problem:

'When I commenced to work on the steam turbine in 1884, with the hope of making it a practical success, it seemed to me, in spite of the fact that many had previously failed in their endeavours, that it was right in principle, and that after a thorough experimental investigation, it should be possible to realize success. In short, I thought it was worth trying. Encouraging results followed, one improvement led to another, and it gradually became an efficient motor. When it had beaten a compound engine driving a dynamo, my old friend Dr. John Bell Simpson said to me one day when we were out shooting: "Why not try it at driving a ship?" To which I replied that I thought the time was ripe for the attempt.'

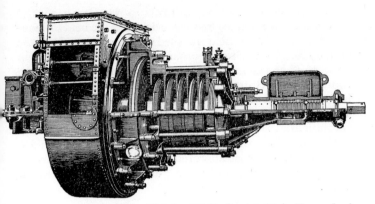

[From *A History of Technology*, Vol. V, after photo Science Museum, London

Radial-flow turbine from the *Turbinia*, 1894

He formed a new company, the Marine Steam Turbine Company, to test the application of his steam turbine to the driving of ships. He believed that the turbine would drive ships much faster and for much less cost than the best existing steam engines. He intended to build a small vessel of $44\frac{1}{2}$ tons displacement. To determine the power required he made many experiments with models, some of them only two feet long, which he towed with a fishing rod and line on a near-by pond.

Then he tested a 6-foot long model driven by twisted rubber cord and worked out the resistance and the efficiency of the propeller. From these early experiments the horse-power of the real vessel, the *Turbinia*, was calculated. On one of these days he wrote to his brother:

'It is blowing hard today. 'I tried the model in a quarry close by; with comparatively big waves – it cut right through them like a knife. The screw did not appear to draw any air. It seemed to go first-rate and nearly as fast as in smooth water.'

There were many engineering problems to be solved – the best type of boiler, the correct pitch for the screw propeller. Eventually the *Turbinia*, 100 feet long, 9 feet beam and 3 feet draught, was ready for her first run. The turbine drove a single shaft with three propellers. Parsons described the trip:

October 3, 1895.

'We had a preliminary run yesterday with the boat to Tyne-mouth and back. The boat travelled very smoothly indeed, and with 60 lb. steam and 9 lb. vacuum the speed appeared to be between 18 and 20 knots. We could only run for a few minutes owing to want of draught, and, in so short a time, the main air-pump could not sweep out the air thoroughly. So far, the screw appears to behave perfectly – that is, up to 1,200 revolutions . . .

'I think, on the whole, the first run is quite satisfactory. The thrust of the propeller appeared to be about balanced by the steam thrust, and there was an almost *complete* absence of vibration.'

This was an advance but Parsons realized that improvements were necessary if real speed was to be achieved. He therefore installed three propeller shafts, each driven by a turbine and each carrying three propellers. There were many difficult problems to solve. The best width of the propeller blades so as to avoid 'racing' was only one of them, but a complicated one. He was working very hard at this time but he got some relaxa-tion from fishing and shooting:

'Spending four days with the Cooksons . . . I got five salmon from 9 down to 5 lb., and in the afternoon had a stalk after a stag which I was lucky in bagging. They said it was the best sport in one day there for a long time. The other days we were not so lucky – on the Monday two salmon, and on the Saturday a high flood.'

The refitted *Turbinia* was now ready for trials. He wrote to his brother:

March 7, 1897.

'My dear Lawrence,
We went out in the *Turbinia* on Thursday, but it was blowing hard with sleet. The wind had shifted from W. to S.S.W. so it was too rough outside. We got a run in the river . . . We estimated that we reached 31 knots one part of the run. Today we luckily got a smooth sea with a long swell and got a long run and measured the feed-water. Altogether we covered 30

Plate 5

A Trade Union Banner

(*From 'Men of Steel' by A. Pugh*)

Plate 6

Original Parsons steam turbo-generator, 1884
(*Lent to Science Museum, London, by C. A. Parsons & Co., Newcastle upon Tyne*)

T.Y. *Turbinia* at speed, 1894

(*Photo, Science Museum, London*)

miles at 25½ knots. Two runs on the mile North and South gave a mean 28·12 knots and the feed was 20·75 lb. per hour at 26 knots . . .

Your affectionate brother,
Charles.

I hope you will excuse the scrawl. Fingers are cold and raw with runs.'

Parsons had now shown that the steam turbine was the most efficient means of driving ships. It had cost £16,000 to build the *Turbinia*. Later in the same year there occurred the famous incident at the naval review at Spithead.

The Diamond Jubilee of Queen Victoria was celebrated in 1897. A naval review was held at Spithead. Parsons had the *Turbinia* brought down from the Tyne to Cowes. The warships, cruisers and battleships were all in line, fully dressed for the occasion. Suddenly onlookers saw the little *Turbinia*, 100 feet long, 2,000 h.p., racing down the lines of big ships at 34½ knots, the highest speed ever reached by a vessel. The Navy put out a picket boat to stop her but she was too fast to be caught and the picket boat was nearly sunk. It was a sensation. In this way Parsons brought home to the Admiralty the new marvel of high speed at sea. (Plate VI, facing p. 240.)

It was in the Navy that the Parsons turbine was used first. The Admiralty was so impressed with the speed and power of manoeuvre that very soon it gave the Parsons Marine Turbine Company a contract for two destroyers fitted with turbines. These were the *Viper* and the *Cobra*. They had their first preliminary trials only two years after the *Turbinia*'s exploit. Parsons wrote:

November 21, 1899.

'The *Viper* had her first preliminary trial today and reached 32 knots with about ¾ full steam and 3 inches water-gauge air-pressure . . . It was a very rough day. Three Government inspectors were out and also Leyland. Started at 10 a.m. Stopped fast running at 2 p.m. The inspectors seemed greatly pleased and said they considered the performance as *most satisfactory* in every way, and that it was the roughest sea trial of a destroyer they had been on. Even Leyland in the conning-tower got wet through. The present screws should bring her up to $33\frac{1}{2}$ or 34 knots on the next trial – and after modification she should do 35 easily.'

June 22, 1900.

'The *Cobra* had a semi-official trial today. The mean speed for six consecutive runs was 34·89 knots and the mean for the three hours, not allowing for turns, was 34·32 knots . . . The Admiralty and Armstrong's officials expressed themselves very pleased and reported the trial as entirely satisfactory. I suppose she is now, therefore, as good as sold to the Admiralty. The next fastest vessel in the Service is Thorneycroft's *Albatross*, $31\frac{1}{2}$ knots.

'It would now appear that the *Viper* will reach a mean speed of close on 36 knots on her official trials, or 5 knots above her guarantee.'

Everything now pointed to success. The turbine would be accepted by the Navy and this would be the first step to its being used by other ships. Yet almost as soon as the Navy had taken over the two destroyers they came to grief. Within six weeks of each other both ships became a total loss. The *Viper* was wrecked in the Channel Isles and the *Cobra* broke in two and sank off the Lincolnshire coast.

H.M.S. *Viper* left Portsmouth at 2 p.m. on 3rd August 1901. Later she ran into dense fog and at 5.25 p.m. she struck the rocks at Alderney. The engine room and the stokeholds filled with water and at 6.45 p.m. the crew took to the boats and the ship was abandoned. No one was lost. The ship broke clean in two.

There was nothing to connect the wreck of the *Viper* with her turbine machinery, but when the *Cobra* sank soon afterwards the two were put together and as a result a big enquiry was made.

The *Cobra* left the Tyne at 5 p.m. on 17th September 1901 and set out for a run of 60 miles. The weather was very bad. A 7 a.m. the following morning the ship began to break in two and both parts quickly sank in fifteen fathoms of water. Out of the ship's company of sixty-six only the chief engineer and eleven men were saved. Parsons, deeply shocked by this calamity, in which he felt his responsibility, attended the court martial into the loss of the ship. At the end of the long enquiry lasting six days the finding of the court was:

'The Court has come to the conclusion that His Majesty's ship *Cobra* did not touch the ground, nor meet with any obstruction, nor was her loss due to any error in navigation, but is attributable to the structural weakness of the ship.

'The Court also finds that the *Cobra* was weaker than other destroyers, and in view of that fact, it is to be regretted that she was purchased into His Majesty's service.'

It was clear that the *Viper* and the *Cobra* were not lost because of their turbines. Still, it was never quite explained why the *Cobra* sank. Parsons felt that a special effort had to be made to get the turbine generally accepted and used in ships. He therefore formed a new company, which built the first turbine-driven passenger ship, the *King Edward*. This ship ran on the Clyde with her sister ship. A year or two later two cross-channel steamers were built with turbine engines. This was the beginning of the victory of the steam turbine in ocean going vessels.

Within a few years the big Cunard liners were equipped with steam turbines. The Royal Navy, however, adopted them enthusiastically before they were widely used by merchant vessels.

During the years before the 1914–18 War Britain was running a race for naval power against Germany. Each country was trying to get ahead of the other. The name dreadnought for a battleship was coined and the popular cry was:

'We want eight (dreadnoughts)
And we won't wait.'

Parsons' turbine played a considerable part in this race.

Another important factor in victory at sea in the 1914–18 War was the use of oil for raising steam. The Diesel engine had just arrived in Germany and there was a danger of its being used by their navy. The British navy was so pleased with steam turbines that it was strongly opposed to oil engines. The great question was – could the internal combustion engine be combined with the turbine principle? A royal commission on fuel and engines was set up to enquire into these questions which were so vital to the Navy. Parsons appeared before it and the following conversation took place:

Engineer Vice-Admiral Sir Henry Oram, F.R.S.: 'We know you have considered the question of the internal combustion turbine.'

Sir Charles Parsons: 'Yes.'

Oram: 'It seems a very retrograde step to go back to the old crank-shaft again; what are your views about that?'

Parsons: 'I do not think that the internal combustion turbine will ever come in. The internal combustion turbine is an absolute impossibility.'

It was only 18 years later when Frank Whittle invented the turbine jet aircraft engine.

Parsons had been knighted the year before this for his achievements in engineering. Many honours were bestowed on him. He became a fellow of the Royal Society when he was forty-two. He was a Doctor of eight universities, president of the British Association and, like F. W. Lanchester whose work is described in this chapter, president of the Junior Institution of Engineers. Four years before his death he received the Order of Merit.

He had many side interests, some of which occupied him more as he grew older. He invented a small device which was fixed to stringed musical instruments such as the 'cello in order to increase the volume of sound and richness of tone. Another subject on which he worked for many years was the manufacture of artificial diamonds, but in this he was no more successful than many others. Yet another of his activities was making optical glass and optical instruments. He was a great fisherman.

In his retirement he travelled round the world. On these cruises he would be found in the engine room where his turbines were at work. On one such cruise he died in his bunk on board ship in the West Indies.

F. W. LANCHESTER (1868–1946)

The name of Lanchester is familiar to all who know about veteran or vintage cars. The last Lanchester car was made by the Daimler Company a few years ago. The first ones were made in the 1890's. Many of the basic features of the modern car originated in those early cars made by F. W. Lanchester.

228

He was the greatest British pioneer of the motor-car. He was also famous, and still is, in the world of flight. He discovered some of the basic theory of flight and was one of the great pioneers of aerodynamics, the science of flight.

Lanchester's father was an architect and his mother had been a teacher. He was the fourth child in a large family of eight children. The eldest boy became a well known architect. Lanchester, however, as a boy, showed a strong bent towards engineering.

He was sent to a nursery school at the age of six and then to a preparatory boarding school in Brighton, not far from his home in Hove. There he got on quickly in mathematics and science but he always found English difficult. By the time he was fourteen his parents saw that he wanted to be an engineer and so they sent him to the Hartley Institution at Southampton. This was then the best place in the south for a scientific and technical training. After two years there he won a national scholarship, worth £300, to the Royal College of Science, London, or as it was then called the Normal School of Science. This college was later on part of London University.

Lanchester was a full-time student at the college for three years. There were, of course, only a few students of engineering in those days, compared with the present day. He made good progress for a time but in the last year of the course he lost interest, and he left without taking the final examination or getting the associateship of the college. This would have been serious for an ordinary man but it was not a disaster for Lanchester.

The reason why he did not finish his course at college was typical of Lanchester. He particularly wanted to study mechanical engineering but it was not included in the course. He therefore lost interest and spent most of his time during the last year in the library. At the same time, on his own initiative, he attended evening classes in workshop practice at Finsbury Technical College. He became, in his own words, an 'average good toolmaker'.

While he was still a student he started his career as an inventor. The first invention was an accelerometer for measuring and recording the acceleration and deceleration of a vehicle. Later on he developed it and used it for car testing.

The second invention was a fixture on the slide rule, to be used for rapid calculations in thermodynamics. This also was manufactured in later years.

When Lanchester left college at the age of twenty he had to find a job. Though he was a good mechanic and draughtsman and had studied his own subjects deeply he had no qualifications, and so he had to take on draughting work at 6d. an hour for a time. While he was doing this he took out his first patent. This was for a draughtsman's instrument for 'hatching, shading and geometrical design', and he sold the patent for £25. He had made a start.

Then he had a stroke of luck. His uncle, a gun maker in Birmingham, introduced him to a small engineering firm in that city, called the Forward Gas Engine Company. He was appointed assistant works manager. He wrote:

'The pay was 20/– a week. The so-called drawing office had at one time been a bedroom in a ramshackle house in a poor district – Saltley, Birmingham. The tap water contained many living creatures, the most interesting of which was a kind of fresh water shrimp about half an inch in length. Of drainage there was none.'

The company, which employed about 50 men, serviced, maintained and manufactured, in a small way, Otto gas engines. It was a lucky chance which took Lanchester there. The experience he gained led him straight to the petrol engine and the motor-car. The Otto gas engine had been invented some years before and thousands of them had taken the place of steam engines all over the world. When Lanchester came into the business inventors were trying to improve the gas economy. His first job at the works was re-surfacing the slide-valves of the gas engines. Within a year or two he was designing and constructing engines ranging between 2 h.p. and 60 h.p. He became works manager.

Lanchester made two useful inventions for the gas engine. When he was twenty-one he invented a pendulum governor which took the place of the centrifugal governor and was widely used. He received ten shillings royalty on each one sold. Next year he invented an engine starter. This was more important. Lanchester wrote:

'Another of our early difficulties was starting. It was the practice for gas engines to be started by pulling over the fly-wheel by hand, and every week or so a case would be reported of a man killed or injured by being thrown over the wheel by a backfire. I took out a patent for a method of starting of surprising simplicity. The starter was initiated by a low-pressure explosion and followed up by a number of low-pressure impulses until sufficient speed had been acquired to overcome the compression. In the days of large single-cylinder gas engines the starter was a godsend and was soon adopted by the leading engine builders of the day.'

He received royalties of about £3,000 for the engine starter, and then sold the patent. When he was twenty-three he resigned from his job in order to visit the United States and sell his patents there. The trip was a failure financially but he learnt much about American manufacturing methods.

Back in England, he decided he would make a petrol-driven motor-car. His experience with the gas engine company had prepared him for this:

'During my early experience I encountered gas engines of all types and had the great educational advantage of seeing them in operation, and in many cases of executing repairs and replacements, often of conducting indicator and brake tests. The Otto and the Langen engine (which preceded the Otto by some few years) was to me a source of great entertainment. In that engine a free piston was shot upward like a projectile from a gun, and, on one occasion when I had the job of installing an old engine on an upper floor, I had to place struts like mine props from floor to floor down to the solid earth to take the recoil.'

He always intended to make a petrol engine while he was still working on the gas engine. He even discussed the possibility of making an aero-engine (in 1890) but a friend told him that if he tried to make an engine for a flying machine people would think him a crazy inventor, and his reputation as an engineer would be ruined.

The position of the motor-car when Lanchester designed and started to make his car in 1894 was as follows. In Germany

231

Benz had made a successful four-wheeled car driven by a horizontal single cylinder petrol engine. The engine ran at a low speed and the speed of the car was about 8 m.p.h. Also in Germany Daimler had invented a vertical single cylinder engine which ran at a high speed, and had put it in a four-wheeled vehicle. Lanchester saw this vehicle at a Paris exhibition and described it as 'having rather the appearance of two bicycles coupled side by side, a body with motor and transmission mechanism bridging the gap between them'. In France, Peugeot had used a V-twin Daimler engine in his own car built like a bicycle. This was all that had developed.

In Britain J. H. Knight, and Austin at the Wolseley Sheep Shearing Machine Company, were both making three-wheeled cars. The real advances had been made on the Continent. In Britain the law still said that there must be a man on foot twenty yards ahead of any horseless vehicle. This had checked development of the car in Britain. Manufacturers in Britain were using foreign inventions and patents. What Lanchester did was to design and build a completely British car. It was original; it owed little or nothing to the pioneers in Germany and France.

Up till then inventors had adapted the horse-drawn vehicle, merely putting an engine and transmission in instead of a horse, and producing a horseless carriage. Lanchester broke away from this, started from scratch, and produced the first car designed and thought out as a car. (Plate VII.)

This first experimental car took nearly two years to make. It was a five-seater. The frame was of brazed steel tubes. Under this was the single cylinder air-cooled engine of 5 h.p. He used electrical ignition, unlike most early inventors, and invented his own low-tension system in which an inductive spark was caused in the cylinder. The carburettor was also his own invention. It was the wick type of carburettor, in which the petrol was absorbed by the wick, air being let in to form the mixture. Lanchester invented his own transmission mechanism; an epicyclic gear-box was combined with chain drive. Tiller steering was used.

Early one morning in February 1896 Lanchester and his brother took the car out on its first run. It was quite dark; they wanted to avoid the law which still required a man to be walking ahead. The car ran satisfactorily but they found that they had to push it up the hills. It was under-powered. They immediately set to work to reconstruct it. This took them 18 months.

This reconstructed model took some time to finish because a new engine and new transmission mechanism had to be

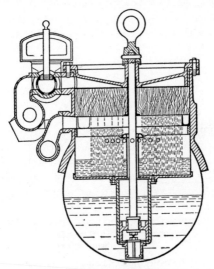

[From *The Complete Motorist*, by A. B. F. Young

The Lanchester wick-carburettor

designed and made. Working in the shops of the Forward Gas Engine Company, Lanchester produced a twin-cylinder air-cooled engine of 8 h.p. In order to get a balanced engine he invented a special counter-balancing mechanism. This had two crankshafts, one above the other, revolving in opposite directions. The two pistons were connected to both crankshafts.

Instead of having the chain drive Lanchester designed a completely new kind of worm drive. The worm was driven direct from the engine shaft when on top gear, and through epicyclic gear for low speed and reverse. In order to make the worm gear he had to invent a special cutting machine. This was used for many years.

The reconstructed car was on the road in 1897. It now ran successfully at up to 20 m.p.h.

Lanchester intended to manufacture cars for the commercial market. However, his next step was to make a second experimental car which was finished in 1898. It was a famous car in its day. It was awarded a special gold medal for design and performance at the trials of the Automobile Club of Great Britain in 1899. Now it is in the Science Museum.

This car, which Lanchester called the Gold Medal Phaeton,

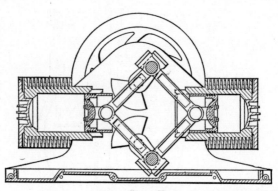

[From *The Complete Motorist*, by A. B. F. Young

The twin-cylinder Lanchester engine

seated three abreast. As with the first car, many new inventions were put in it and these were copied and used in motor-car engineering later. The twin-cylinder engine was completely balanced as before. This made it possible to have higher piston speed than was thought possible at that time. The splined shaft was introduced in this car. For the epicyclic gear-box Lanchester had to make his own roller bearings as no one could be found to make them. The pedal accelerator he invented was now used for the first time. Ignition was obtained through a magnetic generator in which two massive magnets were built into a fly-wheel. Cantilever springs, at the forward end of the chassis, were also used for the first time.

The car proved to be a success. Lanchester and his brother took it out on the first non-stop run of 68 miles from the works in Birmingham to Pershore, Evesham and back. There were no mishaps. They reached 28 m.p.h. without being caught for speeding. The car did many longer runs – Birmingham to London in six and a half hours was one of them.

Lanchester never left off inventing; during his lifetime of 78 years he took out over 400 patents. However, in the next five years he gave most of his energy and time to organizing production of his cars for the market. He was now thirty-one. He was a big man, in appearance, heavily built, and with strong features above a thick dark beard. He remained single until he was over fifty.

When Lanchester had started planning production of the cars he found that even the smallest detail needed thinking out. For instance, he found that the standard Whitworth screw threads were unsuitable. So he produced his own range of standard threads which were used in all Lanchester cars for many years. Another example was oil. In those days every merchant had his own grades of oil so that it was impossible to know exactly what oil one was buying. He therefore built a plant for blending and filtering, and blended his own oils according to his own standards. His biggest achievement in production was to get complete interchangeability of parts.

All the pioneering work Lanchester carried out can be summed up as follows:

Features and devices in the modern car which had their origin in Lanchester practice.

Epicyclic gear, accelerator, magneto ignition, pull-on hand brake, worm transmission gear, pre-selector control, cantilever springing, forced lubrication.

Lanchester's name became famous in automobile engineering. It was all the more remarkable that he also became famous in aeronautics. Aerodynamics, the science of flight, was his earliest interest, even while he was a student. When he was works manager of the Forward Gas Engine Company he started to study the subject seriously. He carried out many experiments with model gliders from a back bedroom and in a meadow behind his house. He spent many hours studying the flight of birds; he took up shooting in order to examine the wings and body structure of birds, and fishing so as to study the stream-lining of fish.

His mind worked so quickly that within a year or two, when he was twenty-six, he had made his great discovery in aerodynamics. This was the *vortex theory* or the circulation theory. It explained the lift which sustains an aeroplane in flight. Modern theory and design of aircraft are based on Lanchester's discovery.

Lanchester was the first to explain that the future of the aeroplane depended on its being stable in the air. The early gliders, and even the aeroplane of the Wright brothers, were kept in the air only by the skill of the pilots, and so many pioneer gliders lost their lives. The planes could not be designed to be stable in the air because no one understood the movements in the air which kept up the aeroplane. After Lanchester had shown that these movements were vortices set up at the wing tips, then it became possible to design stable aircraft. He was the father of modern aerodynamics.

In Britain unfortunately his work was ignored for many years. When he first discovered the vortex theory in 1894 he could not get it published. He was too far in advance of his time; it was ten years before the Wrights flew. It was not until 13 years later that he was able to get published a massive book entitled *Aerial Flight* which contained his vortex theory. During the years between he was busy making the first motor-cars.

Even then scientists in England and France did not accept his theories until after the 1914–18 War. It was only in Germany that they were accepted and there his name became famous. Towards the end of his life he did at last get full recognition. He became a fellow of the Royal Society and the Royal Aeronautical Society and the Institution of Mechanical Engineers gave him its highest awards. But the long delay in recognition of his work embittered him.

Lanchester was a big man in every way. He was very strong, both physically and mentally, often intolerant of people whose minds did not work as quickly as his and sometimes sarcastic at their expense. Besides this he was very versatile. He was as much at home as a scientist in the laboratory as he was as an engineer in the workshop. He loved opera and classical music, which he sang. He invented a loudspeaker which gave better reproduction than any then existing. He also wrote and published a book of poetry. He had a good deal of the artist as well as the scientist and engineer in him.

In his last years Lanchester had barely enough money to live on, and it was only a grant from the Society of Motor Manufacturers and Traders that kept him going. While he had earned large sums of money from the sale of inventions and as a consultant, he had spent them freely, mainly on research. He had always financed himself and had never been able to get much support from business men or financiers, whom he disliked as a body.

Some favourite lines in one of his own poems are:

'His soul was in his work, which, living on, bears fruit:
So doth a soul attain to immortality.'

SIR FRANK WHITTLE (1907–)

Whittle, the inventor of the gas turbine for jet propulsion of aircraft, was born on 1st June 1907, at Coventry. His parents came from a Lancashire family of working people. His father had little education and started work in a cotton mill at the age of eleven. He was a gifted man, however, and by the time Whittle was born he had become a skilled mechanic and had made many inventions.

What Whittle learnt from his father laid the basis of his future career. When he was quite young he was shown how to work on a drawing board. When he was only ten he began to get some experience on the bench and with the lathes. His family had moved to Leamington Spa where his father bought with his savings a small engineering business. This Leamington Valve and Piston Company was very small, in fact it was practically a one man business for some time. This had the advantage that Whittle had to help his father when he was free from school and for this he was paid the appropriate rate.

From five to eleven he was at elementary schools in Coventry and Leamington. At eleven he won a scholarship, as it was then called, or a place, at a secondary grammar school. This school later became Leamington College.

Although at the end of his first year he won another small

scholarship which brought in £10 a year, his school record was not particularly good. This was not because he was not clever but because he was not interested in most of the subjects and could not bring himself to work hard at them. The only school subject which really interested him was chemistry. But there were many other subjects, not taken at school, which he studied by himself. He spent many hours in the public library reading eagerly whatever books he could find about astronomy, physiology and engineering. Already aircraft engineering was his special interest. While the other boys did their homework he studied books on the theory of flight and practical flying. He looked forward to the day when he could fly aeroplanes and he was confident he could do it.

He left school at the age of fifteen: what he lost in cutting short his school days he had gained in learning the basis of his future career.

His ambition was to become an aircraft apprentice in the Royal Air Force. When he applied, however, he was unsuccessful because, although he easily passed the written examination, he was too short by the R.A.F. standard. He was a strong, wiry lad but he was only five feet tall. This was a bitter disappointment but he was determined to succeed. He worked away at a course of physical exercises to improve his physique. Then he asked for his application to be reconsidered but he found that he could not be accepted after having been rejected. He therefore decided to by-pass the official channels; he made a fresh application and this time he was successful. If it had not been for his determination the R.A.F. would not have had the jet engine as early as it did.

Now sixteen, Whittle became an aircraft apprentice at Cranwell. He was there for three years but this was only the first stage in his very long training of different kinds extending over many years. It was this long training which gave him such extraordinary qualifications and enabled him to produce the jet engine.

At Cranwell he was trained as a rigger for metal aircraft. Metal aircraft were comparatively new in 1923. He enjoyed the training as an aircraft mechanic but the strict service discipline, the drills, and the life of the barrack room were not to his liking. Although he disliked this part of the life at

Cranwell there were other ways in which he could use his ability. In the model aircraft society there was the opportunity to follow his own bent. With it he worked many hours, often when he should have been doing other work.

The making of model aircraft was very important in the next step in his training. Not only did he learn a great deal about aircraft but his work on models helped to win him a cadetship at the Royal Air Force College at Cranwell. In fact he thought that the models compensated for his record in the main training course. His experience at school was repeated. He wrote:

'The highlight in connection with my model work was the making of a large model of ten feet six inches wing span powered by a two-stroke petrol engine. I headed the small team which worked on this ambitious project and was responsible for the design of the airframe, the drawings, wooden jigs for the construction of the delicate wing ribs and other parts of the structure, and the fabric covering. The engine was made by a laboratory assistant who was a very skilful mechanic. Only the miniature sparking plugs, of which we purchased two, were not made by us.'

Unfortunately this model never flew. It came to the notice of the commanding officer and the apprentices were instructed to arrange its first flight on the great passing-out day. All the authorities were present on the day but when it came to test the engine of the model both sparking plugs failed, and no flight could be made. It was a great disappointment. Whittle thought that his dislike of piston engines started on that day.

Now began a new life as a cadet; he was all set for a commission. He was one of only five apprentices out of 600 to win a cadetship. It was a big step up for Whittle. Not only would he have a commission but as a flight cadet he would learn to become a pilot. He must have dreamed about the possibility of joining the Royal Air Force College for often, on parade in the ranks of the apprentices, he had watched the cadets march smartly on to the square, different beings from another world.

So, at the age of nineteen, Whittle began his two years of cadet training on pay of 7s. a day, which he found ample. The course was a very wide one and it included a great number of subjects intended to fit the cadet to become an officer. He had to learn about meteorology, navigation, signals, armament, law, and organization. There was a full course of workshop practice for aircraft maintenance. The theoretical subjects included English, history, mathematics, physics and mechanics. Drill, rifle practice and physical training took up many hours. What time was left was spent on games which were compulsory but there was a choice. Whittle chose fencing and in his own words 'became moderately proficient with the foil, sabre and epée'.

Of all the instruction at Cranwell the most interesting to Whittle was flying. He had to be satisfied with model making while he was an apprentice, but this was now the real thing. He became a good pilot; his only fault was entered in his record as follows:

'Over-confidence. This is most marked. He gives aerobatics too much value and has neglected accuracy. Must learn to discipline his flying. Inclined to perform to gallery and flies too low.'

The most important happening, however, during Whittle's years as a cadet was that he began to think about gas turbines. The cadets had to write a thesis on a scientific subject each term. He chose the subject of Future Developments in Aircraft Design. Years later he wrote:

'This task was really the starting point of my subsequent work on jet propulsion. In the course of its preparation I came to the conclusion that if very high speeds were to be combined with long range, it would be necessary to fly at very great heights where the low air density would greatly reduce resistance in proportion to speed. I was thinking in terms of speeds of 500 miles per hour at heights where the air density was less than one quarter of its sea level value. The top speed of R.A.F. fighters in those days was about 150 m.p.h.

'It seemed unlikely that the conventional piston engine and propeller combination would meet the power plant needs of the kind of high-speed, high-altitude aircraft I had in mind, and so, in my discussion of power plant, I cast my net very wide and discussed the possibilities of rocket propulsion and of

Plate 7

The aeroplane designed and constructed by Parsons in 1893. It was propelled by steam or by the vapour of alcohol. Standing by it is his son, Algernon Parsons, afterwards Major A. Parsons, R.F.A.

(From 'Charles Parsons: His Life and Work' by R. Appleyard)

First Lanchester car, 1895, with 5 h.p. engine amidships

(From 'F. W. Lanchester' by P. W. Kingsford)

Plate 8

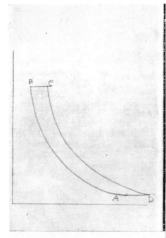

ORIGINAL THESIS ON JET PROPULSION BY
AIR COMMODORE SIR FRANK WHITTLE.

WRITTEN AT THE ROYAL AIR FORCE
COLLEGE, CRANWELL, IN 1928 WHEN HE
WAS A FLIGHT-CADET 21 YEARS OF AGE.

Sir Frank Whittle's Thesis

(Photo, Science Museum, London. By courtesy of Sir Frank Whittle)

Britain's first jet-propelled aeroplane, the Gloster E.28/39, with the Whittle W.1
turbo-jet engine in the foreground

(Crown copyright, Science Museum, London)

gas turbines driving propellers, but it did not then occur to me to use the gas turbine for jet propulsion.'

Thus at the age of twenty, in 1928, he started the train of thought which led to the jet engine (Plate VIII, facing p. 241).

When his time at Cranwell came to an end he passed out second out of about thirty cadets, and he won a prize for aeronautical sciences.

Having received his commission, Whittle's first posting as a Pilot Officer was to 111 Fighter Squadron at Hornchurch. He enjoyed very much the freer life there after the strict discipline of the last five years. He also, at the age of twenty-one, became engaged.

At Hornchurch, after just over a year of instruction and practice in flying, he was good enough to be selected to be trained as an instructor and he was sent to the Central Flying School at Wittering in Sussex. There he had yet another period of training of three months and at the end qualified as a flying instructor. He was then posted as an instructor to No. 2 Flying Training School at Digby in Lincolnshire. Teaching men to fly he found an interesting and sometimes exciting job.

While an instructor at Digby he was selected with another Flying Officer to give the exhibition of crazy flying at the R.A.F. Annual Display at Hendon. This required very skilled flying indeed. The pilots flew as though they had never flown before, did all the wrong things and made it look as if an accident could happen at any moment. Afterwards he was delighted to receive the following letter from the Air Officer Commanding:

'Dear Whittle,
You will see published in Orders an appreciation by the C.A.S. of the work done by all the officers to make the Display a success.

I want to add my personal congratulations on the excellent show put up by you. The crowd appreciated your evolutions very much indeed . . .

Yours sincerely,
P. B. Joubert.'

In the meantime he had got married and his first son was

born a year later. It was not easy to make ends meet on his pay and the allowances for a single officer; he was too young to qualify for a service marriage allowance.

During all this time the idea of jet propulsion took shape in Whittle's mind. His aim was to design a power plant which would propel aircraft flying much faster and at much higher altitudes than were possible at that time. His first idea was to get the propelling jet from a low-pressure fan which was driven by an ordinary piston engine. Suddenly the idea came to him; in his own words:

'While I was at Wittering, it suddenly occurred to me to substitute a turbine for the piston engine. This change meant that the compressor would have to have a much higher pressure ratio than the one I had visualised for the piston-engined scheme. In short, I was back to the gas turbine, but this time of a type which produced a propelling jet instead of driving a propeller. Once this idea had taken shape, it seemed rather odd that I had taken so long to arrive at a concept which had become very obvious and of extraordinary simplicity. My calculations satisfied me that it was far superior to any earlier proposals.'

He had much encouragement from a friend, an instructor at the Central Flying School, in working out his scheme for a turbo-jet engine. After some time he was instructed to report his scheme to the Air Ministry. Unfortunately, some years earlier the Ministry had been advised that the gas turbine was not practicable. Whittle was told that there was no future in developing his scheme because there were no materials which could stand up to the high temperature and high stresses involved. This was true enough at the time but it was possible that such materials could be developed in the future.

Although his scheme was rejected by the Air Ministry, Whittle took out a patent for a turbo-jet engine in January 1930 and hoped that something would come of it. He was then twenty-two. He visited several big engineering firms to persuade them to back his invention but without success. The chief engineer of one of these firms described the great difficulty:

'It seems to me that the whole scheme depends upon obtaining material which will work satisfactorily at a very high temperature. Personally, I doubt very much whether such material is available and this, I think, prevents the development of the internal combustion turbine. I fear therefore that I cannot hold out any hopes that this firm will take any serious interest in your proposal.'

In the meantime he took another step forward in his service career. He was posted to the Marine Aircraft Experimental Establishment at Felixstowe as a float-plane test pilot.

He liked it there very much; there was plenty of scope for technical work. He was mainly engaged on testing catapults for launching aircraft. Experimental work was being done on catapults and Whittle was often the first pilot to try out a new type. In one month he made 47 catapult launches, nine of them in one day. They were carried out at sea from H.M.S. *Ark Royal*.

Another nerve-testing trial he carried out was a flotation test of a land aeroplane. The pilot had to ditch the plane in the sea in order to test the flotation apparatus on it. In two previous trials the plane had sunk almost immediately but Whittle succeeded, as he described himself:

'I brought the aircraft down into the required position and "pancaked" it into the sea from a height of about five feet. As soon as the wheels met the water, the aeroplane buried its nose in the sea and a great sheet of water entered the cockpit. For an instant I thought I had turned right over, but though the fuselage reached a vertical position it fell back. I had no difficulty in inflating and launching the collapsible dinghy which was carried in the rear cockpit. I stepped into the dinghy with an immense feeling of relief and floated away from the aircraft.'

Soon after he received a high commendation from the Navy. In his confidential report for that year he was described as 'a keen and capable young officer'. Resulting from this he began another period of training: he was sent to the officers' engineering course at Henlow. The course was for two years but Whittle did so extremely well in the entrance examination that he was allowed to take the course in 18 months. At the end of the first year he won distinction in every subject except one. His outstanding merit was recognized by the Air Ministry. Immediately after the Henlow course he was sent to Cambridge University to study for the degree in mechanical sciences. And so yet another two years of training were added to his record. He was now twenty-seven, much older than most of the undergraduates.

In the meantime no progress had been made with the jet turbine. In 1935 he had to find five pounds to renew the patent. Quite apart from the money which he could not easily afford, he had practically given up hope of his engine. He realized better than before the cost and effort which would be involved, and he now believed that his invention was before its time.

Then, out of the blue, came a letter which changed everything, and gradually plans for the jet engine began to take shape. At Cambridge, Whittle was attached, as a Flight Lieutenant, to the University Air Squadron. One day in the Squadron Office he was handed a letter from an old R.A.F. friend telling him that a man in an engineering firm was interested in his invention of 'an aeroplane without a propeller'. Whittle felt it was hardly worth replying but he did, saying:

'Nobody would touch it on account of the enormous cost of the experimental work and I don't think they were far wrong though I still have every faith in the invention. However if anybody were keen on taking it up I think it would pay them.' (I did not really believe this.) 'There is no doubt in my mind that as things stand at present, it is the only way to high-altitude flying.'

Whittle and the friend and his partner made an agreement to go ahead. For some time they searched for a financier who would supply the £50,000 they aimed to raise. They were determined to keep away from the big aircraft firms because, although additional patents had been taken out, they did not give full protection to the inventors. Eventually a firm of investment brokers became interested and after long negotiations a company was formed for which they supplied the capital. This was in March 1936: the company was called Power Jets Ltd. and its authorized capital was £10,000. Now work on an experimental jet engine could begin.

The British Thomson-Houston company was asked to prepare design drawings for an experimental engine. The aim was to make an engine which would have enough power for a 500 m.p.h. mail plane, although it would not actually fly a plane. Some idea of what was involved is given by Whittle's own description of such an engine:

'The major organs of a turbo-jet engine are: a compressor, a combustion chamber assembly, a turbine, and an exhaust pipe ending in a jet nozzle. Large quantities of air drawn in at a front intake pass through these organs in that order. The flow through the engine is continuous. In the combustion chambers the air compressed by the compressor is heated by the steady combustion of fuel. The compressed and heated gases then pass through the turbine, thus providing the power to drive the compressor to which the turbine is connected by a shaft. They then pass along the exhaust duct and emerge from the jet nozzle as a high-velocity propelling jet.'

The performance required for the compressor, turbine and combustion chambers was far beyond anything yet achieved. Whittle felt confident about the compressor and turbine but he got outside advice about the combustion problems.

He soon became very busy in discussions with the firms who were taking part in making the engine. This work had interfered with his studies at the University. He was determined to get a first class honours degree and he succeeded by dint of intensive work, although he was unwell throughout the examinations because of overstrain. The question was now whether as an R.A.F. officer he could go on with work on the engine. Fortunately the Air Ministry agreed to his having another year on post-graduate research and this meant he could spend most of his time on the engine.

Work went on rapidly. Whittle went to see the forging of the compressor impeller and of the turbine. Combustion experiments went on for a long time. By April 1937 the experimental engine was ready for the first test run. Whittle's diary records this event:

'Pilot jet successfully ignited at 1,000 r.p.m. Speed raised to 2,000 r.p.m. by motor. I requested a further raising of speed to

2,500 r.p.m. and during this process I opened valve "B" and the unit ran away. Probably started at about 2,300 and using only about 5 h.p. starting power . . . Noted that return pipe from jet was overheating badly. Flame tube red hot at inner valves; combustion very bad . . .'

It was a very exciting moment. As soon as Whittle opened the control valve the engine accelerated rapidly and with a rising shriek ran out of control. Everyone took to his heels except Whittle who remained at the controls. Fortunately the speed went no further than 8,000 r.p.m. and then fell. After alterations some test runs were made but combustion was the main problem. The firm was short of money (money was always the problem) and Whittle decided the engine would have to be reconstructed. Then the Air Ministry began to take more interest and gave a contract to go on with the research and experimenting. Just at this time too the Ministry agreed to this work being Whittle's official R.A.F. work and he was promoted to squadron leader.

Work began on reconstruction of the engine. This was the second model. British Thomson-Houston had decided it was too dangerous to continue tests at Rugby but rented to Power Jets part of a disused foundry at Lutterworth where the new start was made. Much of the original engine was used. One important difference was in the turbine blades, for Whittle made a new discovery that the blades should be set at a different angle and, in spite of the experts, insisted that the engine should be altered accordingly.

Very soon after this model was tested it failed. A weak feature in the design resulted in nine turbine blades breaking off. This was in 1938. Whittle was very discouraged; he decided on a complete reconstruction of the engine. Although he did not know at the time, in Germany the firm of Heinkel were building a turbo-jet engine.

In the third model Whittle decided to have ten small combustion chambers instead of the single chamber in the first models. This resulted in a lighter and more compact engine. He was worried all the time about shortage of money but more capital was found and another contract came from the Air Ministry. The third model went ahead; Whittle was searching all the time for stronger materials. He was still making do with parts of the earlier models which should have been scrapped.

After successful tests the authorities gradually changed their attitude. Whereas they had thought that the work was simply research which might be useful in the long run they now began to think that the result might be a practical aero-engine. Power Jets was given a contract for a flight engine and the Gloster Aircraft Company received a contract for the experimental aeroplane. Thus in July 1939, a few weeks before the outbreak of war, Whittle was working on the design of a flight engine. It was called the W.1. He was told that if war broke out the work was to go on, and a new and more powerful engine, the W.2, was to be designed.

In the meantime the Gloster Aircraft Company were starting on the small aeroplane which was to test the W.1 engine, the Gloster-Whittle E.28/39. At Lutterworth the Power Jets works had an atmosphere which was all its own; in Whittle's words:

'On one occasion when Walker from Gloster's entered my office he found a group of us on our knees studying a blue-print on the floor. This amused him considerably and he mentioned that their people had come to refer to Power Jets as "The Cherry Orchard". I asked "Why Cherry Orchard?" He explained that the atmosphere at Power Jets reminded them of the play by Chekhov in which various characters would appear on the stage, say something quite irrelevant and then disappear again . . . I asked him why he thought Power Jets was like that, so he said that in the first place, Power Jets was quite different from any other engineering concern he had ever seen, and then went on somewhat as follows: "A small boy comes through one door carrying a cup of tea; then you jump up, pick up a rifle and fire it through the window. Next one of your directors appears to ask whether he can afford to have a three-inch gas pipe put in; then the same small boy comes through another door with another cup of tea . . ."'

(The rifle refers to Whittle's habit of taking a shot at stray rabbits.)

Work went ahead but too slowly for Whittle. In January

1940 Power Jets employees numbered only 22 including men on loan from other companies. Air Marshal Tedder saw a test run of the experimental engine and was much impressed. The authorities decided that the jet engine might help to win the war. But Whittle was afraid that if the engine was taken over by the big aircraft firms Power Jets would be squeezed out of business. He opposed the Government policy of handing production over to big outside firms and keeping Power Jets on research work only, obliged to help the outside firms in every way. He did not always find it easy to work with the big firms, and he himself was not always an easy person to get on with. At a meeting at the Air Ministry –

'Sir Wilfrid (Freeman) turned to Tedder and asked him if I was a difficult fellow to get on with, adding: "He seems a reasonable enough being in this office." Tedder smiled and said I was a little difficult at times (in our earlier talk, Tedder had remarked that I had to be regarded somewhat as a "prima donna" – very important, but needing to be handled gently). I said to Freeman that I hoped that time would show that I was not as difficult as Tedder implied.'

While all this was going on the war was developing. Germany overran France, the remnants of the British Army evacuated from Dunkirk, and Britain was isolated. The Chamberlain Government fell and Winston Churchill became Prime Minister. A new minister of aircraft production was set up, with Lord Beaverbrook at its head, and aircraft production began to be stepped up; this affected Whittle. Vauxhall was drawn into production as well as Rover and B.T.H. After making tests with only one experimental engine for three years, Power Jets now had two engines for the all important testing. But they still had to struggle to get the labour and equipment they wanted.

At length in May 1941 the first British jet plane, the Gloster-Whittle E.28/39, was ready for flight. 'Evening – first test flight of the E.28.' This short note in Whittle's diary marked a historic event in aviation. He describes what happened. The pilot was G. E. R. Sayer, Gloster's chief test pilot.

'Sayer was in position at about 7.40 p.m. He ran the engine

up to 16,500 r.p.m. against the brakes. He then released the brakes and the aeroplane quickly gathered speed and lifted smoothly from the runway after a run of about 600 yards. It continued to the west in a flat climb for several miles and disappeared from view behind cloud banks. For several minutes we could only hear the smooth roar of the engine. Then it came into sight again as it made a wide circuit preparatory to landing. As Sayer came in it was obvious that he had complete confidence in the aeroplane. He approached in a series of gliding turns as though he had flown the machine for hundreds of hours. Those of us who were pilots knew that he felt completely at home. He made a perfect landing at the far end of the runway and came to a stop somewhere short of where we were standing – the flight had lasted seventeen minutes. He taxied towards us, stopped, and gave us a "thumbs up" sign. We, of course, rushed up to shake him warmly by the hand.

'It is difficult to describe my emotions during and after the flight – I was very tense, not so much because of my fears about the engine, but because this was a machine making its first flight.' (Plate VIII, facing p. 241.)

This successful flight aroused great optimism, but Whittle was aware that much remained to be done before the factories could go ahead with large scale production of the engine. He felt sure that the turbine end of the engine needed improvement, and as it turned out there was to be trouble with the compressor and combustion chambers before a thoroughly reliable engine was achieved. He wanted much more testing and development work and he was dismayed to find that plans were already made for large scale production.

Trouble with the different parts of the engine still continued during testing throughout 1941. One day the compressor impeller burst and the engine was shattered. There were four people in the test cell at the time. By a miracle no one was killed or even seriously injured. Development of the engine was, all the time, handicapped by shortage of materials and equipment. Power Jets even made blades out of hard wood for testing. Other firms were now brought in by the Government to help in the development work. Rolls-Royce and De

Havilland started designing jet engines. Power Jets supplied the initial know-how throughout.

During 1942 Power Jets at last got a full scale test plant and a new factory at Whetstone, near Leicester, for developing the engine. Whittle paid a visit to the United States and took a jet engine and drawings to General Electric for them to build jet engines. The Gloster Aircraft Company were pressing ahead with the Meteor fighter powered by a Whittle engine, but in the meantime the need for such a plane had lessened. America was now in the war, the Allies were getting on top in the air and so it was less urgent to have a fast interceptor plane operating at high altitudes. There was massive production of piston-engined fighters and bombers. However, Rolls-Royce went ahead with production of jet engines although they were still not reliable, and testing and trials continued.

Under the strain of years of continuous effort Whittle's health began to give way. He was sent on a three months' course at the Staff College for a change, but it was hardly a rest. Then he became subject to a blaze of publicity. He received a C.B.E. in January 1944. Soon after the Government released the news of the jet engine to the Press. He was deluged by correspondence and he became recognized wherever he went. He found this a great nuisance. He could not see any good reason for the Government's action. One result may have been that the Germans made great efforts to produce jet planes. By 1944 they were on the defensive and were trying to stop the Allied day and night bombing raids. The Messerschmitt 262, powered by a Junkers turbo-jet engine, began seriously to threaten the Allied bombers.

For Whittle now began another period of great strain and worry. The whole future of Power Jets Ltd. was at stake. Was the firm built up by Whittle and his helpers to continue as a private company or was it to be taken over by the State? Whittle himself wondered what the future of his firm would be. He therefore wrote to Sir Stafford Cripps, the Minister of Aircraft Production, and suggested that the whole of the jet engine business should be nationalized. This meant not only the research and development begun and carried on by Power Jets but also the production in the hands of the big aircraft firms. There was no reason why the big firms should be able to profit from the research which had been largely financed by public money.

Whittle described the interview with Cripps which followed:

'Sir Stafford Cripps requested me to see him on 11th May, 1943. He told me he agreed in general with the points I had made in my letter, but that his problem was ways and means, because the Government was not a socialist one and the law only allowed him to take over firms if they were inefficient. At this point he gave me a rather penetrating look, and said, "Power Jets does not give me that excuse, does it?" I replied, "No, Sir!".'

The Government decided that Power Jets must be taken over because it was necessary to have a gas turbine experimental station run by the state. The aircraft firms were left as they were. Power Jets was bought by the Government for £135,563; if the firm had not accepted this it would have been taken over without compensation. Whittle felt this was most unjust.

He now had to decide whether he should give up his own money in Power Jets or should take part of the compensation. The value of his shares and rights was about £47,000. It was a lot to give up. He felt it was his duty as an officer in the R.A.F. to give it up, but, although he had offered to do this earlier on, he was now undecided because of the way in which Power Jets had been nationalized. He wrote to the Minister:

'While it is quite true that I have no particular desire to "make my fortune" I think my disinterest in money matters has been over-rated. That may be my own fault. There is always a difference between what one would like to do and what one believes one ought to do. It may be that I have overstressed the latter. The truth is, as I told you in my first interview, that I am sufficiently interested in financial matters to desire sufficient for comfort and to be free from the need to worry about my bank balance and to ensure that my family would not suffer hardship in the event of anything happening to me. You are not therefore to think that this offer was a light-hearted one; on the contrary, I felt it to be a duty – and a painful one . . .'

Whittle did give up the money although he could have kept it.

He resigned from Power Jets in 1946. He felt that he had 'the right crew in the wrong ship'; there was no point in him and his colleagues who were 'engineers who have an intense interest in doing a practical job of work' staying in a purely research organization divorced from engineering. Several members of the unique team of engineers he had gathered together so carefully had already left. Very soon the whole team was disbanded.

In the following year his health broke down again and he spent most of the year in hospital. Because of this it was agreed that he should soon retire from the R.A.F. During that year he was elected a Fellow of the Royal Society.

In 1948 the Royal Commission on awards to Inventors at last considered his case and awarded him the sum of £100,000 free of tax. He retired from the R.A.F. on medical grounds with the rank of Air Commodore and received the K.B.E. He was still only forty-one and he had achieved a revolution in motive power.

He had acted on principle. His great regret was that he had not been able to hold together the engineering team of Power Jets and he felt that he had not been able to live up to their trust in his ability to do that. He gradually withdrew from the whole gas turbine industry. For a time he was still connected with it as consultant to B.O.A.C. When the folly of another world war became possible he worked to help emigration so as to reduce the population of Britain and strengthen the Commonwealth. He wrote his own account of the struggle to achieve the jet engine in *Jet, The Story of a Pioneer*. In 1954 he took a post as adviser to a Dutch oil company at The Hague.

THE ENGINEERING WORKERS (1890–1945)

Parsons's steam turbine revolutionized the shipbuilding industry. Lanchester's inventions were the basis for a new industry, the motor-car. Whittle's gas turbine revolutionized the aircraft industry. The work and lives of the engineering workers were bound to be changed fundamentally by these inventions. Many new products could be made because of the new ideas. The number of workers in the engineering industry grew from a quarter of a million to well over one million. This was a great field for trade union recruitment.

The First World War came half-way through this period. Let us see first the effects on the engineering works before 1914. By then the steam turbine was being used by warships and big merchant ships. The motor-car was still bought only by wealthy customers. The output was about 2,000 a year. In these growing industries, the conditions in the workshops changed and new kinds of skill and work were needed.

The ship and the motor-car became bigger and more complicated, as did the new electrical products. The bicycle was mass-produced. Therefore specialization grew, that is, firms began more and more to make only one product or one part or component. As an engineering worker said in 1900:

'Not only are firms making a speciality of one class of tools or engines but we find them standardizing and confining themselves to a few stock sizes, some firms even confining themselves to the production of a small part. For example, pumps, piston rings, crank shafts, valves, etc., all come from a specialist, ready to drop into place.'

This change resulted in other big changes in the machine shops. New machines, the capstan and turret lathe, the vertical and horizontal milling machines, the surface grinder, and others replaced the old established centre lathe. Many men saw the machines as a threat to their jobs and their wages. With the machines came new methods of incentives. Work was speeded up. The engineering workers, involved in these problems, turned for help to the trade unions, particularly the Amalgamated Society of Engineers.

When an invention like Parsons's marine turbine called for new kinds of work, the workers in different trades quarrelled as to who should do the work. When the fitters and the brass finishers both demanded the work of blading the turbines they turned to their unions to decide this demarcation dispute.

Parsons's turbine for generating electricity gave the power which was required to drive the new machines. These machines also needed better cutting steel before they could be fully used.

High-speed steel was discovered in America and seen first in Europe at a Paris exhibition in 1900.

'Those engineers who saw a lathe turning at a high speed with a tool with its point red hot removing a dark blue chip felt that they were witnessing the beginning of a revolution in tool steel and in machines fitted for its use.'

As output increased products became more standardized. Parts had to be interchangeable. Tolerances came in instead of dead accuracy. 'Go and not-Go' gauges appeared in the workshops. Some of the old work of the fitter disappeared with the accuracy, but the new machines gave him new work to do.

The result was that the organization of the workshops changed. Production was speeded up; it was now necessary to plan in the shops so as to avoid hold-ups and to make the best use of the machines. So planners, progress men and rate fixers appeared, and with them 'work hustlers' and 'speed-and-feed men'. Timekeeping became stricter and time clocks were used. One worker said 'the employers would like to put a micrometer on the clocks if they could'.

The whole engineering industry was being changed rapidly. The work of the skilled craftsman changed, and more semi-skilled and unskilled men were brought in. Apprenticeship was no longer the only way of entering the industry and the union. Piece work or some kind of payment by results took the place of time wages. The premium bonus system appeared. The traditional wage disappeared and many of the older skilled workers preferred the good old days. As one of them in a railway workshop put it:

'A decade and a half ago one could come into the shed fearlessly and with perfect complacence; work was a pleasure compared with what it is now. Now, however, every day brings fresh troubles from some quarter or other. The supervisory staffs have been doubled or trebled; before the workman can recover from one shock he is visited with another.'

Many engineering workers saw that the new conditions and methods of work must be controlled, so that work could still be a pleasure, and realized that they could only do this through their trade union.

The first big conflict in the industry was the lock-out of 1897–98. Before that date the Amalgamated Society of Engineers had reorganized itself. The employers also set up a new Employers' Federation of Engineering Associations. For several years the union had been resisting changes which meant skilled men losing their jobs because new machines, capstan and turret lathes, millers and borers, were operated by handymen. It had also demanded a 48-hour week to offset the speed-up in the workshops. When a strike was threatened the employers locked out all union men in all federated firms. The lock-out went on for six months but, although the union received money from all over the world, its funds gave out and it accepted the employers' terms. The union had to agree that the organization in the workshops was not their business and they had to drop the 48-hour week. It gained, however, from the employers' agreement to negotiate in disputes.

Although the A.S.E. was defeated it kept on coming back to the main issues, right up to 1914, because they were so important to its members. On the machine question the employers claimed the right to train whom they liked for any kind of work. This meant that they could train youths for the new turret lathes while apprenticed turners had to tramp from town to town looking for work. After several years the Employers' Federation did agree to 'recommend to their members that consideration should be given to the case of workmen who may be displaced, with a view, if possible, of retaining their services on the work affected or finding other employment for them.'

However this did not happen often and the union came gradually to see that its best solution was to admit into membership semi-skilled as well as skilled men.

During the First World War, because of the unending demand for munitions, the Amalgamated Society of Engineers increased greatly in size and influence. The membership nearly doubled. The union negotiated direct with the Government. It agreed to give up the right to strike, to allow unskilled men to be on Government work and to remove any restrictive practices which interfered with production. This was only while the war lasted. However, while the trade union leaders agreed to this, the rank and file members did not see it in the

255

same way. They saw big profits being made and the cost of living soaring, so they formed the shop stewards' movement to prevent the trade union agreement being exploited. This meant that, while the union officials worked with the Government, the shop stewards led the members in many disputes. In spite of this the union gained such prestige that after the war it persuaded many other smaller unions to join with it and form the new Amalgamated Engineering Union, with nearly half a million members.

After the 1914–18 War came the years of boom and then slump and unemployment. The engineering workers were not so badly off as many in other industries. Their industry was not so depressed as others, it merely stagnated. For the individual worker it depended what section of the industry he was in. The older sections like shipbuilding, textile machinery and mining were in a bad way. In the newer sections, electrical, motor and aircraft, there was growth and the lot of the engineer was easier. The discoveries of Siemens, Parsons and Lanchester were bearing fruit.

As before, so in these years before the 1939 War there were new tools, machines and materials which changed the working conditions of the engineer. Lathes became more specialized. Special purpose machines – the centreless grinder and the multi-spindle drill – came in. Tungsten-carbide steel and other cutting materials appeared and with them stainless steel and aluminium alloys were used more widely. Work was divided up into more operations. As machining time became less, machine loading and rapid handling of parts became more important. More planning of work in the shops before production was necessary.

All these changes affected the engineering worker. New kinds of work appeared which could be learned by practice rather than by instruction. Apprenticeship declined. It was no longer the main way of entering the industry. Aircraft firms were an exception to this; they kept to the apprenticeship system. But in engineering generally the young man who had become skilled in practice on particular machines, but who was not apprenticed, was upgraded to a skilled man.

The newer trades were in pressing and stamping, polishing, grinding and sheet metal work. Many of the men in them were

256

called semi-skilled. Throughout the industry there came to be more semi-skilled men than either fully skilled or labourers. Wages became very complicated, with many additions to the basic rate. When the worker received his pay packet he found it very difficult, if not impossible, to check. For apprentices, however, the system was put on a more sensible basis. The rates for apprentices were fixed by agreement with the union, as proportions of the rate of the skilled fitter; at 16 years it was $27\frac{1}{2}$ per cent and at 20 years $62\frac{1}{2}$ per cent.

When the Second World War began the engineers, who had been under-employed for many years, became vitally important. Training had been neglected in the inter-war years. Now many more thousands of men were wanted in the industry, and a tremendous amount of training had to be carried out. Nearly three quarters of a million women were employed. All jobs were controlled by the Government. No man could leave his job or seek another or be dismissed without permission from the Ministry officials. The biggest change in the industry was the setting up of joint production committees, at the request of the A.E.U. These were introduced first in Government factories and then in private firms. Composed of managers and workers, their job was to improve efficiency and increase production for the war effort. It was an engineers' war and victory would have been impossible without them.

Additional Reading

R. Appleyard, *Charles Parsons*, Constable 1933.
P. W. Kingsford, *F. W. Lanchester*, Edward Arnold 1960.
Sir F. Whittle, *Jet*, Frederick Muller 1953.
J. B. Jefferys, *The Story of the Engineers*, Lawrence & Wishart 1945.

CHAPTER TWELVE

Trade Unions
1918-1945

ONE way of seeing the growth of the trade unions is to look at their total membership.

Date				Membership of all trade unions
1914	..	..	..	4,145,000
1918	..	..	..	6,533,000
1920	..	..	..	8,334,000
1933	..	..	..	4,389,000
1939	..	..	..	6,298,000
1945	..	..	..	7,875,000
1954	..	..	..	9,949,000

The ups and downs can easily be seen. They were due to economic and social conditions and the success or failure of trade union policy. There was the increase during the First World War. Then came the sudden increase because of the post-war enthusiasm, rising to a maximum in 1920. Then the membership fell to the minimum in 1933; this followed the general strike and heavy unemployment. After that, employment improved slowly, helped by rearmament, and during the Second World War many more people worked in the factories.

Another way of following the trade union movement during these years is to see what their aims were and how they tried to achieve them. How much did their influence and power grow?

Immediately after peace in 1918 business was booming. The unions were ready to press forward on the offensive for higher wages and shorter hours. Many problems had been left over from the war years. After the slaughter of millions of men in the trenches, it seemed that there should be a better life for everyone. The first trade union aim was to shorten hours of work. During 1919 the 48-hour week was obtained in most of the big industries without difficulty, but when the unions tried to get a shorter week than this they failed. Resistance to wage cuts was the cause of the national strike of the railwaymen in that year. The whole system was brought to a stop for nine days and the Government, which still controlled the railways, had to give way. The dockers also, led by Ernest Bevin, made a big advance when they won a national minimum wage of 16s. a day. Very soon the post-war boom in business collapsed. By 1921 there were more than two million unemployed. The employers wanted to reduce wages. For the next ten years the unions were in retreat, fighting a long rearguard action to maintain wages. They were not able to achieve this aim because of the great number of unemployed who were anxious to have a job.

Although the engineering workers were not hit by unemployment as hard as some other industries, still in 1922 the Amalgamated Engineering Union had 55,000 members without jobs. The union therefore took a stand on the question of overtime. It said that overtime should be worked only by mutual consent and not only on the instructions of the employers. A union cartoon of that time said; 'Must I work overtime whilst my mate and his family starve for want of work?' This dispute led to a national lock-out by the employers which lasted three months and ended in victory for the employers.

The struggle by the unions to prevent wage cuts went on throughout industry but it was the miners who were at the centre of it. The coal industry was in great difficulties. Other countries did not want Britain's coal as much as they did before the war and the exports of coal fell, as well as the price obtained for it. The Government handed back the mines to the mine owners and refused to nationalize the industry. The owners then demanded a cut in wages and, when the miners refused to accept it, locked them out. The lock-out lasted for three months and ended in defeat for the miners. They hoped that the triple alliance would come into action on their side. The triple alliance was an agreement made before the war between the railwaymen, the transport workers and the miners that they would help each other in a strike. The two big unions did announce that they would strike in support of the miners but on the last day they backed down and the miners were left by themselves. This day, 15th April 1921, came to be known as 'Black Friday'.

The coal mining industry went from bad to worse. When the French occupied the Ruhr, exports to Europe rose but this was only temporary. The mine owners had not tried to modernize the pits. The only way they could see to make the mines pay was to cut wages. They also wanted to go back to an eight-hour day and repeal the Seven Hours Act of 1919. All this led to the General Strike of 1926.

The miners' slogan in 1926 was 'Not a penny off the pay, not a second on the day'. They stuck to this and called on the trade union movement to support them. The Trades Union Congress agreed to do this because wages were being attacked throughout industry, and because they were ashamed of 'Black Friday'. The mine owners did not mind very much if there was a stoppage, because prices were falling. The Government refused to reorganize the industry.

The General Strike lasted nine days. The T.U.C. called out on strike the railwaymen, transport workers, iron and steel workers, builders and printers. All of them came out solidly and many others too. Only emergency services ran, with the help of volunteers. There were no newspapers, except the Government's *British Gazette* and the T.U.C.'s *British Worker*. The Government enrolled thousands of special constables, called out troops and armour and arrested hundreds of strikers.

The men were still standing firm after nine days but the T.U.C. called off the strike and ordered them to return to work. The T.U.C. was ready to accept a compromise but the miners would still not give up a penny or a second. The miners were, therefore, again left on their own and they continued their struggle for another six months before they were forced back by starvation. They accepted lower wages and longer hours.

There was much victimization after the General Strike. The Government struck back against the unions by passing the Trades Disputes Act of 1927. This Act made sympathetic strikes illegal. It also reduced the trade unions' power to spend money on political action by making it necessary for their members to 'contract in' to the political levy instead of 'contracting out' of it.

The General Strike was a turning point in the history of the trade unions. Direct action on a big scale had failed; the challenge to capitalism had fallen flat. Both sides in industry shrank from a repetition of it. Both sides now wanted to have peace in industry. In the next few years the T.U.C. tried to agree with the employers how production could be increased and in this way raise the standard of living. Together they held a number of conferences but there was no practical result.

As industrial action had been unsuccessful the unions placed their hopes in politics. They were closely linked with the Labour Party. In 1929 the Labour Party won enough seats in Parliament to form a government. Although this government did not have a majority in the House of Commons but depended on the Liberals for support, the unions hoped for great improvements in industry.

Unfortunately this Labour victory came at the same time as the great world depression. Unemployment in Britain soared to three million. The new government did nothing about it. After only a short time it fell because it proposed to cut unemployment benefit, and several of its leaders joined the Conservatives to form a national government.

Trade union membership fell to its lowest point three years later. The unions seemed to be able to do nothing to maintain, let alone improve, the living conditions of their members. Then, as trade gradually recovered and money began to be spent on the rearmament before 1939, there were more jobs and more men joined the unions.

In the meantime the unions were moving towards new methods, quite different from the old ones of challenge. The challenge of the General Strike had failed; so had the conferences with the employers which followed. Industry and work shrank or became stagnant. The unions became convinced that the only way towards recovery of trade and more employment was through state intervention and control. If the Government would either nationalize or control and help industry, so that it could expand and provide work for all, then the unions would be a willing partner.

When the Second World War started the unions got a good

deal of what they wanted. The Government controlled in one way or another practically all industries. The unions were able to say how they thought the controls should be brought in and to help in operating them. In fact they played a big part in doing this. The unions' co-operation with the Government was much greater than in the First World War. There were two main reasons for this. The unions had taken a stand against fascism during its growth in the pre-war years and so in 1939 they were determined that Britain should win the war against the fascist countries. Thus the unions were more united than ever before, at all levels from shop steward to general secretary, behind the war effort. Secondly, from the start the Government set up controls to prevent profiteering, to ensure fair shares, and to limit prices as well as wages. The unions could, therefore, more easily protect the living standards of their members and be freer to concentrate on increasing production for the war. There were no serious conflicts between employers and workers as there were in the First World War.

When Winston Churchill formed his government in 1940 several Labour leaders held important posts in it. Ernest Bevin, general secretary of the Transport and General Workers' Union, became Minister of Labour. Because of this the views of the unions had more influence in helping to operate the controls over industry and labour.

The desire of the unions to increase production during the war had important results. Joint Production Committees were set up. The joint production committee in a factory was composed of management and workers, and its job was to discuss and agree on such matters as changes in production, absenteeism, dilution of labour. It was the engineering unions which first demanded that these committees should be set up. The Government agreed to them throughout the engineering industry and more than 4,000 such committees were formed. This example was followed by other industries and joint production committees were set up in the shipbuilding industries and others. The shop stewards were often the leaders on the labour side in the joint committees.

In this way there was a great deal of co-operation between employers and trade unions in the running of the firms. It was a very big change from the old days when strikes were caused by workers' demands that they should have a say in the way in which they were employed. Now the employers learnt more about the workers' point of view and the workers had useful experience of the employers' problems.

During the later years of the war people again looked forward to a better world. All sorts of plans were drawn up for the improvement of industry and society. In the forces men discussed the plans for a better life and what they wanted the Government to do about them. The Trades Union Congress issued a report on post-war reconstruction. It asked not only for nationalization of the main industries but also that the workpeople in private enterprise should have a much greater say in management. It pointed out that the experience during the war showed that this could be done. The T.U.C. claimed that work-people had a right to share in decisions which affected their livelihood, and that their experience and common sense could be used to improve production.

Thus at the end of the war in 1945 the aims of the trade unions had enlarged a great deal since their early days. In the nineteenth century they tried simply to maintain or improve the wages, hours and conditions of work of their members. By 1945 that was still their object but a great deal more was included. They wanted full employment, through government action if necessary, and to see that work-people of all kinds, wage earning and salaried, had a share in management, so that they could influence the policy and purpose of industry and make sure that industry was run for the common good.

EMPLOYERS' ASSOCIATIONS

The First World War strengthened employers' associations just as it did the trade unions, and for the same reasons. As arbitration in disputes was compulsory, employers had to be represented by associations at meetings with the trade unions; where no associations existed they had to be formed.

At the end of the war many industries set up their own joint industrial councils composed of employers and employees. These were for voluntary negotiation about wages, instead of compulsory arbitration.

While the trade unions had the Trades Union Congress to

represent them, the employers' associations had no such body until the present British Employers' Confederation was formed in 1919. It was just over fifty years behind the T.U.C. Another employers' organization, the present Federation of British Industries (F.B.I.) had already been set up during the war, but it dealt only with problems of trade. At the end of the war the Government established a national Joint Industrial Council for employers and trade unions in the hope that the closer relations between them which had developed during the war would continue. The B.E.C. was formed to represent the employers on this council, and it has continued to be the chief employers' association.

The B.E.C. is composed of federations of employers in different industries. It does not take part in any negotiations or disputes. Its main work is to give the employers' point of view to the government, the civil service and the international organizations.

The engineering industry is largely covered by the Engineering and Allied Employers' National Federation. This was founded as early as 1896 and it has grown ever since. It was this federation which locked out the engineering workers for three months in 1922 over a dispute about overtime. It now includes over 4,400 firms employing nearly two million workers. The federation negotiates at national level with the Confederation of Shipbuilding and Engineering Unions.

Before a dispute reaches national level it has to go through several stages. A question raised by a worker is first discussed with the foreman. If it is not settled the shop steward then takes it up with the management. Next it goes to a works conference or works committee. If it is still not settled the dispute is taken to a local conference composed of local officials of the employers' association and of the trade union. The final stage is the central conference between national representatives of the two sides. In this way it may take quite a long time for a dispute to be settled.

JOINT CONSULTATION IN INDUSTRY

In some factories there are committees or councils of workers' representatives and of management which discuss various problems of running a factory. These problems can be almost anything except wages and hours of work which are usually negotiated between the trade unions and the management. The subjects often discussed at these meetings are – changing methods of production, safety and welfare, training, works rules. This is how joint consultation between workers and management takes place.

Joint consultation occurs far more today than it used to. Fifty or sixty years ago there were very few employers who believed in it or practised it in their works. However, here is one example. In 1892 William Mather, head of the firm of Mather and Platt at Salford, wanted to bring in an 8-hour day. He spoke to a meeting of workers in one of the erecting shops:

'I have invited you to meet me today for the purpose of asking you whether we could not, in this firm, devise some plan by which the hours of labour may be shortened, so as to be a benefit to you, and not disadvantageous to the business in which we are all engaged. You form a partnership with the members of this firm in carrying on a large industry, and the success of that industry is as much your concern as ours. We should therefore endeavour not to allow it to fall away by any mistaken policy or action, whether on your part or ours. Of course, our competitors alone would benefit in that case; you would suffer, and we would suffer.'

It was during the 1914–18 War that joint consultation first became important. Production had to be expanded. Labour was scarce. Managers had to keep their workers and they had to listen to a new kind of workers' representative, the shop steward. Numerous factory joint committees were formed. The Government had to bring together employers and trade union leaders to discuss industrial problems.

In 1917 the Whitley Committee on Relations between Employers and Employed issued a report which aimed at making this change permanent. It said that each industry should set up a joint industrial council and that in the factories there should be works committees. The industrial councils were to deal with improvements in methods of work. They were always to remember the work-people's point of view and to use their practical knowledge and experience. The works committees, the report said, 'should always keep in the fore-front the idea of constructive co-operation in the improvement of the industry to which they belong'.

Immediately after the 1914–18 War there was some enthusiasm for joint consultation and about seventy joint industrial councils were set up, for instance, in boot and shoe manufacture and in printing, and also a number of works committees. However, very soon the slump of 1921 and mass unemployment in the nineteen thirties killed this enthusiasm, and few of these bodies survived the inter-war years. Employers no longer had any need to keep the good will of workers, and trade unions had enough to do trying to stop wages from being reduced.

When the Second World War came joint consultation again became necessary, for the same reasons as in the 1914–18 War. This time it was more widespread. In the engineering industry, particularly, many changes had to be made in the workshops which could only be carried through with the agreement of the workers. Three such changes were: new methods of production; dilution, that is employing semi-skilled or unskilled men on skilled jobs; and control of labour through the Essential Work Orders. These orders made it impossible for men to leave any job which was essential to the war effort. Because of the need to discuss these changes with the workers the shop steward movement became stronger.

Early in the war a new kind of factory committee, the Joint Production Committee, sprang up. The J.P.C.s, as they were and still are called, appeared first on the initiative of the workers in Woolwich Arsenal and the Government ordnance factories. When the U.S.S.R. entered the war the communists wanted to increase the output of arms, and they had much influence among the shop stewards. Soon the trade union leaders made agreements with the employers for J.P.C.s to be set up in the factories. Towards the end of the war the number of J.P.C.s in engineering firms had increased to over 4,000, covering two and a half million workers.

In the coal industry there were over a thousand pit production committees. Nearly all the shipbuilding yards had yard committees, and in the building industry there were many site committees.

There was, therefore, a great deal of joint consultation in various industries during the war. It increased production because there was a common aim – winning the war. The fact that it also enabled managers and workers to understand each other's problems and points of view was just as important.

For the first few years after the end of the war in 1945 there was the same need for joint consultation as during the war itself. There were acute shortages of everything, including labour, and increased production was badly needed. The Labour government arranged consultation between the leaders of both sides in industry, but in the factories the war-time enthusiasm faded away and many J.P.C.s disappeared. Only in the nationalized industries were they compulsory.

We do not know how many production committees or works committees there are today, or how much joint consultation there really is. Many people working in industry will know something about them. Some committees discuss the whole range of management problems and are concerned with the well-being and prosperity of the firm; there is real consultation and it works well, giving satisfaction to both sides. Other committees are limited to discussion of purely welfare subjects, such as the canteen and the washing facilities, and are not so successful.

It is not easy to bring about real joint consultation in a firm, whether it is through a works council or committee or a joint production committee. There are many problems. Both managers and workers may be suspicious of the idea. Managers may think that joint consultation takes away some of their authority. Workers may think that it is a trap to weaken their will to fight for better conditions. The foremen may also have their position weakened if information by-passes them when it is given to the workers by their representatives on the committee. The trade unions may also be afraid that the workers' representatives may be agreeing with the management on subjects which the unions should be negotiating.

Then there is the difficulty of deciding the scope of the committee, what subjects it should discuss. What power should the committee have? Should it simply give advice or should it be able to make decisions and see that they are carried out? The workers will be interested only if the subjects discussed are important to them and to the firm in which they work. If the workers' representatives discuss important subjects which are vital to the firm they need to have full information about finance and future plans of the firm. The management may not like to give this information, or may not be able to.

Many of these problems exist because people in industry have different ideas of what the committees are for. Some people see them simply as a way of increasing production; other people, depending on which side they are, see the committees as a safety valve for the workers to let off steam, or as an opportunity to express grievances. For other people they are a step towards democracy in industry.

Joint consultation can bring great benefits to all concerned. However, while it is growing it has not yet had a big influence on British industry as a whole.

Additional Reading

G. D. H. Cole, *Short History of the British Working Class Movement*, Allen & Unwin 1937.

E. L. Wigham, *Trade Unions*, Oxford University Press 1956.

Index

270